# JIMMY BRESLIN

## THE MAN WHO TOLD THE TRUTH

# JIMMY BRESLIN

## THE MAN WHO TOLD THE TRUTH

RICHARD ESPOSITO

With Reporting by
Ted Gerstein

NEW YORK

JIMMY BRESLIN: THE MAN WHO TOLD THE TRUTH

Crime Ink
An Imprint of Penzler Publishers
58 Warren Street
New York, N.Y. 10007



First Crime Ink edition

Interior design by Charles Perry



Library of Congress Control Number: 2024941962

ISBN: 978-1-61316-577-5
eBook ISBN: 978-1-61316-578-2

10 9 8 7 6 5 4 3 2 1

Printed in the United States of America
Distributed by W. W. Norton & Company

# JIMMY BRESLIN

## THE MAN WHO TOLD THE TRUTH

To Karen

*For Everything*

"Because I came from Queens, which nobody in the history of New York newspapers ever wrote about or even saw, I was reputed to be streetwise and tough. Which was untrue. I didn't fight. I chased stories, not beatings. But I knew where to find people who were somewhat less than our civic best, and so editors clung to the illusion."

—Jimmy Breslin

If it's true, put it in the paper and go have a drink . . . Let society sort it out.

—Breslin to Eric Shawn, Fox News, during the trial of the "Snakehead Queen" following the grounding of the cargo ship *Golden Venture* at Fort Tilden Beach on the Rockaway peninsula, on June 6, 1993, and the death of ten of the 286 undocumented migrants on board

"I don't know what objectivity is. The truth is what's important."

—Breslin to Karen Polk, *Boston Globe,* 1988, following his joining *New York Newsday*

# CONTENTS

# CAST OF CHARACTERS

**James Earle Breslin**
October 17, 1928–March 19, 2017

**Alfred Damon Runyon**
October 4, 1880–December 10 1946

**Rosemary Dattolico Breslin**
1931–1981
Spouse, 1954–1981

**Ronnie Eldridge**
Spouse, 1982–2017

**James, Kevin, Rosemary,**
**Patrick, Kelly, & Christopher**
The Breslin children

**James Earle Breslin, Sr. & Frances**
Parents

**Deirdre Breslin**
Sister

LONE KILLERS
*including:*

**David Berkowitz**
Serial killer

**Lee Harvey Oswald**
Assassin

**Sirhan Sirhan**
Assassin

---

MOBSTERS
*including:*

**Frank Costello**
Prime Minister, the Mob

**Tony Provenzano**
Labor racketeer

**Joe Valachi**
Mob stoolie

**Big Mama Nunziata**
The last Gallo on President St.

**Joe Gallo**
Mob clown prince

**Anthony "Gaspipe" Casso**
Rat

**Joe Magliocco**
Profaci crime family boss

**Jimmy "the Gent" Burke**
Mastermind of the Lufthansa heist

**Burton Kaplan**
Mob associate, government informant

---

GOOD COPS
*including:*

**Bill Clark**
Lead detective, Son of Sam case

**Tony Cama**
Detective, Son of Sam case

---

FBI AGENTS
*including:*

**Steve Cerbone**
Lead agent, Lufthansa heist

**Bill Simon, Joseph Casper**
Frank Sinatra, Jr., kidnapping

### Historical Figures

*including:*

**John Fitzgerald Kennedy**
President of the United States

**Richard Milhous Nixon**
President of the United States

**Malcolm X**
Civil rights activist,
Muslim minister

**Martin Luther King, Jr.**
Civil rights leader,
Nobel Prize winner

**Robert F. Kennedy**
Attorney General of
the United States,
US Senator

**John Lennon**
Musician

---

### Gravediggers

**Clifton Pollard**
JFK Gravedigger

**William Weatroski**
Andrew Goodman Gravedigger

### Breslin's People

*including:*

**Mel Lebetkin**
aka Klein the Lawyer

**Fat Thomas**
known on his arrest records as
Thomas Rand

**Mutchie**
Bar owner

**Pep McGuire**
Bar owner

**Marvin the Torch**
Arsonist

**Un Occhio**
Pleasant Avenue mob boss

---

### Newspaper Owners

**John Hay (Jock) Whitney**
*New York Herald Tribune*

**Dorothy Schiff**
*New York Post*

**Rupert Murdoch**
*New York Post*

ROMAN CATHOLIC CLERGY

*including:*

**Cardinal Bernard Law**

**Father Bruce Ritter**

---

OTHER SUPPORTING CAST

**Joan Whitney Payson**
Owner of the New York Mets

**Donald Manes**
Queens Borough President

**Rudy Giuliani**
Attorney,
Mayor of New York City

**Bernie Goetz**
Subway shooter

**Donald Trump**
Real estate magnate,
TV personality,
future President

**Hugh Carey**
Governor of New York

**Ed McDonald**
Attorney

**Sterling Lord**
Breslin's agent

**Morty Matz**
Public relations man

# JIMMY BRESLIN

## THE MAN WHO TOLD THE TRUTH

# PROLOGUE

James Earle Breslin, 48 years old and at the top of his game, stood in front of the open office door of a newspaper editor named Dick Oliver. He was wearing a blue pinstripe suit with a Countess Mara tie draped under the open shirt collar and around his fat neck, and he slashed the air with a Macanudo Robusto cigar.

"Do Not. Confuse me. With. The Facts. I tell the truth."

Each word was as loud as the crack of a bat in the Bronx.

I stared down the long room with its submarine-low acoustic tile ceiling and saw, hanging down right there, marking the heart of the newspaper and the hours and then the minutes and then the seconds until the presses rolled, the large four-sided clock in its beautiful oak case. It hung, neither ominous nor friendly, more like a Greek god, ruling above the clatter of keys and the *zmmmump* and slam of returns and the cigar and cigarette smoke and the ground-out butts in the carpet and the smell of beer. I was as awestruck as a batboy seeing Babe Ruth step out of the Yankee Stadium dugout.

A cigar smoke plume rose above his black Irish curls as the words came right out of Breslin's big mouth the same way they came out of his typewriter, and that was cleaner and better than anyone else who tried to tell the truth in a 1,000–1,100 word newspaper column.

He leaned in and out with each word, and now it was a boxer dancing or something else you had never seen or even read about in a writer or a poet or a singer unless you were very lucky. I've seen it since, once or twice, when the poetry comes out through the eyes, and the mouth moves and the arms move and the legs move and it is all one thing. It is far bigger than the man himself. Far bigger. Far better too. In Breslin it was the soul of the city rising.

That is my first memory of Breslin, and as good a way as any way I know to begin telling his story.

It is as good a way as any because it is emblematic of Breslin's impact: on the reader, on his family, on his editors and on those individuals who were the subjects of his ire. Nearly everyone who ever met him had a Breslin story.

Pugnacious. Passionate. Profound. Bombastic. Bully. Buffoon. Bellowing. Reckless. Resourceful. Vengeful. Nasty. Gracious. Gratuitous. Insecure. Heavy drinking. Grandstanding miserable bastard.

Better on deadline than anyone.

We all have multiple selves. Jimmy Breslin made it a point to admit—in fact, he made it a point of considerable pride—that he often wasn't sure which of his personae were real or when he was inhabiting one of his subjects or his characters. And of course, he knew and he knew that you would know as soon as you heard it or read it that the whole thing was a conceit. He knew who he was, and what purpose each of those selves was serving. He was, as he often bellowed, "J.B. Number One." A great reporter and a brilliant deadline artist, that was Breslin.

In this and many other things he owed a great debt to Damon Runyon, a debt that he repaid when he wrote his 1991 biography of that writer, *Damon Runyon,* a book that was in many ways Breslin's autobiography. The part that is pertinent here is that when Breslin talked about his confused identity, he could bring a smile to your eyes. In saying of Runyon, "He put a smile into a newspaper, which usually has as much humor as a bus accident," he was writing a sentence that set himself and Runyon apart from many of the other inhabitants of the "literary underworld" that in the twentieth century was an American newsroom. Like Runyon he was a liar, a cheater, a thief, and a tout. But each could put a smile on your face.

As to who the two men were: in each case their multiple selves were at their core neither simply self-centered, nor narcissistic, neither bombastic nor buffoon, neither ugly nor angry, though in fact they included all of those things taken together. No, like the chaos they each thrived in, these traits were the molten lead that each would pour into the typewriter. In Breslin's case the lead would then come out the other side as solid and perfect words.

These columns of words did not disregard the facts. They were, at their best, fact after fact after fact; detail after detail after detail; observation after observation after observation; emotion captured in lyrical simplicity and taken together whether funny or sad, personal or global, harsh or sympathetic; they were nouns, verbs, subjects or objects; and yes, occasionally—very occasionally—adjectives and adverbs. It is what he did with these words that mattered.

His acolyte, his protégé, and his friend, the city columnist Michael Daly, once explained what Breslin strove for in his writing. "Emotional clarity," Daly mumbled. "Emotional clarity."

He had gotten right to the heart of the matter in two words. Breslin often achieved clarity by seeing the world through the eyes of the characters he created or through those of the subjects of his reporting. With charity. With empathy. With an understanding of the essential tragicomic nature of so much of so many lives. He always was ready to duel to the death with the forces arrayed against them. But he was not an earnest crusader. He was a reporter and poet equally. He was able to get you to see and also to feel what the victims of poverty, injustice, and the deceit of the powerful were stuck with. He did this in a way that is one of the hardest: he put you in the scene with them, and he made you see and feel through their eyes what was in their hearts.

In person, Breslin also had a great sense of humor and, when he let you see it, you saw that his own heart was very big.

"He had a hard head, but he had a warm heart." In that, the wonderful and wonderfully precise reporter Barbara Ross said it best. When she said it, she was summing up an encounter she once had with his bluster.

He was, in this hardheadedness and so many other ways, so much of the time, and for so many, impossible to live with. His cyclonic greed for attention began in childhood and was unrelenting. It was, however, alloyed with genuine warmth and love. This made it almost tolerable. You could see this warmth in his eyes, in his joy and in his sadness when he spoke of his mother; his sister, Deirdre; his first wife, Rosemary; his daughters, Kelly and Rosemary, who both died too young; and his wife until the very end, Ronnie Eldridge, saint, safekeeper, chauffeur and gentle nurse to his ego, his conscience, and as time went on, his health. You could see it when he crouched down to play with children.

His affection was not maudlin. His sense of piety had no room for falsehood. This is important too, for piety and faith were at the core of his religious point of view: not the institution of the Catholic Church, which he saw as the husk of these things. In this, as in whatever he saw, he wrote clearly. It is explicit in his book *The Church that Forgot Christ*.

It is expressed a little more enigmatically in the epitaph he wrote for Jack Maple. A bowler hat wearing, spectator shoe shod, and bow tie wrapped New York cop, Maple was as ironic of character as he was cherubic in stature. He was the man who in 1994 invented CompStat with New York City Police Commissioner Bill Bratton. The predictive, accountability-driven approach to policing revitalized its stagnant management and dramatically reduced crime in America. Breslin's chiseled words said less about Jack and volumes more about Jimmy, and the distillation of fact into truth.

BRESLIN SAYS NO, I WILL NOT ATTEND HIS FUNERAL

You should go to jail and visit prisoners
That is a corporal work of mercy
The dead don't know that you're there
So whadda ya go for, the family?
Who knows what they feel about the dirty bastard?

Maple's family and friends in fact loved him. His home city, New York, was in fact grateful to him. Maple, in fact, suffering from cancer, held his own wake in the back room of a famous New York gin mill, Elaine's, while he was still alive and could enjoy his friends arrayed in tuxedos as they toasted him and their world. And Breslin thought highly of him. So what is Breslin saying here? He is saying:

if you want to worship, worship with your feet. This was what his God required.

Breslin, a Roman Catholic all his life, was sure God resided in your heart, and doubted it resided in any church. This belief about faith, mercy, God, and man resonated throughout the breadth of his more than six decades of reporting. Reporting well, for Breslin, could be a penance and it could be a corporal work of mercy. Just do a good job and do it for the living, as Maple did in his police work and when he held his own wake.

* * *

When it came to the subject of crime writing, Breslin had a very high bar, his City Editor at the *New York Daily News*, Sam Roberts, once observed. Even so, there was plenty to go around and he reported and wrote about many crimes—those against the nation, those by police and those by mobsters.

His method, Sam Roberts explained, was simple: "You know what Jimmy said, he said, you know, journalism is a four letter word, W-O-R-K. And that was absolutely true. You couldn't cover it from the office, you couldn't cover it on the telephone, you had to go slap up the stairs of tenements, go up in the housing projects. It was all shoe leather. And it was absolutely true."

Sam was 28 when he was City Editor of the *Daily News*. It was his 75th birthday when he sat down to recount it.

"Seventy five," he began. "Now that's a number. Seventy. Five." Sam, like Breslin, had been laying out pages and writing headlines and stories since before the age of ten, putting together his own publishing operation on his parents' floors.

"I was way too young to have that job at 28. I began and ended every day with Jimmy Breslin," Sam said, identifying something everyone who ever worked with Breslin knew: Jimmy Breslin got up earlier and he worked later than almost anyone in the business. Sam also was a witness to all the doubters to Breslin's veracity.

"All the people who faulted him and said, oh, this was made up or this was fudged and everything—well, virtually everything I saw turned out to be true. You know, yeah, it may have had a polished quote here or there or some characters in some way might have been a little composite." But on the whole, Sam said, it was "wishful thinking" on the part of the doubters. Because the stories only Breslin could get came as a result of long hours and "W-O-R-K."

Breslin, he said, had the hunter's instinct. "He had to get ahead of the story." The John Lennon murder, the Kennedy gravedigger, the perpetrators of the great Lufthansa heist: on all of those things he was way ahead of everybody else. "It was that imagination he had; it was that foresight. That just made him such a special person."

"But as somebody said, if it wasn't true, it was certainly truth," the City Editor recalled. He was at one thing, however, a miserable failure, Sam noted: "He missed virtually every political prediction."

In this last observation, he sums up centralized journalism in its twentieth-century heyday: as an authoritative way to predict the past. During the beginning of Sam's tenure in that era, there were sharp spikes poised near the edge of desks on which to slap the sheets of copy paper on which tomorrow's news was typed or crossed out and retyped. To a reporter, these pieces of paper were rent receipts. They wrote, as Breslin said, for money.

"There were spikes, before OSHA outlawed them, and there were typewriters. I remember when we switched to computers and everybody said, the city room is freaking too quiet and they made the keys chirp. And then somebody said, it sounds like an aviary and they had to turn that off. It was just, you know—as you know, for better or for worse, as I'm sure people said about us at the time, it was a whole different world," Sam said.

Certainly, different from *The New York Times*, where Sam toiled in his mid-seventies, writing beautifully about New York and New Yorkers, and where algorithms measured what was trending, what ought to be moved to the fore, what things few seemed to care about. When Sam was hired at the *Daily News*, Ed Quinn, the head of personnel, told him to not tell anyone he had gone to Cornell University.

"Tell them you went to Tilden High, or something," Quinn told him.

In this world, which would turn out not to be a world without end, the worst crime a reporter could commit, Breslin noted repeatedly, was to fail to find a sensation. He noted in his writing that in 1883, when one publisher new to New York observed that another newspaper had misunderstood sensation and had devoted just three paragraphs to the opening of the Brooklyn Bridge, the publisher, Joseph Pulitzer, knew right then that he could beat these "imbeciles" at this game.

When Breslin arrived at the *Herald Tribune* and observed how columnists wrote what they *thought* mattered, he knew he could beat them at this game. He would actually leave the building and go out on the streets to gather the material for columns that mattered. He knew that if bridge openings and horse racing and baseball could bring some excitement to the reader, it was crime, if the crime was big enough, that was the main event. Because if a crime was big enough for Breslin, it usually was big enough and sensational enough to make the front pages of New York City's rival tabloids—the civic-minded, solidly blue-collar *Daily News*, where he worked steadily in the 1970s and 1980s, and the once-liberal *New York Post*, which from practically the day Rupert Murdoch bought it and promised he would not change anything was transmogrifying into a one-sided comic book that was soon to be a secret pleasure of many Manhattanites.

The crimes of David Berkowitz soared over Breslin's high bar. Berkowitz committed horrible, unfathomable, serial crimes and as he read what Breslin wrote about them he decided that he considered Jimmy Breslin a friend, perhaps a muse, so he communicated with him and taunted him. And let his demons speak to him.

That was just a few months after November 1976 when, to many New Yorkers, "J.B. Number One" seemed to appear full-blown on the pages of the *Daily News*. Of course, like so many who appeared to be an overnight success, his career actually began decades before.

He was born in 1929 to a father who was an itinerant piano player, who walked out the door as Breslin toddled. His father, also James Earle Breslin, left Jimmy, his sister Deirdre, and a mother who was by many accounts a lovely—if alcoholic, and at least one time suicidal—woman, in a state of abject poverty. Poverty, loneliness, desperation, survival, and it ought to be noted, cops—Breslin grew up with cops in his family and lived with an alcoholic uncle who was also a cop—these were part of the fabric of the youth who walked into the newsroom of a local paper, the *Long Island Press*. By 18, in his first bylined article for that paper, he demonstrated that while he might not always be the first on the scene—he was writing this time about the first television set to be installed in a local bar, and there were plenty of TV sets in plenty of bars already—he would be among the first to provide insight into what it meant. In this case, he demonstrated through the vivid portrayal of the bar's occupants how it changed the nature of bent-elbowed conversation forever, except in those few establishments that valued words so much that TVs were banned or kept off except during a World Series, when the sound was turned down, and for presidential debates, when it was turned up.

He went on from that long-gone newspaper: other newspapers, press associations, sportswriting, books—his first was about horse racing, which, he explained, was all he could know about, growing up in the shadow of a racetrack, and therefore all he should write about. Then, somehow, full-grown and chubby and cocky, he arrived at the *Herald Tribune*, where he joined a company of journalistic revolutionaries and demonstrated a talent that few—even in that newsroom, and it held plenty of talent—could match.

There was, of course, the future novelist Tom Wolfe, who when he walked in with his PhD—and his genius, he recalled to an interviewer modestly—looked around and said, *I can beat these guys.* A few months later he found himself sitting a few yards downwind from the cloud of smoke that enshrouded someone who thought exactly the same way: Breslin. Essentially, that was how the two of them changed journalism. They knew, like Runyon, that they could beat this game. They could change the rules.

* * *

Long before his arrival at the *New York Daily News*, Breslin had written about John F. Kennedy's murder and his last rites in the emergency room in Dallas. He had written about Kennedy's gravedigger. In these two pieces he changed not just the form, but the substance of how news was reported. He had traveled to London and poignantly written of the death of an aged and bedridden Churchill. In this, he showed us the tears on the faces of Blitz survivors as they recalled the moments when a flawed man punched above his weight for his nation. He had already become known to the all-knowing literati, and the novelists and press critics, as a shoe-leather member of the founding group of this thing they called (though he would not) "The New Journalism."

He had lived in Harlem to write about riots. In this, he followed the great tradition of muckraking reformers. He wrote about heists that claimed the lives of heisters through mistrust and incestuous murder. In this, he showed how sources could inform and betray—just like him. He had captured the glint of the diamond vanity ring of a corrupt labor racketeer facing the judge and jury. His palette was richer than that of a courtroom artist. Retired Mob boss Frank Costello, crazy Joe Gallo and his lion, Joe Valachi, the Mob rat, and crime on the streets of New York; he had written about all of these. It was portraiture at its best. And there was Joe McCarthy, the senator who destroyed lives, stymied art, gutted government departments through his nastiness and his campaign against what he saw as communism. He had lampooned LBJ, tasted the jungle dirt of Vietnam and put you in the courtroom as Watergate verdicts were read.

His overnight success at the *News* came after more than 720 newspaper columns for the *Trib* and the *Post* as well as numerous Sunday feature articles and numerous magazine articles. It came after four books, one of which had been made into a very successful movie, a comic Mafia bouffe called *The Gang That Couldn't Shoot Straight*. That book shared one remarkable feature with Runyon's *Guys and Dolls*, which Breslin knew was a marquee trait: "He made the gangsters so enjoyable that they could walk off a page and across a movie screen."

But the *News* was the tabloid of record. The blue-collar bible had more readers—even as it slid down from its peak paid circulation to around a million daily and close to two million on a Sunday—than several of Jimmy's past homes at newspapers and magazines had when combined.

And now it would have Son of Sam. Subway cars were filled with the sound of tabloid pages turning. Sam had captured the fevered imagination of an imperiled imperial city—a city by now dubbed "Fear City." And it was Sam who chose Breslin, whose prose he admired. So it is with Sam that we begin to widen our aperture to capture the personas of James Earle Breslin.

## SAM

For David Berkowitz the killing began at around 1:10 A.M. on July 29, 1976.

Donna Lauria, eighteen, with dark brown hair, was stepping from an Oldsmobile car owned by her friend Jody Valenti when an assailant described as a short, stout, white man stepped from the darkness, the only light provided by a thin crescent moon. He pulled a one hundred-and-fifty-three-dollar revolver from a paper bag and killed Donna Lauria with a bullet that came with the first loud bark of the gun.

Her last known words were believed to be "Now what is this—" which sounds about right, as that is the way people still speak in some parts of the Bronx.

Lauria had been training to be an emergency medical technician. Valenti, nineteen and a nursing student, was shot in the thigh. A third bullet missed them both and was found by police lodged in the Oldsmobile's body.

The young women had been sitting, double-parked, in the blue Cutlass on a quiet street in the pleasant Pelham Bay enclave of the Bronx. They had been talking about their Thursday night at Peachtree's, a discotheque in the Westchester suburb of New Rochelle, which was on a hot nightlife strip a little over six and a half miles north.

This sitting in cars—for conversation, for romance, for the kinds of sex that such space permitted—would figure prominently in the reporting of what would happen in the twelve months ahead. During that time six young women and men were killed and nine were wounded. Many of the victims had been in parked cars, others were hunted as they emerged from discos and one was a student, her arms filled with books, shot in the face after she stepped up from the subway.

As the shootings continued and the evidence developed, police could see where the killer hunted: the Bronx and Queens. They could identify locations where he might strike: near discos, on darkened side streets. Another possible piece of the puzzle, as the evidence emerged, was the fact that like his first victim, Donna Lauria, most of the victims were women, and all but one of them would have long brown hair. The survivor and witness descriptions of the assailant varied in nearly every way but for this one fact: the killer was a white man. A white man who had emerged from the dark, said not a word, and opened fire.

Another important part of the witness testimony was the stubby gun that survivors described. Ballistic evidence and a lack of shell casings pointed to a revolver. A powerful one. The deformed slugs seemed to be .44 or .45 caliber. Thick and ugly things. Soon after the student was killed, ballistics tests would show that the same gun had been used in prior incidents. But as the months went on, detectives seemed no closer to catching their killer.

Investigations are very often built on the simplest things. The ballistic evidence is, of course, very useful and is part of this. The witness description of the suspect also can be helpful, but is often woefully inaccurate. But the other facts gathered through the shoe leather of dozens of police officers on the street—sometimes scribbled on matchbook covers, in notebooks pushed into a detective's suitcoat pocket, or on some scrap of paper under a patrolman's hat—can be the most helpful of all when they are later pieced together in some room smelling of sweat and coffee and lunch.

It would soon become clear from the canvassers that none of the victims knew each other. None of them were robbed. Finally, the victims came from two boroughs—the Bronx and Queens—that were separated by deep water spanned by three bridges. Where he killed would not provide much help in figuring out where he lived.

There is also the luck that comes with this hard work. In the end, it would be luck—in the form of a parking ticket—that would bring an end to the killing in this case.

But for now, we go back to about 3 A.M. on that July morning in 1976, when it is time for Donna Lauria to step out of the car that was parked right in front of her building at 2860 Buhre Avenue and go upstairs to her family's apartment. Her parents were home. She had seen them arrive a short while earlier. And she was just a few yards away from her front door when Sam struck.

Just moments later, her father emerged to walk the dog and saw his fallen daughter. He ran to her, but it already was too late even as he gathered her into his arms and tried to race her to the hospital. This would be in his memory forever: the last time he would see the brightness of his daughter, it was cooling down on the dark street.

The bullet that killed their daughter also killed the Laurias' chance at a normal life. They never recovered from the senselessness, from the grief.

For the cops, though, for the moment, this was another random shooting in a city that was violent, burning, and broke. It was added to the big pile of uncleared cases at the New York Police Department's Detective Bureau.

In the months that followed there were three more shootings that the evidence indicated appeared to be linked: one in October, one in November, and one in January. The shootings claimed five victims: one dead, one paralyzed, one shot in the head, one in the neck, and one with less critical injuries.

For Jimmy Breslin, the story of the killings began a few months later on March 8, 1977, with the murder of a young woman that hit very close to home.

A Columbia University School of General Studies Russian major, Virginia Voskerichian, 19, born in Sofia, Bulgaria and already in less than one generation, with parents still struggling with the English language, was attending the best of colleges America could offer. She had just made the Dean's list. Now with her arms filled with books, she had stepped off the subway at the Continental Avenue stop in Forest Hills and begun her walk home when a man stepped in front of her and pulled his weapon from a brown paper bag. She raised her books, but her speed was no match for a heavy, soft lead-tipped bullet.

The heavy bullet left residue on her books but ruined her young face. She fell across the sidewalk and died with her head in the bushes in front of 4 Dartmouth Street. She had been wearing a peasant blouse, a skirt, a jacket made in Paris and tall boots.

The gunman, as he fled, made sure to scare off any witnesses by emptying the other four cylinders into the no longer quiet night. Virginia Voskerichian was about two and a half blocks from her home at

69-11 Exeter Street when she died between 7:30 and 7:40 P.M., as near as the detectives could determine.

She also was about 100 yards away from where another young woman, Christine Freund, 26, was killed on January 30, five weeks and three days earlier. Christine Freund had been hit by two bullets. Both went into her head. She had been sitting in a car with her boyfriend, John Diel, 30. You could call him lucky in that he was physically unharmed. Another brunette with shoulder-length hair killed.

Virginia's death was also about three minutes away from the Breslin home at 52 Deepdene Road, where a wife and two young daughters—Rosemary, with her brown hair, and Kelly, whose was blonde—resided. This made it personal for Breslin, who thrived on the personal.

Throughout his career, any attack or slight perceived, any fear felt or illness survived, or any wound to the heart, whether real or imagined, would fuel his prose. Making it personal was also a trait that helped make him, in the words of one editor, the "miserable man" he knew. The editor, Dick Oliver, claimed that the rumpled Irish tabloid bard would be the first to acknowledge this.

Much of the time he served no one except his readers. That he did well. He called himself, proudly and loudly, "J.B. Number One." But he was an often miserable man.

But in this instance, what fueled his prose was his fear for his daughters. The same fear that, once he put it on the page, you would now have had for yours.

The two bullets that took Freund's life were 246 grain, .44 caliber Winchester Westerns. Ugly things with soft lead tips. They would turn out to be the same kind as the one that went into Virginia

Voskerichian, shattering her teeth and searing through her brain into the spinal column.

It would later be determined that they came from a Charter Arms .44 Bulldog revolver, a five-shot revolver manufactured in Connecticut's Gun Valley. They left something of a unique pattern on all their expended rounds.

Now, instead of wearing a cap and gown and stepping into the upper ranks of America's educated, Virginia's valediction would be that of a victim, and would be told in black ink and halftone pictures on the dull off-white pages of a big city newspaper. A beautiful, dead, dark-haired young woman rubbing off on our fingers.

Breslin's first attempt at telling the *Daily News* readers what was occurring that day in New York City began:

> The morning after the murder, Tony Cama, who is a detective of homicide, was out on the street looking for the killer. Tony was in his cop clothes: brown checked jacket, formless blue checked pants, cocoa shirt, wine red tie, olive raincoat and red face. He held a spiral notepad and a hand radio. On the sidewalk at his feet the sun glistened on the dried blood of the girl who had been killed the night before.
>
> A woman came along the street and Cama smiled at her. "Excuse me, ma'am. Police Department," he said.
>
> "Oh, yes," the woman said. "Is this where the murder was last night?"
>
> "Oh, yes," Cama said. He pointed at the blood on the sidewalk.
>
> "Oh," the woman said. She stepped back.
>
> "Isn't this—right where the first one was too?" she said.
>
> "Right over there," Cama said, pointing past the corner.

The man—and it was a man on the copy desk—who wrote the headline over the column did what good copy desk persons do. He had summed up the topic of Breslin's writing in a few clear words:

What Breslin did under it was classic crime reporting, spare and vivid.

> "Do you think the same person could've done both murders?" the woman asked.
>
> "We're in a lot of trouble if it is," Cama said . . .
>
> "They're checking down in the morgue now to see if the bullets are the same," Cama said, "If they are, we got a nut to put up with."

Clear. Matter of fact. The scenes sharply defined through dialogue. Here was the fifteenth paragraph of the column on Virginia:

> A workman began chopping down pine bushes that lined the sidewalk.

And here were the end of the eighteenth and the whole of the nineteenth:

> She walked along the row of pine bushes.
>
> Somebody shot her in the face and she pitched into the pine bushes and died.

Here was someone who could, just like a team of skilled detectives, take a pattern of facts and using his thick, fat fingers, tell you—his audience of one—everything you needed in order to actually see what had happened. The night before you read it, he had used this gift to hammer out the story. Rat-tat-tatting and slamming—powerful, fast heavy-fingered key strikes—sweating, smoking, crumpling pages into balls that cluttered the desk and dropped onto the floor. All the while he was selecting the details that would evoke with great clarity what you, specifically you, needed to understand.

In this case, that was what the city's police detectives and the city's parents were facing. He had to put you right there in their heads and in their shoes. No other young woman's head would fall into those same bushes. You could see the sadness of a life cut down, requiring bushes to be cut down. The tragic. The counterpoint. You could wonder where the next victim might fall. What you could not see were all the words he had tried and then rejected and crumpled into balls before he had what he needed to simply put you where he knew you needed to be. In Queens. On a street. With the beginning of an adulthood that would now be an incomplete story. A treasure spent by someone who stole it.

What you could not see was the cursing, the smoking, the picking up and banging down of telephones and the impatience of the editors he had to fend off.

"His was a one-on-one with the reader, not writing for a lot of people—it was one on one. And so, consequently as an editor, he's talking to you," explained Oliver, who was the Metropolitan Editor of the *Daily News*, and the burly cigar-smoking man responsible for Breslin. "And as an editor then, you're able to come up with some questions . . . sometimes come up with some—to flesh out what he's writing. But really it was not a big deal to edit Jimmy Breslin. It's a big deal to get him on time. And he was always, always late, always."

The *Daily News* had a very good team of police reporters, the best in New York City, covering this young woman's death. They could see the larger story unfolding. But a beat reporter at a blue-collar tabloid was constrained. The inverted pyramid convention laid out the facts with an orderly "who, what, where, when" insistence, but largely eliminated any narrative. There were the one- and two-sentence paragraphs. The sentences with few or no commas. The very short lengths.

"Tabloid" was not a bad word. The word itself sounds tainted now, but actually it was a format—a compact one that could be read without taking up the whole kitchen table, unlike a standard broadsheet newspaper. One that could be read while hanging on a strap on a crowded bus. Accuracy was prized. A little sensation would not be refused. But a tabloid was simply a mass circulation newspaper, with plenty of pictures, aimed at the working-class reader.

Breslin's work however, was not constrained by the usual conventions. He was allowed a column length often of 1,100 or more words. His narratives were novels for a tabloid audience.

> On the corner, detectives stood in groups and looked over mimeographed forms. They split up, like groups of door-to-door salesmen and started for the houses on the block.
>
> "What they gave me," Cama was saying, "was to come out here and stand here and ask anybody, if they saw anything."
>
> "For how long?"
>
> "As long as they tell me. This is the only way you do it, you know. Legwork. Stand and ask. Go knock on doors and ask. This isn't a television show. This is a murder."
>
> "How many murders have you been on?"
>
> "My own cases, I've had 13. I cleared 11 of them. You clear them this good, some guys say they're grounders. You know, easy things to pick up. I say I make them grounders."
>
> A man came up and Cama said excuse me, and began talking to him, making notes. Taking the name and address: the drudgery of solving the highest crime.
>
> "I hope this isn't the same person who did the first murder," the man said to Cama.
>
> "So do I. Because we'd be in some trouble."
>
> He stood in the sunlight and asked his questions and waited to hear about the autopsy.

And this is how Breslin allowed the story to unfold. It was a story about a serial killer who soon would have a name, but for now did not. A serial killer who despite the police sketch artist's efforts did not yet have a face. A serial killer who a task force of detectives had already begun to quietly hunt. Who a homicide detective named Cama already had the instinct to fear. Because who is it that kills two women for no money and with no apparent connection between them? A madman. Suddenly the idea of motive must take you to a very dark place. But so far, the clues were still thin, and the city's residents, with a lot of other crime to contend with, had not yet paid close attention.

When Virginia Voskerichian's death was told in this way, the subways became crowded with fear as well as elbows, sweat, and open newspapers. The arc of the story that Breslin had begun to own was one that would emerge over weeks and weeks and finally months until there was a year-long serialization of fear. The sensational aspect of the story would also grow, and in this the tabloids knew something too: *Punch in the gut to capture your audience. Aim for the heart. Not for the head. The audience is probably smarter than the editor.* But they have even less time.

There was something else to note here—an aside in the story of Sam, but important to the story of Breslin.

His portrayal of the dedicated detectives and their work would put the lie to the later accusations that he hated cops. He didn't. He hated sloppy cops. He despised racist cops. He was insulted by corrupt cops. Most of all, he was angered by cops who took the paychecks but did not take the time to understand the city and the residents they were sworn to protect.

* * *

And the audience was now in fear for their daughters' lives. For the parents of the low-rise neighborhoods of New York where the *Daily News* readers lived, where Metropolitan Editor Oliver came from, where Breslin himself came from, this was far more important than a city budget, or the political landscape of Washington, D.C. These murders in the Bronx and Queens could drive people from the city.

Breslin was born in one of these boroughs of New York—in Queens, a sprawling place with more residents than almost any American city—and raised in a rundown detached house. It was a borough of New York City where there were far more buildings with stairs to climb than with elevators to ride. Where low-wattage lightbulbs often left those stairwells in gloom.

He was painting a picture that could tell his readers what they were up against.

The first clues worth very much to Breslin were those that Cama was thinking about and talking about. They were the ones that pointed to the bullets and to the gun.

In Cama's mind, the gun almost certainly was in the hands of the most frightening of men: a serial killer. And the *Daily News* audience had now been so informed in Cama's own words.

The Bulldog was a gun with a short barrel and a heavy round, and it took a lot to control its power. Recoil would make the 21-ounce gun jump, and it could hurt the hand. But the killer certainly seemed to know how to handle it. The descriptions of him, though they varied widely, did include a couple of mentions that he had crouched, used a two-handed grip, and even rested his elbow on his thigh for stability.

This led, of course, to theories as to his training and background. A soldier, a cop.

Like many of the physical descriptions, almost everything explored would turn out at least partially inaccurate. Slowly these things would be ruled out. Breslin would explain this as he began to write after going to the crime scene and speaking with Detective Tony Cama. But that is the way of investigations. Sam himself would later say, when he had been caught, that at first he fired one-handed, and was very inaccurate. Later he would change his stance and his grip on the gun.

Breslin, it is worth noting, sometimes moved his lips as he wrote his columns. And sometimes he tried the words and phrases aloud. He was certain you moved yours as you read. The sentences were short. But they were, as they came one after another, a kind of poetry you might have read if Auden or Yeats had written for a person who drove a cab.

"He was quite a plus for the *Daily News*—to have a powerhouse like him," Oliver said. As Editor, "you're thinking constantly of what's breaking, what's going on, but Jimmy would probably be on the phone before you. He was tuned in to virtually everyone. By that, I mean, somebody could know something was going on—Jimmy would be talking to that person."

This was the reporting that the poetry conveyed. This was why, Tom Wolfe explained, there was no one better than Jimmy Breslin on deadline. He had witnessed that as long ago as 1963, when they were young stars in the firmament of the *Herald Tribune*.

"He always reminded me of three or four different-sized bowling balls stacked on top of each other," Wolfe said in an interview in his impeccable and sunny Fifth Avenue apartment.

"He was the greatest writer on deadline . . . he was about 30 feet from where I sat and there would be these bowling balls with smoke coming out of him."

Wolfe wore a white suit, of course, and diamond-patterned black socks. He was trying a new kind of black shirt, collarless, and he wanted to know if the interviewer liked it.

"Yes," the interviewer replied.

Wolfe expanded on his observations. "And he got to a point where he would go up to the City Desk and say . . . what have you got for me today, and if there was a story he thought was interesting he would take it, he won't just do a column on the story— That's the story."

Standing near the blood that had dried on a street in Queens, Breslin knew now he had that story.

When a president died, there would be pages and pages in *The New York Times*.

When a Donna or Virginia died, *The Times* could have a lot less room and the tabloid a great deal more.

Breslin and the *News* reporters knew who they wrote for, and they knew what the reader needed to know.

Already, on February 1, five full weeks earlier, *The News*, on Page Five, at the top, across the page, in fifteen paragraphs, had told its readers there was now a task force of detectives numbering fifty. That is a police number; those numbers often count cops who might or might not be doing other things, or who weren't essential to the investigation. Still, the police wanted the public to know they were making a big effort to solve several murders and shootings that could be linked.

> More than 50 detectives are investigating possible links between the mysterious murder of Christine Freund in Forest Hills, Queens early Sunday and three episodes last year—two in Queens and one in Bronx.
>
> Two young women have been killed and three were wounded, one of them seriously, in the four incidents.
>
> "We are leaning toward a connection in all these cases," said Sgt. Richard Conlon of the Queens 15th homicide zone.

They were keeping this thing calm as they could.

"In each of the cases a single gunman acting without apparent motive emerged in the early morning darkness to shoot down his unsuspecting victims." It was the same single gunman each time, police came to believe. Though in years to come, theories would emerge that others were involved.

What is interesting, looking backward more than forty-five years at this point, is that the headlines on the stories were large and black—not simply for sensationalism, although that would be true too, but because they were meant to sell papers on newsstands. Just like the title of a book was meant to be read in a bookstore by someone standing several feet from a shelf. It was graphic design, not itself sensationalism. Until Sam himself started writing, most of the prose was not breathless—far from it, it was understated and clean. At this point, no one was publicly calling this a serial killing. Not yet. But the list of victims was growing:

- Donna Lauria, dead July 29, 1976, Bronx
- Jody Valenti, wounded, same day, same car, Bronx, in front of the Lauria building
- Joanne Lomino, shot in the spine, November 27, Queens
- Donna DeMasi, shot in the neck, same car; these last two right in front of the Lomino home, Floral Park, Queens
- Christine Freund, 26, dead, Forest Hills, Queens
- John Diel, 30, same January 30 incident, superficial injuries; Diel was not struck by any of the three rounds that entered the parked car. He and Christine would have been engaged in fifteen days on Valentine's Day.

The sketches the police artists prepared convey the uncertainty of witness testimony much better than courtroom scenes in many television shows of that period. One shows a young man with Elvis-plump lips and thick curly hair, the other a square-jawed man with a part in his light-colored hair. Taken together they might help. But so far they hadn't and the investigation was not making much headway.

## SAM SPEAKS

I AM DEEPLY HURT BY YOUR CALLING
ME A WEMON HATER. I AM NOT.
BUT I AM A MONSTER
I AM THE "SON OF SAM."

And so it began on April 17, 1977. A new chapter. Two more are dead. Bullets and victims are no longer enough. Now there was this block-printed, four-page letter left in an envelope in the car where his latest two victims had been kissing when the killer found them and fired three shots through the glass of the driver's side window. Now there was another blood-splashed love. Now there was another dead brunette, and this time a dead boyfriend. And now the killer had a name: "Son of Sam." And police had a clue.

Breslin had been writing. The police had been circulating their sketches, and they had announced that the task force had expanded and was now canvassing two sections of the city—the Bronx and Queens. The best detective commanders in the department, Captain Joseph Borelli and Inspector Timothy Dowd, were in charge.

Sam had been reading.

MR. BORELLI, SIR
I DONT WANT TO KILL ANYMORE
NO SIR, NO MORE BUT I
MUST, "HONOUR THY FATHER."

At the time it was called a taunt. It certainly directly addressed the police captain. It certainly explained the twisted logic of this demon.

> I AM A LITTLE
> "BRAT"
> WHEN FATHER SAM GETS DRUNK
> HE GETS MEAN. HE BEATS HIS
> FAMILY SOMETIMES HE TIES ME
> UP TO THE BACK OF THE HOUSE.
> OTHER TIMES HE LOCKS ME
> IN THE GARAGE. SAM LOVES TO
> DRINK BLOOD
> "GO OUT AND KILL" COMMANDS
> FATHER SAM

"He wanted, he wanted the recognition," said Bill Clark, a lead detective on the case. "It wasn't just the killing itself. He wanted to get the recognition." Letter-writing and killing, that was how he would get it.

The double homicide occurred at about 3:00 A.M. Valentina Suriani and Alexander Esau were leaning into each other, kissing, in a car parked on a Bronx street paralleling the Hutchison River Parkway—that meant more privacy for the young couple, as there were houses only on one side. It meant more privacy for the killer.

> I LOVE TO HUNT. PROWLING
> THE STREETS LOOKING FOR
> FAIR GAME—TASTY MEAT

"Fair game." Clever prose, it would seem.

Suriani, 18, was hit by two slugs and died immediately. Esau, 20, hung on at Jacobi Hospital for a couple of hours, while his father,

Rudolf, kept a bedside vigil in the intensive care unit, the *Daily News* reported.

By now, the ballistic evidence was already in. All the past murders and shootings had been linked to the same gun. Serial number 212922, it would turn out.

On Tuesday, April 19, the *News* printed an article by William Federici, their matinee idol-handsome star police reporter, and Paul Meskil, a top rewrite man who had some very odd habits, including at one point the wearing of yellow leather pants with bright red suspenders.

> A handwritten note, taunting the police and warning that "I'll do it again," was left by the psychopathic .44 caliber killer in the car in which he murdered his latest victims.
>
> It was found on the front seat of the auto in which Valentina Suriani, 18, and her boyfriend, Alexander Esau, 20, were fatally wounded early Sunday a block from the girl's Bronx home.
>
> The couple had parked in front of 1878 Hutchinson River Parkway. The killer apparently leaped in front of the 1969 maroon Mercury Montego and, without warning, fired four shots through the windshield, hitting Miss Suriano once in the head and Esau three times in the head. Then the gunman tossed his previously prepared letter through the car window.
>
> Detectives said yesterday that ballistics tests indicated that the .44-caliber bullet used to shoot the couple had come from [the] . . . gun that killed three young women and wounded four others in Forest Hills and Floral Park, Queens and in the Bronx.

The demon prowling the streets was without a doubt targeting young women. Daughters were locked in as securely as if in a medieval convent.

Two young women dead in the Bronx. Two dead in Queens. One dead young tow truck driver, Esau. Two young women badly wounded; one would become a paraplegic. One young man with a plate in his head.

> I SAY GOODBYE AND
> GOODNIGHT.
> POLICE—LET ME
> HAUNT YOU WITH THESE WORDS;
> I'LL BE BACK!
> I'll BE BACK!
> TO BE INTERRPRETED
> AS BANG, BANG, BANG,
> BANG, BANG—UGH!!
> YOURS IN
> MURDER
> MR. MONSTER

His spelling wasn't much. Soon, his use of the semicolon in a second letter would be noted as pretty impressive. It seemed Sam could write. Five bangs. Five bullets. One gun. There were no longer any doubts.

Still later, with thirty years' worth of storytelling behind him, Breslin would use his gift of compression to retell the collection of the ballistic evidence prior to the shooting of Virginia Voskerichian this way:

> And all day over in Police Headquarters there was a guy hunched over a machine. And he had one slug here on a spoke and one slug here and he turned it slowly . . . He did it all day.
>
> Late in the day finally he said he had a match. You could look and see that the lines on the shells from the barrel of the gun when they were shot matched. They came from the same gun.
>
> And now you know you had trouble—you had a serial killer.

This was how Breslin wrote about crime. He likely would have had to have been in Queens, with the detective at the crime scene, and in Manhattan with a lab technician who had a bullet on a spoke with Breslin over his shoulder. Could he put in all that shoe leather in one day, and then get back to a desk to sit down and write it? If any reporter could, it would be Breslin. Even his most passionate critics—often his colleagues and cops—would not disagree. The facts? The truth? Breslin would always use the former, heavily and well, but use regularly the prerogative that came with a black-lined box that separated the columnist from news coverage to allow him to get to the latter.

Some would call this the heart of the New Journalism. Not Breslin. Breslin described it as the old journalism, saying that the only thing he and his colleague Tom Wolfe had discovered was that storytelling had been lost in journalism. Runyon. Westbrook Pegler. He identified these as prelapsarian examples. He was modest for once. What he did. What Wolfe did. What Gay Talese did. They told human stories.

"Any movement, group, poetry, program, philosophy or theory that goes under a name with "New" in it is just begging for trouble. The garbage barge of history is already full of them," Tom Wolfe wrote in *Esquire* magazine in 1972. "Nevertheless, the New Journalism was the term that caught on eventually."

# SAM'S LETTER TO BRESLIN

The tabloid war simmered with the knowledge that the killer had sent a letter taunting police. The police did not release that letter, but without a doubt, this was a sensational story. The coverage had been ramping up. Soon it was a story the *News* would come to dominate—because Berkowitz wrote a second letter and he sent it to Breslin.

Now Breslin was typing his reply. Tie undone. A black bowl of curls. Beefy black sideburns. Rat. Tat. Tat. Tat. The people around him walk on eggshells. He needs the tension. He needs it and he needs chaos. His demons. Sam's demon. They connect.

Over at the *New York Post,* they would read, and begin their campaign to get into the game. To match. To increase the fear. To add sensation. To bring the city to a boil.

Breslin was writing for the *Sunday News*. Don Singleton, the mutton chop sporting keyboard artist whose demeanor was as calm as Breslin's was volatile, on Friday had effortlessly slid his carriage back and forth with deft keystrokes and smooth shifts into reverse made by pulling the return and had alerted the readers to what was coming in that thin edition that slipped off the presses Friday nights and early Saturday mornings. The Saturday paper was an appetizer. If you were a horseplayer, a Mets fan, couldn't sleep, or stayed out late, the Final Edition slid you into Sunday. And if you had a daughter, you might have checked in on her.

The Mets fans who read the final editions were also rewarded with news of a 1-0 loss to the Philadelphia Phillies in a night game at Shea Stadium, with 20,013 in attendance. But there was no doubt about what story mattered most.

The headline on the Four Star (****) Final:

> .44 KILLER: I
>
> AM NOT ASLEEP
>
> "Don't think because you haven't heard from (me) for a while that I went to sleep. No, rather, I am still here. Like a spirit roaming the night. Thirsty, hungry, seldom stopping to rest; anxious to please Sam. I love my work. Now, the void has been filled."
>
> The letter, addressed to News columnist Jimmy Breslin, was examined in the police laboratory, and . . . handwriting analysis confirms that the letter was written by the same person who wrote the first message.
>
> In the new handwritten note the killer warns that he cannot stop himself. . . He adds that he looks forward to meeting Breslin "face to face someday or perhaps I will be blown away by cops with smoking .38's."

The killer closed his note: "I will see you at the next job. Or. should I say you will see my handiwork at the next job."

Now it was Breslin's turn for handiwork. A reply to Sam. His audience, one man. "Son of Sam." In a city of newsstands, a city on edge, the reply was as big a piece of work as Breslin had ever been given.

Here is the letter from Sam to which he would now reply:

Hello from the gutters of N.Y.C. which are filled with dog manure, vomit, stale wine, urine and blood. Hello from the sewers of N.Y.C. which swallow up these delicacies when they are washed away by the sweeper trucks. Hello from the cracks in the sidewalks of N.Y.C. and from the ants that dwell in these cracks and feed in the dried blood of the dead that has settled into the cracks. J.B., I'm just dropping you a line to let you know that I appreciate your interest in those recent and horrendous .44 killings. I also want to tell you that I read your column daily and I find it quite informative. Tell me Jim, what will you have for July twenty-ninth? You can forget about me if you like because I don't care for publicity. However you must not forget Donna Lauria and you cannot let the people forget her either. She was a very, very sweet girl but Sam's a thirsty lad and he won't let me stop killing until he gets his fill of blood. Mr. Breslin, sir, don't think that because you haven't heard from me for a while that I went to sleep. No, rather, I am still here. Like a spirit roaming the night. Thirsty, hungry, seldom stopping to rest; anxious to please Sam. I love my work. Now, the void has been filled. Perhaps we shall meet face to face someday or perhaps I will be blown away by cops with smoking .38's. Whatever, if I shall be fortunate enough to meet you I will tell you all about Sam if you like and I will introduce you to him. His name is "Sam the terrible." Not knowing what the future holds I shall say farewell and I will see you at the next job. Or should I say you will see my handiwork at the next job? Remember Ms. Lauria. Thank you. In their blood and from the gutter "Sam's creation" .44 Here are some names to help you along. Forward them to the inspector for use by N.C.I.C: "The Duke of Death" "The Wicked King Wicker" "The Twenty Two Disciples of Hell" "John 'Wheaties' – Rapist and Suffocator of Young Girls. PS: Please inform all the detectives working the slaying to remain. P.S: JB, Please inform all the detectives working the case that I wish them the best of luck. "Keep 'em digging, drive on, think positive, get off your butts, knock on coffins, etc." Upon my capture I promise to buy all the guys working the case a new pair of shoes if I can get up the money. Son of Sam

One man who read J.B.'s work. Who called him Jim. Who reminded him that soon it would be a year since he killed Donna Lauria, the first brunette gunned down. Who was, it would seem, himself not a bad writer at all. Not bad at all.

The letter had come into the paper several days earlier. According to Sam Roberts, it came in to Breslin's secretary, Ann Marie Caggiano. She brought it to the City Desk.

"I was holding it in my hands," Roberts, the City Editor and the youngest senior editor at the paper, said. He noted that one could write a book on the letter itself.

The paper alerted Breslin. A copy was delivered to his home in Queens. According to his son, Kevin Breslin, his father had sent him to the office to pick it up and then rush it back home.

"Jimmy was genuinely scared. I know for his family because it was getting a little too close to home," Roberts said. When a serial killer makes you his pen pal, there is every reason for concern. He could be—and at one point, in Breslin's case, might have been—watching your house.

Meanwhile, there was a discussion among the senior editors about whether they should rush the letter and a column by Breslin into the paper right away or alert the authorities. In the end, the *Daily News* turned the letter over to the New York Police Department.

"Then the cops came to examine it. They had to come twice to do elimination prints on it," Roberts recalled. Prints determined to come from the killer—ones that matched the prints on the earlier letter to Captain Joseph Borelli, which the killer had dropped onto the seat of the car of two of his Bronx victims—were obtained. They would be useful forensically; they could be useful as evidence after the killer was caught; but they could only immediately be useful if they matched a set on file with authorities. That was not to be the case.

Frank McLaughlin, who until recently had been a reporter at the *News,* was now the Deputy Commissioner for Public Information at the New York Police Department.

"They gave us at least a day," he said. "But they wanted us to tell them that we thought the letter was genuine right before they published it, and we did tell them the letter was genuine because the fingerprint was on it. The print on the letter matched the fingerprint that came off the one in the car in the Bronx."

"The police thought publishing it might somehow help," Roberts said. And, he acknowledged, it would sell papers.

At the beginning of the column Breslin wrote, he recounts his own reaction when he first examined it.

*"He's a pretty good writer," somebody at the table said. "Yes, he is," I said. The letter was from the person who calls himself 'Son of Sam.'"*

Unlike most of his work for the *News*, Breslin had more than a day, not hours, to think about how he would tell the story. When he first wrote about crimes large and small for the news reader and earlier in life when he wrote for the sports reader, his work was informed by the requirements of immediacy and scores and results. He now used the extra time well and put all of that accumulated skill to work, creating that immediacy and the same human frame that captured a pitcher failing to twist himself backward on his mound fast enough to stop a double play, or a jockey cheating a horse by standing in the stirrups, to capture the emotion of something far more important:

> Donna Lauria was the only victim mentioned by the killer in this letter, which was sent to me at my newspaper in New York, the Daily News. So yesterday, I took the letter up to the fourth-floor apartment of Donna Lauria's parents and I sat over coffee and read the letter again and talked to the Laurias about it.

You can feel the silent reverence in those footsteps. You can feel him watch the pain form and reform on the faces. If you were to read all of the Facebook encomiums posted on his death, you would find he had educated so many younger men and women on which stairs to climb and how to climb them in order to achieve this kind of reporting. The story, he explained, was always at the top of the stairs. When you find it, tell it. And in this case, the reader would feel the Laurias grow old.

In this case, Rose Lauria, the victim's mother, now growing old, gave an insight as good as any and better than most of the theories circulating through the city and among the police detectives:

> We took out the page that mentioned her daughter and gave Rose Lauria the rest. Her large expressive brown eyes become cold . . . On the wall behind her was a picture of her daughter, a lovely brown-haired girl with the mother's features . . . "He's probably a very brilliant man, boy, whatever he is," she said.
>
> "His brain functions the opposite way."

The next part of the column tells a different part of the story of Breslin. Here he is the tabloid showman, even while writing about great grief and pain, about fear stalking the city itself. He inserts himself into the column in a way that he had rarely done in the past. He had long played the buffoon and the bully. He had been an arrogant, difficult, and entitled man-child. He wrote bullying or cajoling memos to his editors. He bragged about his movie money. He made threats to his competitors. And every day he lobbed shattering telephone calls into the otherwise thoughtful early mornings of his editors' lives. He would not learn to drive. He would not do his expenses. Everyone around him was a bit player in the drama of his life.

Here, it seems, he was at a pivot point. With Son of Sam, Breslin knew he was ready to become even bigger, to become larger than life to an audience of millions. Larger than life to radio listeners, readers of the print ads, TV viewers and to New Yorkers who watched as the black *Daily News* delivery trucks raced by with bundles of wire-tied papers inside the panels that bore posters with their own larger-than-life images of Breslin.

> The only way for the killer to leave this special torment is to give himself up to me, if he trusts me, or to the police . . . If he wants any further contact, all he has to do is call or write me at *The Daily News*. It's simple to get me. The only people I don't answer are bill collectors. The time to do it, however, is now. We are too close to the July 29 that the killer mentions in his letter. It is the first anniversary of the death of Donna Lauria.

Now when he sat disheveled on a corner barstool, drinking too much, in the kind of place where he years earlier captured the arrival of the first television in a Queens, New York, bar, he could look up and marvel at something he truly loved: his own face on the electronic barroom wall. He had become, if not famous, a celebrity.

They were close, he noted, to July 29. "It is the first anniversary of the death of Donna Lauria," he wrote. And with that sentence, you get the frame for how the tabloids now would be covering the Son of Sam.

Sam provided the tabloids a basis for massive sensationalism and the hope of greater sales. Although the editors of the *News* would by now have half-convinced themselves that the massive coverage was simply a public service, the headlines were: WANTED; COPS: .44 KILLER "IS TAUNTING US"; *Breslin to .44 Killer:* GIVE UP! IT'S THE ONLY WAY OUT

Breslin, tormented by the story, by the always-looming deadline, by his own being, would run around the *News* yelling "Fuck, Fuck, Fuck," his friend, the writer Pete Hamill, recalled. He would go desk to desk chiding reporters, "He writes better than you," and "If we had [Sam], we wouldn't need you." Always the outbursts. Always the creative genius married to the miserable man.

> These days, every day is the worst day in Jimmy Breslin's life. So today is no exception. If anything, it is worse than the worst. It is Monday, June 27, the day after Son of Sam's attack on a young couple with a .44-caliber Bulldog revolver on a dark street in the borough of Queens, New York City.
>
> Breslin thumps into his seventh-floor office at the Daily News at 10:30 A.M. His blue-striped tie is undone and his white collar is open. He is very hung over, and his face looks like it was used to catch fly balls the previous night.

Denis Hamill, the younger brother of Jimmy's good friend Pete Hamill, wrote this for *MORE* magazine. You can feel all the sweat, and hard work, and misery and insecurity, that went into the making of the poetry.

> The phone rings and Breslin snatches it up.
>
> "Yeah." Breslin says. "No, I'm the copyboy. What can I do for you? Oh, you saw the killer in your dream, hah? Good, go back to sleep and ask him his name and address and call me back later I'm trying to make a living here and I'm just about doing it, guhbye." Slam . . .
>
> Another call.
>
> "She says it has to be an Armenian because of the way he crosses his t's."

Another.

"He says it has to be a shipping clerk."

This goes on for three hours . . . the callers have told Breslin that Son of Sam must be a state trooper named Sampson, a Jew because of the way he spells Beelzebub, a parochial schoolteacher who must have tried to put the make on one of the female students but was rejected, someone who works in a car wash where he spots all the victims, a priest, a rabbi, and a sewer worker . . .

"I'm tellin' you it's nuts," he says. "The biggest story in town is not Son of Sam himself. It's the fuckin' unanimous insanity of the fuckin' general populace. The whole town, all the citizens, have gone fuckin' nuts. I'm tellin' you. And every one of them prefaces the call with the same phrase: 'This isn't a kook or a crank call, but I think I know who he is . . . And the worst part is that any one of them could be right so I just pass the information to the cops. I must send a full box of letters and phone messages over to homicide every week."

Hamill might have been the younger brother of a good novelist and a dashing man about town who dated Jackie Onassis and Shirley MacLaine, but he lived in no shadow and would soon be writing his own City Column.

Breslin, in one of his many columns on the killer, wrote: "He's the only person I know who understands the proper use of the semicolon."

To which a writer friend of Breslin's recently remarked: "Jimmy doesn't have to understand the proper use of the semicolon. He writes simple declarative sentences. He learned how to write them from studying his collection agency letters."

"One of the cops on the case called me up and said to me that he writes better than most guys on the police force," Breslin said. "I said,

> 'Fuck the police force, he writes better than most of the reporters in the city.'"

Hamill's firsthand observations, recorded as the events were unfolding, have an immediacy all their own, and insights that you cannot get even if you use a telescope to look back at the past.

> He finally rolls a sheet of paper into his Olympia typewriter (He doesn't use an Olivetti like it says in the ads.) This is how Jimmy Breslin types: BAM. SLAM, BANG, BANG. BANG. KABOOM. BANG, SLAM. And then tears what he has written out of the machine, balls it, flings it at the glass partition and walks out of his office. "It's all over," Breslin yells. "I'm old. I'm fat. I'm over the hill, nobody reads the shit I write. I belong in pajamas watchin' The Price Is Right all afternoon, eatin' Raisinettes, and sluggin' some kind of diet soda shit. I gotta give up drinkin'. Today. When I went home last night, they had the house locked up like the fuckin' Bastille. Son of Sam would need a tank to get in there. I banged and banged on the door but none of the kids or my wife would answer the door. It was like a reprieve because I had to stagger up the block to the saloon to make the phone call to get into the house. I didn't make the call until an hour and a half after I got into the bar."
>
> He yanks the bifocals off the bridge of his nose and walks defiantly back to his typewriter. He sits down and rolls the paper into the machine again. He clamps the glasses onto the peak of his nose again and begins to write. Slam. Bang. Boom . . . when he writes he actually speaks the story aloud like this:
>
> "The detective walked down the street . . . nah. fuck it," he says as he backspaces and x's out the last word. "Make it the avenue, it makes it sound bigger, right? Yeah, avenue. The detective walked down the avenue. That's better."

This is what it is like in a smoke-filled, glass-walled cage, pacing and pounding and trying to ignore the knowledge that the clock in the oak case down in the center of the city room cannot wait. He will make it wait. He wants every word right. Or as good as he can get them in the time he has left. Denis Hamill describes what it is like to watch a fragile ego ballooning.

> Deadline at the *News* for the columnists is 4 P.M. It is 3:30, and Breslin is on take five of his eight-page story. A copyboy is sent in to pester Breslin for copy.
>
> "Please, hah, it's the worst day of my life," Breslin tells the copyboy. "Get me two Sankas and I'll love you for a son. I'll buy you a drink." Breslin pulls out a pocketful of change and dumps it on the table. "There, that's the whole bankroll. Big-shot reporter and all I got is change. Go next door and get greens off Pete Hamill. He's got all the money. I don't make any money. I got six kids and a wife and take car service everywhere so I'm broke. And bring me in one of those green vouchers for the mad money. Tell Sam Roberts I need money and tell him it's the worst day of my entire life."
>
> Breslin is punishing the typewriter now, trying to put his fingers through the keys. The paper he is typing on is punctured with holes where the o's should be.
>
> When the copyboy returns with the two Sankas he tells Breslin that Sam Roberts said he can't get a money voucher until the column is in . . .
>
> He finally gets the copy in at 5:05 P.M. Now he wants his voucher for money from Sam Roberts. When Breslin learns that the cashier is gone for the day he goes berserk. Charging through the city room, he overturns chairs, kicks waste baskets, throws papers in the air, shouts obscenities, and threatens to blow up the building.
>
> Roberts, half amused, begins a frantic collection to calm Breslin down. Once Breslin gets his money he starts for the Exit.

You can see why Son of Sam picked this guy. You can see why Sam knew they understood each other. You can see how the story infected the city and how Breslin's paper had begun to use it to drive circulation and take circulation away from its rival, the *New York Post*.

Looking back at when he was young and a City Editor, Sam Roberts on his 75th birthday offered: "Well, we unabashedly milked that story for everything it was worth now . . . but eventually we're running out of things to do. We even ran the postmark on the letter to say, you know, does anyone recognize this post? We were going to run the gum on the envelope. If we could have, you know—uh, I mean, this was shameless after a point. Oh, but we had the story, we owned the story."

That is much of what you need to know about the tabloid wars. One paper—the *New York Daily News*—owned the story and combined two things that were key to the blue-collar tabloid's credo: inform and entertain. To sell newspapers. That could be read and could inform in the space of a subway ride.

Then there was the other paper, the *New York Post*. It had just undergone a gender change from the liberal left, socially conscious paper run by Dorothy Schiff with a history going back, mostly proudly, to Alexander Hamilton, to a paper now in the hands of Rupert Murdoch, an arriviste who was a brilliant proprietor and who knew one thing: Win. And a second thing: how to make a newspaper sing. And a third thing: side with the powerful.

He had learned his craft in Australia, a place few in New York knew much about. In turn, he did not have any connection to the city, its audience, or what they cared about. What he cared about was power. Stories in the front of the paper served power. Soon pictures of women sunbathing also would grace its pages. Those who worked at the *Post* during the period after the change affectionately called it a comic book. The mantra was, "There is one side to every story and if we like you, we leave you out." It is easy now to see this as prophetic of the divisive world that Murdoch's Fox fueled several decades later.

But at that moment, Murdoch was getting beat. He called on Steve Dunleavy. Straight from the docks of Sydney, not known for any intake of solid food, wearing leather and his black hair swept back from a pompadour wave to a ducktail. If Joseph Conrad had scripted their lives, Dunleavy, forever loyal to "The Boss," was Murdoch's Secret Sharer. Murdoch conquered the boardrooms, Steve the streets. Each had attained a kind of wisdom. And each fought, even as they aged, as ruthlessly as when they were young.

A testament to Murdoch's loyalty to Steve—just one, there are several at least—came at the Aussie's memorial service. It was held in the basement of a large Irish-themed bar off Times Square. Murdoch was there. So were his empire's editors from around the globe. So were the reporters, editors, cops, and flacks who had worked with Steve. No grand valediction by Murdoch. A short, "Steve was a good guy," he muttered into the mike, then Murdoch receded. And he stayed. Through the night. With the rest of his hacks.

Dunleavy pulled every cheap trick he had—and he had plenty—out of his sleeve, from behind his back, wherever he hid them. The best came later, well after Berkowitz claimed his final victim, Stacy Moskowitz. But until then he never beat the *News*, its reporters or Breslin. They continued to own the story.

In the case of Stacy Moskowitz, Dunleavy recalled in an interview, he did, however, get to the family of the victim before Breslin. But he was unlucky. It was a Sunday morning. The next editions of his newspaper would not be until the following afternoon, when the *Post*, which was an afternoon newspaper, next appeared—well after Breslin's morning newspaper.

"And I was saying, 'My God! Dear me!'" He knew what he had. "But Jimmy Breslin turns up. Now he did what all of the other reporters should have done. He just walks in, says, 'How's it goin'.' And he got a story and it appeared before mine."

By the time Breslin got there, Dunleavy recalled, there were about "fifteen to twenty people" from the family of Moskowitz and her boyfriend, Robert Violante, gathered in an area of the hospital that the police and hospital security had cordoned off for the families. And the reporters were all waiting on the other side of the cordon. Such pack mentality was mystifying to Steve.

"And up till that time I was the only reporter there. Now, Jimmy comes in. He walks right past the cordon," and they have a Monday morning story. "So, I had all this tremendous stuff but Breslin would appear first. I mean, I wished I could have appeared first because I had so much, much, much more than Jimmy had."

## SAM SLEEPS

The 29th of July came, and then it went. To call it or the days that came between the letter and the anniversary of Donna Lauria's murder uneventful was to be very selective.

Sam Roberts, the 28-year-old, energetic, needing-little-sleep City Editor—there should be no old ones—years later, in a piece published July 1, 1999, in *The New York Times*, summed up that Summer of Sam:

> In the summer of 1977, New York lost its mind. A mountain climber named George Willig scaled the World Trade Center. Terrorist bombs linked to Puerto Rican nationalists exploded at Manhattan office buildings and department stores. The temperature hit 104 degrees, nearly breaking the record high. A Consolidated Edison blackout triggered looting that resulted in more than 3,000 arrests. Elvis Presley died. Studio 54 opened. The Bronx's most dysfunctional family, the Yankees, revived their legendary World Series rivalry against the Dodgers. Abe Beame was struggling to avoid being the first elected mayor in more than half a century to be defeated for a second term. And, oh yes, a psychopathic serial killer armed with a .44-caliber revolver and dubbed Son of Sam held New York hostage as no crime figure had done in the decades since a disgruntled former Con Ed worker, George Metesky, periodically vented his rage as the folkloric Mad Bomber.

But he did not strike on July 29. The anniversary came and went.

The killing came on July 31. And this time the victim—and she would turn out to be the last victim—was blonde: Stacy Moskowitz, 20.

She had been watching the moon over Gravesend Bay in Brooklyn, where the view is unobstructed, police said, with her boyfriend Robert Violante, also 20.

He lost the sight in one eye. She was shot in the head and neck and lingered a little while in critical condition before she expired on August 1.

Between killed and wounded, the tally was thirteen for Berkowitz and his demons. Six were dead. But Stacy Moskowitz was to be his last victim. Berkowitz had used his own car. He had gotten a parking ticket, and now it would lead detectives to his Yonkers home. The world would now learn that Son of Sam was a postal worker. The details of a dog's demonic bark, of a neighbor named Sam, of the signs of madness that painted his apartment, all that would now come out. And David Berkowitz would come out in handcuffs, smirking.

Bill Clark, who was the lead detective on the case, said that although the department told the public there was a task force of fifty hunting Sam, in reality, there were a handful of key detectives on the case: six, he recalled. In an interview for this book, he explained how the arrest of Berkowitz actually happened. Detail after detail.

"The last shooting . . . He went around, parked his car, and fired, shot the two of them. He came back, got in the car, drove away. I started doing a canvass.

"The next day, the woman in this one house says, uh, you know, this guy, he was parked right in front here. He had, he got, a parking ticket. Nobody at that point is looking.

"Now I go back to her, I said, 'you sure?' She said, 'Yeah, I'm sure you gave a summons out.'"

Clark checked with everyone in the Police Department and even in the Sanitation Department and of course the parking enforcement agents, who might have given a summons out. "No record.

"I go back and talk to her again the next day she says, listen, when the shooting happened, she said, my boyfriend came to the house to see what happened.

"'And I told him, don't park there because I saw a car get a summons there earlier when this happened.' She said, 'I know it.'"

Clark again calls the cop who had been assigned to that sector and again he gets a denial. But the woman, "She's adamant, you know," Clark said.

"This cop was an Italian American who was on Staten Island. So, I got an Italian American detective to call this guy in Staten Island and tell him, listen, nobody's looking to hurt you if you forgot to turn the summons, it was a busy night.

"He gives it up. We go to his locker, get the summons up, check it. David Berkowitz, 35 Pine Street, Yonkers."

But even before that arrest on August 10, the shamelessness of a tabloid war was in high gear. In the Sunday, August 7, editions, the *News* produced a pullout centerfold section reprising Breslin's work:

> No story in recent years has touched a deeper nerve among New Yorkers than the murderous saga of the Son of Sam. And no writer has been closer to that story than News columnist Jimmy Breslin.
>
> From the moment last winter when police discovered a pattern . . . Breslin has been on the job.
>
> He has reported the horror and the tragedy, and the hard, slogging work of the detectives. And when the killer eventually decided to speak from his personal darkness, he wrote a letter to Breslin.

> [With that letter] . . . the name immediately joined those of Jack the Ripper and the Boston Strangler in the gallery of big city monsters. Today, The News reprints the major pieces . . . They provide a chilling, comprehensive narrative of the events that have brought fear to the streets of an entire city.

It was a perfect segue.

On August 10, the spree was over and soon the fear on the streets would dissipate. One version of Breslin's August 11 column on Page One began:

> "Who is Sam," the man was asked?
>
> "You know Sam," he said.
>
> "I don't know him," the detective said.
>
> "Sure you do," the man said.
>
> "Gee, I'm sorry but I don't," the detective said.
>
> "Sam can do anything," the man said. His eyes started to water and his chest heaved as if he were about to cry.
>
> Somebody shut the door and now there was no way to listen anymore. Inside the room, the short, chunky guy, with the pleasant young face, kept talking. His name was David Berkowitz and he told cops he was the .44 killer who used the name Son of Sam.
>
> Now, a detective came out into the hall and walked down to the end.
>
> "Who was Sam?" he was asked.
>
> "Berkowitz says he's a dog. The dog lives in the house behind this guy. He says the dog commands him. That's the word he used. Commands him. He says he understands the dog. The dog commands him to kill.
>
> "To hell with the dog," says the detective. "Do you know what he was going to do tonight? He was going to Riverdale first and get somebody. Then he was going to drive out to Hampton Bays to a discotheque there . . ."

A discotheque where he intended to commit mass murder.

This time, he was armed with a .45 caliber weapon that looked like a submachine gun—the assault rifle of the time—and, he said, he had planned to go out in a blaze of glory. This kind of killing lends itself to thoughts of Columbine, Virginia Tech, Sandy Hook, Uvalde, Buffalo, St. Louis, Lewiston, it seems. Lone gunmen. Mass casualties. But not the night stalking of Sam and his Bulldog gun, the subsonic thud of its rounds and the knowledge that he was out there. Somewhere. It would have earned David Berkowitz the notoriety of the mass killer.

Detective Bill Clark had been relentless. He had made a wrong guess or two along the way but stuck with it to the end. He liked to point out that hard work did create its own luck. But he did not admit to being the unnamed detective in Breslin's column. However, in walking through the case more than forty-five years later, and after a long and successful second career working with the creator of *Hill Street Blues*, Steven Bochco, in Hollywood, he certainly recalled his meeting with David Berkowitz. He recounted his interview of the suspect this way:

"So, I go right next to him and cross the little table from him, and I start talking to him. And he took me to every one of the shootings and exactly how and why and everything, you know, and he was talking like, he would be talking about making dinner, you know? So, I was the only one that ever got to talk to him [take a statement from him]. Nobody was ever allowed before or after that to talk to him. But he was talking about these shootings as if he were talking about, as I say, just a job, you know, nothin'."

Berkowitz explained to Clark "that it had started out because he started understanding this dog that was yelling for blood. Yeah. So, he just started driving around and he told me like the, one of the first shootings, 'I think it was two girls in the car.'

"'Yeah. Donna Lauria,' I said. He said, 'You know, I passed this car and I saw the two girls.' And he says, 'I went around the block,' and he says, 'I saw a parking space.' He says, 'That was my sign. I knew this was it.' So, he parked, he shot the both of them, then he got back in the car and drove off. I mean, that's the mentality, you know? Not personal."

Another version of Breslin's column reports it like this:

> So now I say to him, "Let's talk. You know, you're a likable guy." He sat there and he said, "Likable." He kind of mused . . . I said to him, "You liked Donna Lauria. Why?"
>
> When I asked him that he said, "She's a very nice girl." I said, "Do you know her?" He said. "No." I said, "How do you know that she's a nice girl?" And he said to me, "I can tell a nice girl. I only shoot pretty girls."

The detective in the column told Breslin he thought he was taking a very good statement, one that was legitimate—the suspect had been read his rights. One that would be very good in court. Then the detective realized, "The guy is never going to be in court. They're arraigning him today and they'll put him into Kings County [hospital] for mental observation and that'll do it. They'll find this guy to be completely out of it. He lives in a couple of worlds . . . He has the world in the room with you and then he has this world of voices. No, I'll tell you. I'll never see him again in my life."

Bill Clark says plenty of people stopped by to talk with Berkowitz but he was the first, the last, and the only one to take a statement from Son of Sam.

It was over for Sam, but for Breslin and Dunleavy the final chapter had not yet begun. Here, according to a man who helped supply that chapter, the tabloid wars led to behavior that was beyond a disservice. It could be called reprehensible as well as sensationalizing. Here the other part of Breslin emerged: like Sam, he needed to be a big shot. Rat-a-tat-tat. The keyboard was his weapon. The victims, this time, were his and Dunleavy's.

Desperate. Conniving. In need of a front page. Dunleavy didn't walk so much as he flaunted, and minced, and conducted his sales pitch, wagging his finger in the air in a way that somehow felt decadent and charming. Brilliantly downmarket, he got his sustenance largely from Guinness. He went to Morty Matz, a great public relations man, to ask for help. Matz, who represented the Corrections Officers union, asked one of their number to visit Berkowitz in the Kings County maximum security hospital ward in Brooklyn, where he was being held, and ask him to write a letter to Dunleavy. He was 99 years old in 2023 when he finally revealed his role.

"I then went about trying to get a letter for Steve Dunleavy because I had the Correction Officers Benevolent Association for many years and I knew everybody . . . I contacted them there and they got a letter for Dunleavy."

It was prosaic and demon-free, a letter that suggested a medicated inmate, or a man whose demons were resting. But it was finally a win for Murdoch. How it came about has never before been reported.

"So then Jimmy wanted a letter," Matz said, and he got it for him. He doesn't recall how exactly that message got to him—whether Breslin called direct, which Matz thought was probably unlikely, or someone else made the call. Breslin got his letter.

> Dear Mr. Breslin, it has come to my attention that you wish to speak with me. Well, all you have to do is come to my home at Kings County Hospital at this time I am unable to visit you.

Again: Prosaic stuff.

"I am quite disgusted with how the press has been spreading lies," Berkowitz wrote. "This is like a circus event with clowns and criminals. Please bring a beer when you come." He had a sense of humor, it seemed, and an awareness of what he had created.

The dog, certainly, was no longer in charge. Matz, Dunleavy, and Breslin were.

The staid hold-up-the-coffee-table *New Yorker* made the mistake of biting the dog. Breslin, the big dog, bit back.

### THE *NEW YORKER* LOOKS FOR SAM ON A DEAD-END STREET

> In the *New Yorker*'s July 25 report on the blackout, for example, the magazine devoted one page to Diana Vreeland (a French-American fashion columnist who died in 1989 having made the Best Dressed List Hall of Fame) having dinner in Greenwich Village and expounding on blackouts: "In Paris when I opened my desk at the Crillon (a five-star Paris hotel that in 2022 prices had some cheaper rooms at around $2,000) it was all candles." The *New Yorker* did not print a line about Bushwick where so much of our city fell apart.

The *New Yorker* had written at length on the sins of the tabloids, taking particular umbrage at Breslin's July 28 column that wondered if, as Son of Sam alluded in his letter to Breslin, he would strike on the next day, the day when Sam killed Donna Lauria: "Journalism schools could use these paragraphs as examples of journalistic irresponsibility."

Breslin's simple answer was not the "fuck you, fuck you" bluster he would have used at one of the bars he frequented. Instead, he wrote:

> In the world of the *New Yorker* writer . . . everybody [is] sitting around talking about this Son of Sam stories and these grubby people on

tabloids—tabloids!—who receive letters from killers. Letters they reveal to the public! God, isn't there one of us left to retain some taste?

The *New Yorker*'s grasp of the city's realities was as wan as its grasp of The New Journalism was when the magazine attacked Tom Wolfe in the 1960s and Breslin sprang to his *Herald Tribune* colleague's defense when he called the fabled editor of that magazine, William Shawn, to a bar. When Shawn arrived, Breslin told him what he could do to stop Wolfe from eviscerating the magazine.

"Burn it down," Breslin bellowed.

Wolfe's work, which he had thought might be met with a sense of humor by the literati, did not. But it did run in the *Trib*, where it entertained a few hundred thousand readers.

Now summer waned, any trial was far away, and the frenzy began to die down.

By December 5, Breslin had written dozens of other columns—on Jimmy Carter and his tightfisted response to the city of New York's finances, on Mayor Abe Beame's political obituary after one term of trying to rein in the city's debt and crime, and on the very real question of whether the city was spinning out of control. While Sam had been the Demon, the serial killer who both captured and captivated, haunted and hunted, Breslin and the city, Sam was not all-consuming. Breslin had his eyes wide open and his heart wide open too, in order to alert and inform his readers to the insidiousness enveloping New York.

One of those columns, "Dies the Victim, Dies the City," captured the cheapness of life in the death of one young man, by a shot to the back of the head from a killer who had demanded and already had received his winter coat. A cold murderer. A cold murder. The young victim's two friends ran away as fast as they could. No shots followed. The killer already had his coat and his victim. If you had to ask Breslin which was the more important story to him, then the day you asked, the time of day you asked, and the mood he was working himself up into when you asked might determine your answer. But if you read the bulk of his work, the determination is easy to make. It is there: the Victim. The City. The Nation. That was important. Celebrity. That was fun. And it paid the bills for six children, a house, a heavy drinking habit, cigars and good suits.

And it would, he knew, bring in more stories.

Dunleavy and the *Post* put the coda on that frenzy when they smuggled a camera in and photographed Berkowitz sleeping on his prison cot. "Sam Sleeps," read the caption.

"And then all hell broke loose," Morty Matz said. "Obviously he (Dunleavy) screwed it up for everybody. Somehow, he knew to get out of town real quick and he got Murdoch to send them to Cuba for thirty days."

And Sam—well, years later he had a little more to say.

# SAM WRITES

David Berkowitz #78-A-1976
Shawangunk Correctional Facility
P.O. Box
Wallkill, NY 12589-0700
March 28, 2023

Dear Mr. Esposito:

Sam began, his punctuation as good as ever.

"I have two letters from you. I apologize for being slow in replying. I am familiar with you from the media and I know you have impressive credentials.

You mentioned writing a book about the late Jimmy Breslin. At the time of the crimes I believe I was not in my full right mind. It took years for me to come to terms with this and to stop living in denial of my then mental state. For me it has been a long and winding road.

Point being, looking back I don't even know why I reach [sic] out to Mr. Breslin in the first place. Today I vaguely remember him or any of his many stories. I don't even remember much of anything that he write [sic] concerning the Son of Sam case.

> I do however have continual remorse and sorrow over what transpired in 1976-77. God knows that if I could go back in time and change the course of history, I would. We know this is not possible, but I do continue to pray for the families of those who lost a loved one, and those who were wounded.

The letter is neatly typed as well as cogent. He goes on to decline the offer of a visit and an interview.

> I do not wish to be interviewed and I wish to decline your offer to visit. This is not in any way rejection. I simply cannot deal with this anymore and I remember so very little of those days.

The letter was signed in blue ink in a neat hand, "David" followed by the typed full name: David Berkowitz.

It is considerably different, after more than forty-five years in prison, than his first letters. Now he was contrite. When he was caught, he smirked.

"If you ever noticed when they were bringing him outta police headquarters, the night he was arrested, the look of happiness in his face," Bill Clark said. "He was longing for the day that he would get the recognition of being the Son of Sam. It wasn't just the killing itself. I really believe that one day he wanted to get the recognition."

# BECOMING JIMMY BRESLIN

Four women were essential to Jimmy Breslin throughout his life. These were the women who protected him, stood by him in his insecurity, tolerated his bellowing and self-involvement, raised his children, and shaped who he became and who he could be—and helped him in his final infirmity.

His mother, Frances, was the first. His wife, Rosemary, was the second. His patron, Joan Whitney Payson, was the third. His wife following his widowerhood, Ronnie Eldridge, was the fourth.

They were co-authors of his public personae as well as at least one of his private selves.

His mother, Frances, was a heavy drinker, as Jimmy would become, and a schoolteacher at Grover Cleveland High School in Queens. Later she became a welfare worker in East Harlem. There was so little money after her husband, the first James Earle Breslin, abandoned her and her son—who she called Jay, not Jimmy and certainly not James—and her daughter, Deirdre, that she bicycled to work. This was not yet in fashion.

"I think Jimmy, because he was raised by women [Frances and his aunt] actually had the better of us," said Pete Hamill. The writer, who was closer to Breslin than almost anyone, recalled that "she couldn't afford even the subways.

"She was one of these people that the welfare department had to check to see if you were really secretly wealthy, meaning—did you have a phone."

Breslin, late in life, claimed that her welfare job was helpful to his work.

"She was head of the East Harlem office, which was a good place to be because [it had] all the mobsters that I was to grow up with and, you know, write [about]," Breslin said in a previously unpublished interview with Martin Dunn and Marie McGovern, formerly of the *News*, who recorded it for a TV series set in the era in which the sun had begun to sink beyond the horizons of a popular press. They kindly shared it.

Breslin loved his mother but there were, as with her son and his multiple selves, layers to her. She could be distant and unapproachable.

"[She was] the nightmare in the family, 'Fran', never Grandma Fran," recalled Kevin's twin brother, James Breslin. "She refused to be acknowledged as that. She would come over and ask to see her son Jay. Kevin would ask her why she calls him Jay when his name is Jimmy. She would just sit with an icy grin. Kevin thought she was the devil. She refused to talk to Jimmy's wife, Rosemary. Fran resented Rosemary the Italian wife." She felt, her son said, that Jimmy Breslin had married beneath his station.

In fact, "the former Rosemary Dattolico," as Breslin characterized her in some of his work, was an amazingly tolerant and loyal wife, mother, editor, expense account auditor and partner in crime. The former Rosemary Dattolico kept a watchful eye on everything from their six children—James and Kevin (twins), Rosemary, Patrick, Kelly and Christopher—to the disaster Jimmy attempted to make of the family finances. In the early years the milkman had to be convinced to deliver when his bills had not been paid, the grocer had to be convinced to provide credit, the electric company had to be contacted before power was turned off because the bills had not been paid; many other bill collectors had to be fended off.

Jimmy's bluster would not work, she knew. These tasks fell to her. In this chaos, he demanded silence, and he wrote. As his wife, she was on overwatch from December 26, 1954, until her death on June 9, 1981. She was his great love and she would come to coauthor the path to his destiny as a chronicler of crimes great and small.

"I think Rosemary felt real responsibility for Jimmy," Pete Hamill said. "She knew that behind the tough guy bullshit façade there was a wounded guy living there and she did what she could do to ease the pain—mostly laughter. Mostly jokes."

Rosemary, Hamill said, was "a very caring human being, she had a sense of irony, she could make jokes based on the absurdities of life, you know? But she had a real sense of responsibility for her life—she had all those kids. She had to take care of them. I'm sure Jimmy was useless in the great tradition of his own father."

Michael Daly, 71 in 2022 when he was interviewed, was Jimmy Breslin's young protégé, and his cellmate on columnist row at the *News* in the late 1970s. He has captured much of the art that was in Breslin's newspaper work and has used it to tell his own stories with his own diction, in his own style. He describes his own mother, Mary, and Rosemary attempting to put Breslin's expenses in order: "My mother and Rosemary the elder sat down at the kitchen table and they aged paper with cigarette ashes and coffee stains. And they created all these receipts. They had a little cottage industry of creating receipts."

Later, great illness would strike Rosemary: breast cancer.

"Seven or eight years. It was a pretty long run, and it was harrowing," Kevin Breslin recalled.

Now Jimmy Breslin would again face great loss—not the boy's loss of his father, but a sensitive man's loss of his wife, and with it the loss of the order she brought. For all his posturing, all his difficulty, he loved Rosemary and was not sure how to live and raise a family and write, without her.

"My father in his worst days, screaming and yelling and bucking and going to a hotel to write, saying fuck this, I don't give a fuck," Kevin Breslin explained. "He was a bombastic man. Then you'd be in the kitchen, they'd be hugging each other and was always saying, 'Remember this is how much I love, I love your mother.'

"She brought out a whole different side to him. And in the kitchen he would say, 'Watch this, little boy. Dad loves Mommy.'

"Thank God, you know, because the joint was wild. She was him; he was her. It's like, it didn't matter if the world's caving in. They were like a team. He'd be inside pounding. She'd be right there calling it into the desk.

"But he maintained the highest level of work throughout her illness, and that would be more pressure than most people can handle. Six kids, all not even teenagers. Not only did he maintain the highest level of work, he proved that he could be the caring, thoughtful husband."

Breslin was a person whose hunger, ambition, and career drove him from crisis to crisis and he always met them head on. Now this flawed man proved he could rise above himself when the greatest personal crisis struck.

Rosemary died at Lenox Hill Hospital on June 9, 1981. She was fifty years old.

Breslin had always written of her with affection. The last column would be a love sonnet.

> She ran my life and those of her children almost totally. She leaves us with a tradition of decency that we must attempt to carry on. Her strength was such that even if those of us here today stumble now and then, I think the Rosemary Dattolico line of decency will reveal itself time after time in whatever generations there are to come.

In Breslin's bifold life, there next was Ronnie Eldridge, political operative, New York City councilwoman and Upper West Sider. They married on September 12, 1982, and she took him from the low-rise borough of his birth to the rarified precincts of Manhattan's Upper West Side, in essence from the blue-collared shadows of places like Aqueduct racetrack and the sticky summer excitement of Coney Island's Luna Park Cyclone roller coaster to the shadows of famous buildings like The Dakota and the shade of Central Park. The 20-block radius of her liberal-left life. By the 1990s, he described getting his exercise by swimming in pools in the sky overlooking the city. "I swim in the sky," he said.

From the outset, which came well before their marriage—perhaps all the way back to the era of Bobby Kennedy—she helped refine his politics. She became his wife and protector from September 12, 1982, until his death on March 19, 2017.

Pete Hamill, as close to Jimmy as any man, his friend and his colleague, was at their wedding.

"I remember the day he got married to Ronnie I went in the morning I found Ronnie outside, before we go inside the synagogue—they will marry in the synagogue and a church. And I said, 'Ronnie, please listen to me, don't marry him. Adopt him.' And she laughed out loud."

One of her roles would be—like Rosemary, his sons, and at least one of his friends who became the basis for a character in his columns—to serve as his driver.

"Because he had to be married to a woman . . . who could drive." Hamill, lying back on a couch in his final years of infirmity, had not lost his laugh. He used it now. "At one point my daughter Deirdre worked at the *Arizona Republic* out of Phoenix until she got laid off a few years ago with the whole slew of other people, but she gets a call one day from Jimmy; 'I gotta go to an Indian reservation.'

" 'Yeah Jimmy what can I do for you?'

" 'Drive me!'

"You know, and she did. Cause she loved him. You know, when she had a brain problem, Jimmy called every day at the hospital."

Hamill paused here. A technician needed to take his blood.

A few years later, Pete said, when Breslin himself was hospitalized, Ronnie was there to bear the brunt of the storm.

"I remember I heard that he was in the hospital up [at] Langone, and it was right near Christmas, and I decide to go up and see him. I went in the ground floor, nobody knew. 'Where's Mr. Breslin?' They said, 'Try the seventh floor.' So off I go to the seventh floor, it's totally deserted, nobody there, and I'm walking around looking, no nurses in the nursing station—nothing. And then I hear, 'Get me the FUCK OUT OF HERE.' And I knew I was in the right place . . .

"Ronnie was there that day, and she was sitting outside, exhausted by Jimmy's anger at being in the hospital and she could hear him bellowing down a few doors down and she says to me, 'Why is he like that? Why is he doing that?' and I talked to her a little bit about what I just talked to you about—you know, the wound of the departure of the father and all that. Because in those days in neighborhoods, working-class neighborhoods, you never heard of somebody getting a divorce, or the woman being the person that ran away, it was the man.

"Some guys ended up in jail, that was a different kind of case, because it had shame attached to it; but there was also shame to the disappearance of a father. And so, he creates this mask that makes him sound like a tough guy, and he's not really. And I think that's why my friendship was always little different. I wasn't asking him to perform the bullshit tough guy . . . But the tough guy persona, he used it well . . . You knew he couldn't fight his way out of an empty lot." He laughed. "He's not going get into fistfights."

This father was another great coauthor: if Frances was his first love, and Rosemary was his great love, and Ronnie was his last love, his father was the love he never had.

"The way I understand the story when the father finally died the word got to Jimmy, Jimmy had turned the guy down," Hamill said. "He wanted to meet with Jimmy. Because Jimmy was famous for the beer commercials and stuff. Jimmy said, no. Too late. But when the word came that he had died, Jimmy paid for the funeral, the way I heard the story."

And then there was the aristocratic Joan Whitney Payson, who in 1962 became the first woman to buy a major league baseball team "without inheriting it from a spouse or relative," according to MLB.com. Payson bought the Mets, a brand new team, and in Breslin's book on their disastrous and wonderful 1962 season, *Can't Anybody Here Play This Game?*, he captured with great affection this woman who was happiest when known as a fan, cared little or less about getting her own name in the newspapers, and gave credit for the team's later pennant races and championship seasons to the players and the managers and coaches.

> Recently Mrs. Payson was talking . . . while sitting on a couch in the parlor portion of her personal Pullman car, Adios II. It was hooked to the rear end of the Florida East Coast Champion, which was swaying through the icy weed stalks of the Jersey marshes . . . Mrs. Payson was heading for her annual two-month stay at Hobe Sound. Two dachshunds slept on the couch next to her. A brass spittoon was off to one side on the carpeted floor. It is for decorative purposes; the lady does not chew tobacco. She rested her feet on a huge felt turtle which bore a New York Mets' insignia. "I just received him today as a present," she said. "So I had them sew a Mets' insignia on him right away. The tortoise and the hare. That's the Mets . . . She had a glass of No-Cal ginger ale in her hand, but she saw to it that a Scotch and water, a stiff one, too, was produced for her visitor. She is a large, pleasant woman with light hair. She had on a green blouse and gray skirt and only one bit of jewelry. Which was enough. It was a ring big enough to shake up the Van Cleefs. Her first name is Joan and she is a Whitney. She is of the world of the Social Register and charity drives and art museums and chauffeured Rolls-Royces.

But of course, she was to his keen mind as an important an element of the story of this team as the players and the manager, Casey Stengel himself.

> So this is not a woman who came to be a nice happy loser. At the same time, she's not about to cry. This one knows the game. She is not somebody who merely sits off with her cash and looks at life from the window of a private Pullman car.

And she stayed long enough, until her death in 1975, to see the Mets through another remarkable season—the one that was to come in 1969, a championship season earned by a phenomenal team.

But it was her team's first expansion club season, and the reason the loser team packed the stadium that was the main subject of the book, of course:

> Nearly everybody was saying it by mid-June. And nearly everybody had a good reason for saying it. You see, the Mets are losers, just like nearly everybody else in life. This is a team for the cab driver who gets held up and the guy who loses out on a promotion because he didn't maneuver himself to lunch with the boss enough. It is the team for every guy who has to get out of bed in the morning and go to work for short money on a job he does not like. And it is the team for every woman who looks up ten years later and sees her husband eating dinner in a T-shirt and wonders how the hell she ever let this guy talk her into getting married. The Yankees? Who does well enough to root for them, Laurance Rockefeller?

This woman then took that slim, brilliant book—*Can't Anybody Here Play This Game?: The Improbable Saga of the New York Mets' First Year*—with its wonderful demonstration of this young man's clarity, humor and understanding of how to tell the truth that was at the heart of a story, to her brother, John Hay "Jock" Whitney of Groton, Yale and the Social Register, and told him he must hire this brash young man for his newspaper, the *New York Herald Tribune.* He had bought the paper in 1958 and made himself publisher in 1961. Whitney, one of America's richest men, had a plan to take the once-staid *Herald Tribune* and turn it into something bright and special, using dozens of his millions and a small army of bright young men—and a smaller number of such women—to do so.

Rosemary guided Breslin, Ronnie protected him, and Joan Payson, who was without a doubt to the private Pullman car born, arranged the trajectory of this young sportswriter's career who, equally without a doubt, had been to the losers' locker room born.

"Breslin is one of those fortunate men who have learned the most important things from women," Pete Hamill wrote in the April 25, 1988, issue of *New York* magazine. "His father, James, was a piano player who went out for a pack of Camels in 1936 and never came back." He didn't even leave a sample of his handwriting, Hamill said.

And this is how Breslin, his mother, Frances, who was the first woman, and the one who raised him, and his sister, Deirdre, became the first crime victims found at the top of a flight of stairs. His father left Frances impoverished and alone. He left Breslin with the indelible memory of pain, poverty, abandonment and injustice: the stab that helped give him a real understanding of what it was like to be a powerless victim. His father gave Breslin his dark shadow.

"He was, not doing good against my, my mother. In fact, he found the street more [appealing] to him than the house. He could stay out on a street and if he got hit by a car going across 101st Avenue, where we lived, it would not start any wailing." He walked out the door, across a worn-out covered porch, down a few steps, and disappeared, Breslin said.

Much later in his life, the father, James Earle Breslin, in need of cash, called his by now famous son, who helped him out and then said, in his version—which is of course different from Hamill's, and probably from his own the next time he told it—"Next time, kill yourself."

In this image, Breslin once again found a parallel with Damon Runyon. In his biography of that newsman and famous author, he noted, "As far as he was concerned, his ability was the result of immaculate conception." Breslin quoted Runyon as saying, "Anything I have, I worked hard for. I sure didn't get any help from anyplace. The only thing I ever got was a wire asking for money."

From Runyon's mouth, the angry words come out from the side and you can taste the whiskey in the sound. Breslin's version also reveals an ugly anger and comes out as it was poured into the man's foundation by a piano player's hands at the age of four. When he was a child, he was betrayed. It was the hand he was dealt.

Often, across the years ahead, when he was at his worst, betrayal was the hand he himself dealt to others. As a betrayer, he would, it seemed, outstrip Runyon who also had a rap sheet for that crime.

# BRESLIN BECOMES A BIG SHOT

A few years after his father walked out, the time came that he was able to walk by himself out down those same front steps of the 75-by-100-foot property at 134-02 134th Street, out that same front door, and then around the corner onto 101st Avenue.

When he did, among the things he would find were the friends who later became the basis for his characters.

Breslin would populate columns across the decades with these characters. Among other things, they would provide a respite from the hard-edged reported columns that made up the bulk of his output. What Breslin did through his body of work was essentially invent a genre that became known as the "City Column." He was widely emulated, but rarely equaled. His rogues would commit arson, make bad bets, feed their Mob enemies to wolves, practice the frayed-cuff law of the criminal courts.

His engraving of these lives captured the truth in ways that would bring a smile, or a knowing nod, to the subway rider. Breslin gave the subway conductor, the cop and the bus driver, the housewife and the court officer and the stenographer short stories premised on his knowledge earned since boyhood of the lives of the hapless who plied their trades—arson, gambling, the practice of law that could often have used an opened law book, and organized crime in its petty, insular, and vulgar ways. These characters were well understood by the reader. They and the writer had grown up on those same streets where the reader lived, with the same hopes each of the characters had of escape. They would populate his columns when he felt the need to relieve the reader of the diet of crime, blackout, political scandal, and the economic injustice of his city and instead entertain. Writing this way, crime could, if only on occasion, be used to entertain.

His entertainment with its racetracks, bookmakers, criminal courts, and arsonists was in many ways also the remainder of the *Guys and Dolls* model of his great inspiration, Damon Runyon, where the criminals had hearts and the crimes were, well, ones that the reader forgave if they even needed forgiveness. Because in the New York where Breslin wore out his shoes, any warmth that might have existed was often gone and Times Square and Broadway were places where tourists were yoked and their purses and jewelry were stolen. The boroughs of Brooklyn and the Bronx were scarred by fire and the ice of knives, and Staten Island, the offshore island, was not only the home of Italian Americans, the children of Irish emigres, cops, firemen, vertical slums and the remnants of Sandy Ground, the home of free Black oystermen of the distant past, it was a bastion of isolation and racism and all the crimes of the heart that came with that.

And then there was Queens, the borough of his birth and, by the time he had achieved the height of his powers as a reporter and columnist, the province of corrupt and petty politicians; the ugliest mobster in memory, a man named John Gotti; and a form of racial brutality that could not be excused by ignorance. From Queens would come some of his great crime writing.

If four women and one absent father were in many ways coauthors of his story, it is important to remember that his own was Breslin's one story without an editor or an immediate deadline. He kept pulling the sheets of paper from the typewriter and crumpling them up as he constantly revised it, varying any element that he thought needed a tweak or two to make it right. The number of years he went to college, the facts of his high school career, why he was fired from a newspaper, and the writers and reporters who were his greatest influences in terms of the art of storytelling—all were pliable. He altered everything that he saw needed to be better, and that included, it seemed, the amount of time he spent in Vietnam covering the war. He was polishing that in some of his final interviews decades later. This was his way. He was always sweating over this story as he did over every other thing he wrote, in order to get it right. To make it "Marvelous" and "Fabulous" as he continually created the character "J.B. Number One." "Beautiful!"

When he died, he left a manuscript, 255 single-spaced pages. He had been working on it, going to the machine each day to type. And plenty of it is good. Pretty good, he would say. As good as it could be against the deadline now looming.

"There was noise in the front and here came a crowd in from the Rockaway Beach bus."

That was what he wrote toward the very end. He was still polishing it.

Through all the years and across all the decades of his career he kept polishing, buffing, and trying out different parts of himself. Seeing what would sound and feel the best. At one point, in one version, at first glance there did not appear to be a college, although he did, he would sometimes admit, attend.

> I'm at John Adams High School. In the second year there, I took only two courses cuz I didn't like the rest of it. And the, the, uh, teacher and head of the history department . . . stopped me in the corridor at the school one day and said, why don't you get outta here cuz you don't wanna stay in a school . . . So, get out and get something and get going.

In this version, he heads right to the *Long Island Press*, which he at some point did. Though it appears, looking at the somewhat murky record, that he did finish high school. He played the trumpet in school and at some point joined the newspaper. In another version of his life, working at the paper gave him the motivation to go to college, simply because he was informed that he would need it to get ahead there. On the day it closed, more than two and a half decades later, he vehemently described it as having been jail.

But none of his versions explain the military academy yearbook picture of him with the caption "Bugler." This was inconvenient. It didn't seem to fit any of his narratives, and it is mentioned in no interview that can be found. Michael Daly recalled that he was mortified when confronted with the evidence of it by his secretary at the *Daily News*, Ann Marie, a woman from the boroughs like Jimmy.

Like Daly, the Yale Art History major who liked to mumble away that fact in the nasal intonations of the boroughs, Breslin preferred to be everyman and, increasingly over the years, talked to his colleagues and editors in a profanity-laced version of the language of the city streets. Bugler? Nah.

But this everyman had a portion of a Yeats manuscript framed and running along a wall at the entrance to his and Ronnie Eldridge's apartment. And Pete Hamill, snooping, when Breslin was not around, once found a volume of W.H. Auden's poems in his desk at the *News*. He was literate, he was well read, and his grammar would have made his mother and his sister Deirdre, herself a schoolteacher, proud.

Inconsistency was baked into the crust of Breslin's landscape: his imagined world without end that rolled right into the gray-green surf of the North Atlantic, where he would sit looking out over the spindrift. Beneath the crust were the fissures, the angry ones of his childhood and the ones caused by heartache that came to include the nation's great losses—the Kennedys, King, the young soldiers in Vietnam; the loss of Rosemary and the deaths of two other women, his daughters Rosemary the younger and Kelly.

Many parts of the story would come later, but the first crime was his father walking out, and the first story came soon after at about the age of ten when he and another neighborhood kid, Al Hansen, published a pretty well-done newspaper called *The Flash*.

A faded yellowed copy of *The Flash* was in the possession of Breslin's family, and they shared it. This copy began with a letter from the editor, young Breslin, apologizing for the fact that the paper had not been published in two months.

> Dear reader due to unstoppable circumstance The Flash has not been coming out for a month or so. Beginning now it will come to you 2 times a week. The Management

It also contained the first known example of his crime writing, an illustrated story stripped out like a cartoon and headlined "Dude Killed. Star Witness Against Murderer Killed!"

"Well, I had a newspaper. From age, I don't know, 10 years old or something. *The Flash*. We used to print it by hand and pass it, get it mimeographed in the insurance office across the street by a woman there. And we took it out and sold it and it got around the neighborhood that way." He explained all this to Martin Dunn, who in the 1990s had become the Editor in Chief of the *Daily News*.

> Martin Dunn: What was in *The Flash*?
> Jimmy Breslin: Oh, any accident we could come up. Or anything with the neighbors. There was a couple of the women that always had something at that time . . .

> Martin Dunn: You sell it or give it away?
> Jimmy Breslin: Oh no, we sold [it]. I don't know . . . for 10 cents, a nickel, anything . . . we wanted whatever we could get."

He also discovered a tabloid truth: Sex. Sells. He told another interviewer that one of the stories he wrote, and the one that might have caused the lapse in publication—through censorship—was of a woman in the neighborhood who would take her sweater off in front of her window. He described the excitement of a ten-year-old Catholic boy when she lifted her sweater over her head.

It is not in the tattered pages of the surviving copy of *The Flash*. But another thing that Breslin learned from *The Flash* would inflate his ego for the rest of his life.

"When I wrote something, I got good reception more than I'd ever have if I didn't write it. So that I was a big shot."

In 1927, shortly before Breslin was born, Philo Taylor Farnsworth, age 21 and the Bill Gates of his age, was credited with inventing electronic television. Even as *The Flash* was selling for a nickel or a dime in the Queens neighborhood of Breslin's childhood, the first of the sets Farnsworth envisioned decades before, in a log house in Utah with no electricity, were hitting the market. You plugged them in and the images appeared. They had been turned into electrons that flew over the airwaves and into your home.

And shortly after *The Flash* was making a small splash in Queens, a man—Sarnoff, David, whose name is presented as it would be had he been arrested—was trying and failing to prove he'd invented the medium, demonstrating it at the World's Fair. He was caught and ordered to give Farnsworth some money. Sarnoff went on to make millions and millions with a company he founded named NBC. Farnsworth never got his money.

In 1939, cars cost $750 or so, according to public reports, and the television sets shown at the World's Fair in New York that April cost just a few dollars less. So it started out slow. That would change.

The world in which *The Flash* was published by 10-year-old boys and most everyone who could read got their news in newspapers was gone. By the time Breslin was 18, millions of Americans owned televisions, a number that would grow exponentially.

Breslin had taken the teacher's advice and arrived at the *Long Island Press* where he toiled as a copyboy, whose job description was right there, a boy who ran with copy—pages of words—from desk to desk as it made its way through the newsroom. And like copyboys everywhere he was supposed to bring reporters and editors their cigarettes and their lunch, make sure their shoes were shined—whatever they wanted—but from the beginning he spent weekends in the sports department writing what they offered. And as the ambitious are expected to, he also did whatever he felt like.

One day he walked over to the desk of an editor named David Starr and dropped something in front of him.

"We, the paper, decided to publish a section about a new phenomenon called Television and I was assigned to put the section together to gather copy about this new thing . . . I started collecting stuff and I spoke to people on the staff to ask what they knew about television, et cetera, I'm immersed in this thing, this copyboy named Jimmy Breslin walks over to my desk and drops some pieces of copy paper on the desk. *'Mm-hmm,'* he says out of the side of his mouth. Cause that's the way Jimmy generally spoke. *'Take a look at this. Tell me what you think.'* It's a piece of copy. About television in a bar.

"I had never even thought about television in a bar, but this is a description of a bar that is around the corner from the newspaper, and how it has this TV set hanging on the wall. And how the people in the bar react to it. Oh my God, that's great. It's a wonderful piece of copy written in Jimmy's inimitable style.

"So I, I walk over to the City Editor. 'Take a look at this.'

" 'That's pretty good, who wrote it?'

" 'Jimmy Breslin, the copyboy.'

" 'Copyboy? We don't run copyboys.'

" 'Yeah, but you said it was good.'

" 'I don't care. I'm not gonna run something by a copyboy.'

"I went back to my desk. And I kept on talking to him about it, and finally he agreed that we would run it and it ran in the section.

TV SETS OFF SQUABBLE, BUT PATRONS LOVE IT

*By Jimmy Breslin*

"Sorry Mac you gotta make room for him so he can see the television screen . . . he's a regular here and I mean, after all, I gotta take care of him."

"It ain't bright enough . . . brighten it . . . and don't ring the cash register . . . it makes everything go waving around."

"What time is the game on?"

"Game! We're getting the fights tonight!"

"Fights! . . . Game . . . With Milton Berle you guys want that stuff."

. . . That is about what you hear on the average night in a Long Island tavern. It's 1949 taproom conversation . . . television style . . .

. . . The ball games, movies, Milton Berle, horse shows, newsreels all parade right across the screen for the corner fraternity, "Boy you can't beat them new inventions, can you?"

That is about it. You can't beat television. Sure, it makes it as tough as going through an obstacle course to get your hand on a glass of beer or two . . . but as the guy says, "You can't beat them new inventions."

The piece by Jimmy Breslin, copyboy, is in no collection of his work. David Starr is not mentioned, either. But he gave Breslin his first break as a columnist and was his first known newspaper editor.

A wunderkind editor who himself had started as a copyboy, covered cops and courts, and later went on to become the Starr in the firmament of the Newhouse media empire and editor-in-chief of the *Long Island Press* newspaper by the time it closed in 1977. Starr gave Breslin a big second break, too. He fired him.

Breslin loved to tell that story. He told it if you asked about it. He told it to Pete Hamill, who printed it in *New York* magazine in 1988, and he told it to *Daily News* readers on April 27, 1977, in a column filled with the residue of long-ago slights that was published the day after the *Long Island Press* turned off its lights, "Finally."

In all Breslin's variations, his firing was preceded by a very long beer-drenched day that began when he got off work in the morning from the newspaper and continued until 5:00 P.M. when he walked out into a rainstorm to head back to the paper, where he was due to start again in the sports department at 7:00 P.M.

> Once it seemed beautiful to drink of a summer morning: standing at a bar watching people go to work, with the sunlight cascading through the windows changing the beer in your hand into a glass of shining gold. There was a fine sense of wrongdoing.

That was how the column began. By the body of the column the reader learns that Al Camera, in the art department, was hard at work retouching photographs needed for the engagement pages of the Saturday paper. Pictures of "delicate virginal daughters . . . engaged to young men . . . who were awaiting the call from the Fire Department."

This photo retoucher would then do something that could be viewed as a predecessor to deep fakes: he would use his airbrush to enhance the cleavage of the young women. "A front the likes of which you do not see on Times Square for money," Breslin noted. "No flat chested girls get married while I'm around, Al Camera always said," Breslin reported. He added that as the evening's work was slow—even for someone typing with one hand while the other held a blanket in place—he fell asleep.

> Sometime later, I don't know how long it was, the sound of the sports department door opening woke me up. Walking in was a woman who held a studio photographer's photo of her daughter. The woman walked up the stair and, instead of going across the hallway to the women's department, she walked into the sports department by mistake. Walked in with these prim Rosary Altar Confraternity manners and her lovely, virginal daughter's picture.
>
> I forgot where I was and I jumped up. The car blanket fell to the floor. I stood in front of the lady, stood there with whatever I was born with and smiled politely and said to her, "Can I help you ma'am?"
>
> And that is exactly how I got fired from that job, from the Long Island Press newspaper, which finally folded yesterday.

"Finally." He wrote this in a column in which he described the owner, S.I. Newhouse, as a tightfisted tyrant and the place itself as a jail. If it was a jail, he had thrived in the general population where copyboys ran.

According to David Starr, whose memory was of events nearly seventy years in the past when interviewed, but who does not have Breslin's reputation as an unreliable narrator, the firing did not happen "exactly" that way at all. In Starr's version, there was no matron, there was no virginal daughter, and there was no women's department. The outcome, however, was the same.

"To the best of my recollection, it was a Friday night and Jimmy came to the office dressed in an overcoat, and then underneath it, an Indian blanket. He walks into the city room and sat down. Whether he fell asleep there or not, I was not there.

"But I got a phone call from a young reporter, a clerk who was in the darkroom printing out pictures. She told me in tears that she opened the door of the darkroom, walked out into the city room, and Jimmy was there, and he opened his blanket. And then closed it, and this little young sweet Catholic girl was really shocked and called me at night and in tears. I've gotta do something.

"And on Monday I called Jimmy and I said: there were two reasons why I think you and I should part company. One is your social behavior. And the other one is you're not a good sports editor 'cause you don't know how to lead people." (Though Breslin was a copyboy during the week, by now he was working in Sports on the weekend as an assigning editor, Starr said.)

"You let them do anything because you are not really a boss. And he looks at me and says, 'You are right.' And he left. I'm sorry. I don't mean to laugh, but it's just, that's Jimmy . . . he was a nice kid. He didn't wanna do any harm. He was, he was just Jimmy. He clearly [had] been drinking."

When he was day drinking in the bar on Fire Island and getting sober in the offices of the *Long Island Press*, he held in his hand a glass of shining gold. When he wrote about it some two-and-a-half decades later, he was the gold and he needed to get out before the buffoonery, the boozy prose, the mess of the heavy drinking life got the better of him and the by-then tarnished gold would have to be pawned off by an unlucky editor. He was no longer a pudgy youth but a mature man with a sweep of hair, good suits, and columns that sometimes began—and often ended—in bars.

Of course, when he wasn't posturing or actively drinking, he did some of his best work. Like Runyon's, the era of his most notable work began in Times Square. Breslin's began in 1963 when he walked into a West 40th Street bar and was offered a job at the *New York Herald Tribune.* Soon he would get a desk in a fifth-floor newsroom where he would meet a cast of characters, including Tom Wolfe, who were beginning to create a good deal of what became modern twentieth-century journalism.

## MORE THAN ONE I IN TRIBUNE

Tom Wolfe had walked into the shabby wreckage of the *Trib* newsroom for the first time in 1962, looked around and thought, *Yeah, I can beat these guys*. "These guys" were the writers engaged in what he called the secret competition in "the main Tijuana bullring" for feature writers. In less than three years that would come true and, as *Vanity Fair* reported in 2015, soon he would become a cult figure. The white suit he purchased out of necessity—he had no suit, it was summer, all the paper's writers wore suits, and white was what you wore in the summer back where he was from in Virginia—would become a trademark.

The *Trib* offices were at 230 West 41st Street and the fifth-floor newsroom was a collection of mismatched chairs—some with straight backs, others with half-broken backs, some on squeaky wheels, others on scarred legs. This could be a description of the collection of writers hunched over black Bakelite phones, already on their way to becoming antiques, many in white shirts, most with sleeves rolled up. Cigarette smoking was encouraged, it seemed.

The paper was the Darwinian result of the 1924 merger of Horace Greeley's *New York Tribune* (est. 1841) and James Gordon Bennett's *New York Herald* (est. 1835). The papers had been born at a time when the vying voices that came off the New York presses were as cacophonous as those of the twenty-first century's digital battlers. Among them were Hearst's *New York Journal,* Pulitzer's *New York World,* Jarvis's *The New York Times.* The *Trib* would survive for another 42-plus years.

By the time Wolfe walked in, envisioning that he would be the brightest star in the firmament, the firmament, it seemed, had already been home to everyone who was anyone in the press, from John Steinbeck, who worked as a newspaper reporter long before he became a Nobel prize winner, to Judith Crist. From Homer Bigart to Walter Kerr and Red Smith. Novelist, movie critic, war correspondent, theater critic, sportswriter, big names then at a good, solid, and unfailingly Republican newspaper. Though the writing could be bright and powerful, the paper was as dull and gray as the grimy newsroom.

By the time Breslin walked into the paper's first-floor Rathskeller, a bar named Bleeck's at 213 West 40th Street, he was carrying the reputation he was earning from his book on the Mets baseball team and the arrogance that had started to swell inside him to proportions that were inverse to his sense of insecurity.

Waiting inside was one of America's richest men, John Hay Whitney—or Jock, as he was known—the proprietor of the paper that he had purchased in 1958 and intended to reshape in look and feel and make a home to vivid, intelligent, sharply honed journalism. He had read the book, he had the recommendation of the Mets' owner, his sister, and he had a very thick checkbook.

"You can't afford to pay me enough," Breslin nonetheless dared. He met the paper's editor, Jim Bellows, and of course he took the job. Soon enough he would be making more than $125,000 a year.

The personalities at the paper where Breslin and Wolfe intended to take on the world would become marquee names in news in their own right.

*Dick Schaap*: Schaap came to the paper as a sort of batman to General Breslin, who he began working for when he was fifteen and his general was twenty. He became a fabled City Editor. Then he surrendered that all-important helm and went and slid down into a broken chair where he began a career that would include writing or editing thirty-three books and winning six Emmy awards. He would memorialize himself later in a book he titled *Dick Schaap as Told to Dick Schaap*. The book, his IMDb entry notes, is in some ways a tribute to his habit of name dropping, containing 531 references to celebrities.

*Don Forst*: Forst was a son of the 1930s and the Crown Heights, Brooklyn, Jewish middle classes. An assistant City Editor and the husband of food critic Gael Greene, Forst later would claim to the author of a profile that he got into journalism because of a "pretty girl" at the enrollment table at the University of Vermont. While at that university, he exposed a student rite of performing in blackface. Later in life, when he was an Editor-in-Chief, but still a man who liked to break the furniture, he would ask his own City Editor to tape a particular picture of him to the underside of his top desk drawer, to be used if needed for his obituary. It featured Forst in bellbottom pants with a wide belt and a mop of brown hair. It very much looked as he looked during this era—a moment in time. He carried the mop of hair with the flip of a bang until the end, the way some men might wear a jacket that they purchased at the height of their powers.

*Dick Wald*: Wald, the paper's final managing editor, was hardly shy. He had as a junior foreign correspondent taken on the paper's editor-in-chief at a party the Whitneys hosted at the Paris Ritz. In a fight over coverage, he shouted down the innovative Editor, John Denson: "You don't know how to edit." According to Richard Kluger, the biographer of the *Herald Tribune*, the full charge was that John

Denson diminished the role of his own correspondents by using wire copy that provided more sensational accounts of the news. Denson was the penultimate innovative editor at the paper, trying every magic trick he had to boost readership. The combative Wald was not fired for the outburst. The young man was already a favorite of Whitney, and they developed a lifelong friendship. Wald became the last living senior editor of the paper.

*Jim Bellows*: The man who succeeded John Denson as Editor was unquestionably a gifted one, as summed up in the title of his autobiography, *The Last Editor: How I Saved* The New York Times, *the* Washington Post, *and the* Los Angeles Times *from Dullness and Complacency.* The title was cheeky, but not entirely tongue in cheek. Working at the *Trib*, the *Washington Star*, and the *Los Angeles Herald Examiner*, his stewardship of these lower-circulation papers pushed the market leaders to be more creative. The title, it was quipped, also may have been the longest complete sentence ever composed by Bellows, whose gift was creating the atmosphere for success through vague, stuttering oracular half-phrases that encouraged massive confidence in the writers he hired.

*Clay Felker*: The man who would transform the newspaper's Sunday magazine, *New York*, was, were you to believe Bellows's facile sentence, hired because he was a man about town. He was one. He was also as gifted an editor as he was tall, handsome, and seductive. He was known for a booming tenor, he was described as "superhuman" in his animation, and he just happened within a few short years to completely change the face of American magazine journalism in the twentieth century. Felker loved to dance through the corridors of society and power. He loved the canapés of trends that he could turn into journalism. He had sharp cuffs, perfect collar points, and an amazing smile. He used them all. When they failed to win him the editorship of *Esquire* magazine and he lost the corporate in-fight, he took Bellows's offer to come and help figure out how to bring life to a stale Sunday magazine.

There was a quiet man in the newsroom, too. His name was David Laventhol. He sniffled a lot. He would replace Schaap as city editor, he would be teased by Forst and Schaap for his lack of knowledge of New York and would take his sniffle with him and go on to become the publisher of the *LA Times* and the president of its parent Times Mirror Company.

He told one of his city editors once that it was the best job he ever had. He declined an offer to trade his stock options to get his old job back. He was busy, having helped give birth to the next great innovation in American newspapering, *New York Newsday.*

They of course saw themselves, collectively, as a hot burning sun that would shed heat and light on the world. They actually were reimagining a paper that already had shed plenty of light, if sometimes that light peeked out from its dull overall layout.

*Trib* alum Homer Bigart, who won two Pulitzers and was a brave and powerful frontline war correspondent, left for *The New York Times* in 1955. He summed up the paper's effect on its inhabitants, according to Sam Roberts, who once had been a campus correspondent for the *Trib*:

> When Homer Bigart, a famous World War II correspondent and another *Trib* alumnus who joined *The Times*, died in 1991, Clifton Daniel, a former *Times* managing editor, recalled: "It seemed to me that he always looked down on *The Times*, even when he worked there. Its main fault, in his eyes, was that it wasn't the *Trib*."

Sam, who recalled earning $20 as a campus correspondent at that paper, wrote this in March 2013, at the moment when the *International Herald Tribune* was to be renamed the *International New York Times,* ending the last vestige of what Greeley and Bennett had created. Bigart's paper was *The Paper,* as Richard Kluger aptly titled his book on the *Herald Tribune*—as if it were the only one, even before all the innovations. A writer's paper. A citizens' paper. A democracy's paper.

These "I"-minded newspaper reporters and editors were simply the new kids in town, brought in by Jock Whitney. Whitney, if any one person apart from the editors and reporters, deserves much of the credit for saving the *Trib* from complacency, and for highlighting the quality of its writers. It was, ultimately, his vision. Through his new editors and writers, he found new readers. He drank with his writers and pushed them to use their vocal cords. They did this even as the *Trib* headed toward that thing its linotype operators looked out for as they turned the words on the flimsy copy paper into the lead that would be inked and turned into the paper's columns: *-30-*, the sign that a story was over.

John Hay Whitney, publisher and owner, had an ego on par with that of any of his editorial stars. He was one of the ten wealthiest men in the world. He romanced Tallulah Bankhead, Joan Bennett, Paulette Goddard, and Joan Crawford. But, it was said, his greatest love and the one on which he lavished the greatest attention was his newspaper.

He was a champion polo player. He made one of his homes on the Green Tree Estate on Long Island's Gold Coast, had one ancestor on the *Mayflower* and another who arrived in America late, in 1635. He invested in Technicolor; contributed half the money, according to published accounts, to option *Gone With The Wind*; and with Benno Schmidt, Sr., founded the first venture capital fund. Jock Whitney also would turn out to be one of the best newspaper owners in US history.

He wasn't quite hands-off. He had a vision. It was one of quality. He aggressively sought those who could help realize it. Then he did not meddle as his team executed it, even when his team and its antics riled members of the establishment to which he and his long list of private clubs firmly belonged.

Together they invented this thing later called "The New Journalism." What they thought they were doing was taking a dull, if well-considered, newspaper and proving (as one of the paper's advertising slogans said) that a good newspaper did not have to be dull. Every day they tried to put out a good, interesting newspaper. They were creative. They were aggressive. They were storytellers.

"I've already talked about the special brilliance of Tom Wolfe and Jimmy Breslin," Bellows said in his book. "They appealed to two different kinds of New Yorkers—Tom reached the avant-garde and the sophisticates. Jimmy reached the middle class and the people who didn't have representation.

"Jimmy's was visceral writing . . ."

This paper, then, was Jimmy Breslin's spiritual home. It was the place where he was encouraged to tell the truth. It was a place where his repeated tantrums and outbursts were tolerated and where they grew. Where he became known in some circles as an *enfant terrible.* In the world Breslin wrote about, he more probably would have been known as a "juvie recidivist," a young career criminal.

"I don't think he lacked for ego . . . but other newspapers would never let anybody work that way . . . like Jimmy . . . because the results were always horrible . . . it required talent . . . you couldn't just say, 'write what you want,'" Tom Wolfe said.

"He was the greatest writer on deadline. And I see him . . . he was about 30 feet from where I sat and there would be these bowling balls with smoke coming out of him. He would always . . . and he got to a point where he would go up to the city desk and say, what have you got for me today, and if there was a story he thought was interesting he would take it, he won't just do a column on the story. What Breslin wrote *was* 'the story.'"

"Jimmy was a really good . . . he did five days a week—his column. These were reporting columns. I never remember him speaking off the top of his head—unless it was about his wife," Wolfe told an interviewer.

"He would start the week with two or three good ideas . . . he said Thursday, 'I was really sucking air,' and he said 'On Friday I would just open a vein and let it splash on the paper,'" said Wolfe. Like Breslin, Wolfe could steal with both hands and he did not credit Red Smith, the great sportswriter who also worked at the paper, with the phrase.

In a 1972 article in *New York* magazine (a magazine that arose out of the by-then long gone *Herald*'s Sunday magazine, helmed by Felker and midwifed by Breslin, who held the lofty title Vice President) titled "The Birth of 'The New Journalism'; Eyewitness Report by Tom Wolfe," Wolfe explained this thing he, Breslin, Gail Sheehy, Gay Talese, Pete Hamill and Murray Kempton did this way:

> I doubt if many of the aces I will be extolling in this story went into journalism with the faintest notion of creating a "new" journalism, a "higher" journalism, or even a mildly improved variety. I know they never dreamed that anything they were going to write for newspapers or magazines would wreak such evil havoc in the literary world . . . causing panic, dethroning the novel as the number one literary genre, starting the first new direction in American literature in half a century . . . Nevertheless, that is what has happened.

Wolfe wonderfully explains how these aces often went into feature writing as if they were checking into a motel on the way to that dream in the tournament of champions: The Great American Novel.

> And yet in the early 1960s a curious new notion, just hot enough to inflame the ego, had begun to intrude into the tiny confines of the feature statusphere. It was in the nature of a discovery. This discovery, modest at first, humble, in fact, deferential, you might say, was that it just might be possible to write journalism that would . . . read like a novel. *Like* a novel, if you get the picture. This was the sincerest form of homage to The Novel and to those greats, the novelists, of course. Not even the journalists who pioneered in this direction doubted for a moment that the novelist was the reigning literary artist, now and forever. All they were asking for was the privilege of dressing up like him . . . until the day when they themselves would work up their nerve and go into the shack and try it for real . . . They were dreamers, all right, but one thing they never dreamed of. They never dreamed of the approaching irony. They never guessed for a minute that the work they would do over the next ten years, as journalists, would wipe out the novel as literature's main event.

Wolfe goes on as only this master can do. He spells out his confidence in Gay Talese's reporting in his account of Joe Louis growing older, and swats away all the protestations that these new journalists were "piping" their quotes, sucking them out of the opium pipes of their imagination. He singles out the columnists of old for having been good reporters turned as a reward by their editors into bad columnists who ingested *The Times* and then pundited out their words. And he goes on so beautifully and gets back to Breslin:

> Breslin made a revolutionary discovery. He made the discovery that it was feasible for a columnist to leave the building . . . Breslin would go up to the City Editor and ask what stories and assignments were coming up, choose one, go out, leave the building, cover the story as a reporter, and write about it in his column. If the story were big enough,

> his column would start on page one instead of inside. As obvious as this system may sound, it was unheard of among newspaper columnists, whether local or national . . .
>
> Breslin worked like a Turk. He would be out all day covering a story, come back in at 4 P.M. or so and sit down at a desk in the middle of the city room. It was quite a show. He was a good-looking Irishman with a lot of black hair and a great wrestler's gut. When he sat down at his typewriter he hunched himself over into a shape like a bowling ball. He would start drinking coffee and smoking cigarettes until vapor started drifting off his body. He looked like a bowling ball fueled with liquid oxygen. Thus fired up, he would start typing. I've never seen a man who could write so well against a daily deadline.

That was Wolfe on Breslin and New Journalism.

Breslin, as he preferred, was succinct and used no four- or five-syllable words. At various times he cited John O'Hara, Paul Gallico and others who were great storytellers. But he always got to the point: He said journalism had simply forgotten storytelling and he and Wolfe and Talese "We were first at bringing back the past."

"The idea that he and Wolfe started something new makes Breslin shake with laughter," Mike O'Neill, then Editor-in-Chief of the *New York Daily News*, wrote in 1984 in *The World According to Breslin*. "So it was typical of him to reject any credit for a new journalism which he said must have been developed about the same time as the typewriter . . . 'But no one was doing it when I started. That's why everyone thought it was new.'"

# THE NEW JOURNALISM, & THE OLD MOB

If there is one kind of person who thinks about crime day in and day out more than anyone except perhaps a cop (and a very active cop at that), it is the shoe-leather New York news reporter. That was true in 1963, when Jimmy Breslin joined the *Herald Tribune.* It was true in the 1980s and 1990s when Times Square was a lair for thieves and prostitutes, the Port Authority bus terminal a sad first or last stop on a runaway's journey, and murder in New York City topped 2,000 cases a year. And it was true yesterday whether it was at a solid online publication, at a linear television outlet, on a podcast, or within the diminished world of local newspapers. As Sam Roberts put it, this thinking was best done not behind a desk, but out on the street, where your feet slapped up and down.

And if there was anyone who knew how to walk down the city's darkened streets and come back with the heart of the story or enter a funeral parlor where the gunned down lay in state and return to help you understand the world the gunned down had left, it was Breslin. If there was anyone who could walk into to a courthouse and walk back out and into a bar or a cafeteria and return to his desk and turn into words both the seriousness and the entertainment value of what he had seen—in other words, turn it into a short story, into literature—or who could sit across from a man who had been the Prime Minister of the Mob in America and bring you into the world of his retirement, it would be Breslin.

When he first set foot in the offices of the *Herald Tribune* in 1963, Jimmy Breslin was on the cusp of fame. From the *Long Island Press*, where he began his apprenticeship in sportswriting, he had turned to sports full time. Of sports reporting, it has been said, the best turn when they are young. It molds them, but their writing defines it as much as it defines them. Breslin wrote for the NEA syndicate (Newspaper Enterprise Association), for *Sport* magazine, for the *Saturday Evening Post*, for the *Journal-American*. He covered everything from Little League to "midget baseball" to college baskets to Willie Mays. At the *Journal-American,* one reporter remembers that listening to the "Rat-a-Tat" of Jimmy's typing was like "watching Gene Krupa on the drums."

But on the whole, as a sports reporter he was largely a journeyman.

While he credits, in one retelling of his influences (to Pete Hamill in 1988), Harry Grayson of the NEA with teaching him how to go to the loser's locker room, what sports definitely taught him was how to write fast, against the clock.

Then he quit. It was 1960, and the *Journal-American* was a jail.

"He wasn't there long . . . He left because he wasn't doing what he wanted to. He wanted to write, but he wasn't writing," his *Journal* colleague sportswriter Dave Anderson said.

But before he quit, his sportswriting, free of daily tedium, had already begun to emerge in his magazine work. In May 1958, *True*—what was then called a "men's magazine"—published under the headline "Racing's Old Reliable," a marvelous story that began like this:

> The Thoroughbred horse racing capital of the nation is not at Calumet Farm, whose soft, sloping acres catch your eye, nor is it at ramshackle Churchill Downs, which catches your throat, or palatial Hollywood

> Park, which catches your bankroll. It is at 91-41 Chicot Court, which is a six-room house in an unpretentious section of New York City called Ozone Park.
>
> The house has a cement backyard the size of a beer coaster and the driveway defies you to squeeze a car through without scraping the house next door. In the front, two tiny plots of grass border a brick walk. At 6:15 each morning, James E. Fitzsimmons starts down this walk as his son, Jim, pulls to the curb in a car.
>
> Mr. Fitz is 83, and arthritis has bowed his spine so that he walks like a man carrying a keg of beer on his back and he uses an aluminum crutch under his right arm.

He began writing books. Sports books. The first of these was *Sunny Jim*. In this book his remarkable ability to synthesize detailed reporting with vivid, novelistic writing gave an example of what The New Journalism would become. The book and his next book, though he didn't see them as such, were successors to the novel, as Tom Wolfe later in part defined this emerging journalism.

His first had to be *Sunny Jim*, the story of a horse trainer. Breslin exclaimed: "What else was I gonna write about. I grew up near a racetrack. It was all I knew." Reading the book, you knew James Breslin was himself a thoroughbred.

> On the Monday after Gallant Fox won the 1930 Kentucky Derby, the sun was just starting to gleam on the short-cropped, wet grass of Aqueduct's infield when Mr. Fitz came to the rail, stop watch in hand, while Petee Wrack who was being pointed for the Suburban Handicap, bowed his neck against the exercise boy's hold, and started to thump down the track to begin his workout. This is the way of the professional. Mr. Fitz had just won a Kentucky Derby, but here he was at work, first chance after it, just as he would have been if he had lost. The glamour and excitement and handshaking is for amateurs who have to be told

> that they are good. The big guy doesn't need it. He goes back to the job. You don't find much of this. For an obvious reason. Most people are amateurs.

All you needed to enjoy this book was to enjoy reading. You would learn everything you needed to know about horseracing along the way, as you became immersed in the life of James Fitzsimmons.

His second book was the successful and humor filled *Can't Anybody Here Play This Game?* It delights as it recounts the hopelessness of the first season of the New York Mets, a team that since that day has had enough haplessness to continue to bring a smile to the fan who can identify better with that than with a drawer full of World Series rings.

This is the one that took him from sports to what he called, in his Runyon book, "the main event."

> The night gave Runyon material . . . He got it the only way you can, by hanging out with people for long hours. Through so many decades in the city, only a couple of people ever came around with enough guts and energy to do a thing like this, and then at the end of the night they came up empty because they couldn't write well enough to do a travel pamphlet.

The main event was news, and most often news involved crime and dark streets, amber saloons or rooms whose walls were thick with municipal-grade paint.

He gave you a view of the judge that you could only see from the worn defense table or through the eyes of the defendant, and a view of the proceeding that could only be found at the bar across the street from the courthouse, where you could listen as the defendant held court. The way he vividly brought you there was in the lyrical rhythms of short sentences, the kind that transport you until you lift your head, shake it and head for the doors as they open to the white tile and cement platform of your subway station. This was Breslin. When he achieved clarity, found irony, or in some other way made his point he would summarily say: "Beautiful!" Inhale. And leave the old joint, heading for the newspaper's EXIT sign and turning his face toward tomorrow.

He started his day on the phone earlier than most. He ended it later than many. He usually used more shoe leather and worked as hard as or harder and gathered his facts as well or better than any reporter whose front-page beat was the cops, courts, jails, and the victims of the streets of New York. Then he returned to his desk, tie undone, cigar bitten to shreds and gave his editors exactly what they needed: something special.

He wrote millions of words. He spent many thousands of hours across sixty years of newspapering, mostly; magazine writing, which paid good money sometimes; and book writing steadily. Working the phones, walking the streets, stalking the halls of justice, and most of all climbing to the stories at the top of the stairs. The dream—always a deadline out of reach—was the same dream as that of those feature writers at the *Trib* so many years earlier: to be a novelist. That would probably have been a waste of his real talent. And he knew it.

He was, in fact, as the cable TV company HBO described him in the title of a documentary, *A Deadline Artist*:

July 13, 1963—"Tony's Fluke Day"

August 13, 1963—"A Way of Life: Mourning a Gunned Down Man"

September 27, 1963—"Valachi: A Flashback"

September 29, 1963—"A Retiring Frank Costello"

October 1, 1963—"An Intensive Hunt for Kidnap Clues"

October 22, 1963—"The Last Gallo Living at 51 President St."

November 13, 1963—"The Visitors"

These seven pieces of crime writing span the first year he spent at the *Herald Tribune*. His byline began appearing in 1963 and continued appearing through 1967, when that paper—with its originally vertical layout of gray type in six to eight columns, including shipping news and timetables—ran its presses for the final time and closed its doors, the victim of a labor dispute led by a man, Bert Powers, who thought he was a union leader but who cared little for writing and less, it seemed, for the city of New York, where he and his members earned their living.

It was a time when news, for many, continued to be delivered in ink. It was a time that could be viewed as a beginning to the end of an era in organized crime, a time when a redeeming quality could be found or imagined and put into prose. A time when crack dealing, beheading, and setting fire to whole families were not the most salient traits of gangsters. When they killed each other quietly, to send one kind of message, or left a body on a doorstep to send another.

In the first of these pieces, "Tony's Fluke Day," we join Jimmy Hoffa's confidant in the powerful 180,000-member Teamsters Union. Tony Provenzano, boss of the 13,000-member Local 560 and head of the 80,000-member Joint Teamsters Council, was in federal court in Newark, New Jersey, for his sentencing.

> It did not seem like a bad morning at all. The boss, Tony Provenzano, who is one of the biggest men in the Teamsters Union, walked up and down the corridor outside of this Federal courtroom in Newark and

> he had a little smile on his face and he kept flicking a white cigarette holder around.
>
> "Today is the kind of a day for fishing," Tony was saying. "We ought to go out and get some fluke."

That is how the story began, with you in the halls of justice with the troupe of players—labor racketeers, it would seem—as they got ready for their star to go on stage.

> It was a very good way, this fooling around yesterday morning, to kill time while they were waiting for the judge to send somebody out and tell them that he was ready to sentence Tony Pro for extorting money from a trucking firm.

There, in 120 three-syllables-or-less words (if you don't count Provenzano), six commas and five periods and no contractions, you had all you needed to know about the play you would see through Breslin's eyes.

But what makes for a masterful piece of work—and is seen in all the pieces that follow, written by a 36-year-old man who has come into his powers almost fully now—is what happens next, which is the element of time: the clock on Tony Pro's life.

> On June 11, a jury convicted Provenzano of extorting $17,000 from the Dorn Trucking Co. Provenzano . . . generally is regarded as the Teamster most intimate with Jimmy Hoffa, the union president. Tony Pro makes $80,000 a year. He stands to blow it all.
>
> Now, he sat at a brown wooden table desk, with two lawyers on his left, and he folded his hands in front of him and waited. The courtroom was silent. The clock on the wall in the rear made a loud click when it hit 11:15. The courtroom has white granite walls broken up by brown

> wood and red drapes with gold wreaths on them. Four brown pillars, red drapes between them, formed the backdrop for Judge Shaw . . .
>
> The two United States Attorneys who prosecuted Tony Pro sat alone. They were young-looking and expressionless.
>
> "They look like the kind of kids you used to copy off in school," Danny Rubino, one of Tony Pro's closest friends said.

And it is this touch that captures, even better than a courtroom artist, the plight of Tony Pro.

These kids were the timekeepers. And they recommended to the judge what time might fit the crime that the jury had found.

> "Mr. Provenzano," the judge said, "if you have anything to say at this time I will listen to it."
>
> Tony got up and walked to the lectern in front of the Judge. He had on a gray sharkskin suit and gray tie. He is a short, heavy-set guy who has the puffed eyelids of one who used to fight. Drops of sweat sat on his upper lip. Tony took out a handkerchief and wiped them away. Then he clasped his hands behind his back and talked to the judge like he was a kid back in school and trying to answer a question.
>
> "All I care to say is that I told the truth in the stand and I stand on the truth I told with my hand on the Bible."
>
> Nervousness made him stammer a little. He does not talk too well, but you do not need an elocution course to run a Teamsters Union. You need muscle, and Tony has plenty of that.

But none of it would matter now. His entourage of muscle was a troupe of extras relegated to the back rows.

The simplicity and speed with which Breslin captures time, speeds it up and slows it down in short sentences that sparkle like Tony's ring, is what matters now. It was just 11:15. Between then and 11:30 the judge sentenced Tony to seven years and of course the federal insult of a fine on top—$10,000, which was certainly more than he would earn for even seven years of prison labor. And this now is where Tony's gold wristwatch would be replaced by roll call, chow time, yard time, lockdown time, and all the other kinds of government time that are part of prison.

> "The time has come to serve notice on those who show no respect for the rights of others that such action will not be tolerated. Extortion is a vicious type of crime. The penalty should be appropriate to deter others of like mind . . ." the judge said.

Time. Time in the hall. Time before the judge. Time on bail. Time for an appeal. Time in prison. All this time, which Breslin could make you feel as if you were seeing things through Tony's eyes and hearing things through Tony's ears.

> The room was silent. The clock made a lot of noise when it hit 11:30.
>
> Tony Pro's two lawyers were at the table, right at his elbow, and each had a hand against his forehead and they were busy taking notes as the judge talked. And all of Tony's guys were back in the seats behind him. But yesterday morning Tony Pro was all alone as he stood in the courtroom, because the words were for nobody else . . . The judge was talking only to Tony Pro and it was bad. The sweat formed all over Tony's face. He was alone no matter who was in the room with him.

Then he stops the clock and tells the reader, you, because like the words between the judge and Tony, Breslin is only talking to you, what it means:

> This is how it comes to all of them. They can bluster and laugh and everybody slaps them on the back, but at the end they have to stand alone and nobody can do anything for them.

It is a moment of emphasis that will reappear in other columns: the real sentence—whether prison, divorce, or death—is that the person at the center must endure this fate alone. Every reader understands it.

And then we are out of the court and across the street at "a bar called the Red Coach . . . [where] The bartender put a portable radio in front of Tony, so he could listen to the radio tell him his sentence."

Breslin is there, a place where only the confidants can be, observing them as they listen to the radio make it real. The crime and the sentence and Tony's fate are now available to anyone who could listen.

> At the bar, he is pleasant company. You can't buy a drink around the guy. Picking up checks has always been his reputation. Everybody in Jersey who stands with Tony Pro always tells you that.
>
> "When I stopped driving a truck 12 years ago," Tony was saying, "I got $6.40 a day. Now drivers here get $26.20.
>
> "I'm going to play cards," Tony said.
>
> He picked up his change and shook hands good bye and left in his union-owned Cadillac.

And now it's time to leave. This ending would have been enough for even the best reporter.

At this point, the article is approaching the final tally of 2,360 words. It's a feature report of a length perfect for a standard-sized newspaper like the *Trib*. It was already maybe twice as long, or even a little longer, than the tabloid columns of the next phase of his newspaper career. But the Rockefeller Republican audience of the *Trib*, even the reinvigorated *Trib* where he worked, was an audience that rode the commuter trains in from the suburbs, and not so much the subway trains in from the distant reaches of Rockaway Beach, Far Rockaway, Brighton or Marine Park or Broad Channel or Woodlawn and Jerome, way up in the Bronx on the border to the suburb of Yonkers. Those trips could be a crowded hour or more with not enough elbow room to neatly fold back the pages of a paper set up as a broadsheet like the *Trib.* The trip on the commuter trains often had a comfortable seat, and even when crowded a bit more elbow room. And that is precisely how the story was written. With a bit more elbow room, for an audience that did not move its lips when it read.

And now, as their ride came to an end, so did the story: Everyone has gone home, the courthouse has emptied, and the bartender has wiped down the surface of the bar. Breslin has not left, for there is one last thing to leave you with.

> Three blocks away, in a cafeteria that you had to go two flights down to get into, Richard Levin, who was one of the United States Attorneys who prosecuted Tony Pro, had lunch on a tray—scallops and a fruit salad and iced tea.
>
> He is only 31 . . . He didn't even have a handkerchief in his pocket . . . He never would make it with Tony Pro . . . Nothing on his hand flashed. The guy who sunk Tony Pro doesn't even have a diamond on his pinky.

And this is how it comes to all of them. They can bluster and laugh, but in the morning when the other reporters wake up, Breslin will have stayed longer, gone to greater lengths, and told a better story. This intelligent tenacity, unlike some of his storytelling mechanisms, is not learned in schools and cannot be taught there. This is how to write about crime in a newspaper. It is seen in each of these examples of crime writing that followed.

This crime writing certainly fit the *Herald Tribune* ethos as a writer's paper. It had long been known as one, well before the arrival of Jock Whitney and his money, the stable of Young Turk editors with their energetic new page layouts and the writers and their "New Journalism." They fit the ethos, but they went well beyond what had come before. Theirs was the kind of portraiture that broke down forever the false wall of objectivity that had stood between the reader and the events. It brought the audience into the drama. Breslin closed the distance by moving back and forth between author, omniscient narrator and character who you could touch and feel and who could himself touch and feel. Breslin *was fully present.*

> The old lady came in as old Italian women always come when they have to see the dead.

That is how "A Way of Life," which appeared in the paper one month later, begins.

"Valachi: A Flashback" appeared in the paper on September 27. It begins like this:

> It was a big, new Cadillac and Joe Valachi admired it. He had it parked on 116th St. near Pleasant Ave in East Harlem on this afternoon in 1953 and he was standing in front of a candy store talking to a couple of kids in their early 20's, but he kept his eyes on the car while he talked. Joe was sure he was a big deal because of the car. A gangster without a Cadillac didn't even qualify in his book.

"A Retiring Frank Costello" comes just two days later, on August 29. It is simply brilliant.

> At 10 o'clock, when the waiter brought another round of anisette and coffee, Frank Costello looked at his watch and said it was going to be the last drink of the night.
>
> He had to be up at 7:30 in the morning so he could take his poodle for a walk along Central Park West.

Costello, by 1963, had come a long way from the streets of East Harlem and the shelves of grocery store that his father established before summoning his son and the rest of his family from Sicily.

He had become the Prime Minister of the Mob and prided himself on diplomacy and restraint, and it was often noted that he never had carried a gun. This is not to say he didn't have rivals and opponents killed. He did. But when his boss, Lucky Luciano, was sentenced to Sing Sing, it was Costello who took control of the assets of the Lucchese crime family and who created the commission that brought order if not peace to the Mob's lucrative trade in gambling, labor racketeering, and vice.

And now, twelve years after he had walked out of the Mob hearings held by Senator Estes Kefauver, he was a detached observer of the hearings at which Joe Valachi was the star witness. Just a few days earlier, for the editions of September 27, Breslin had written:

> Cadillac and all, Valachi was only a little guy in New York when he was around. But right now, he is a lot more than that. Today, Joe Valachi is big thing in this town.
>
> Because of him New York is the hottest city in the country. There are so many wiretaps on phones around town that people in several spots around the city would be better off making calls on a network television show. They would have fewer people listening to them.

Now Valachi was a character brushstroked into a portrait of someone who was as important to the Mob as a Medici was to the city-state of Florence.

> Costello was sitting with a couple of friends at a table in this East Side restaurant and nobody else in the place seemed to notice him.
>
> Which seemed strange because now, with crime hearings on in Washington, you automatically thought of Frank Costello. In 1951,

when the first Senate crime hearings were held, Costello was the name which put the show over. Day after day, the television cameras showing only his hands, Costello sat in a Federal Courtroom at Foley Square and faced the Kefauver Committee's questioning. But there is to be no Frank Costello in Washington when the hearings resume today and the old star was saying that he may not even look at them on television.

"My agent told me not to go this time," he was saying. "The last time I never got any of the re-run money. The residuals. They've been showing the same film off and on for 12 years and I never got a check yet."

Costello had on a gray pin-striped suit and dark heavy-rimmed glasses. He fingered a box of English Oval cigarettes and he said he did not want to talk even about the weather, but when he was asked about Joe Valachi, he nodded his head and said, yes, he knew the guy.

"I knew him as Cago," he said. "I knew him from when I was on vacation."

"Where was that?"

"Where was that?" Costello repeated. "Vacation, you know, when I was away." He waved a hand in the general direction of Atlanta.

"I tell you," he said, "I never knew the guy before I saw him there. I didn't know anything about the guy. Just that everybody down there called him Cago. Now a couple of weeks ago I see his pictures in all the papers and they say his name is Valachi."

"He talks about you," Costello was told. Valachi has testified that Costello was the head of the crime syndicate in New York until Vito Genovese replaced him.

Costello shrugged. "I can't stop a man from talking," he said.

"One thing he is talking about is all new to me. This Cosa Nostra. I tell you the truth, I never heard anybody use that expression. But you ought to use it. It sounds colorful."

And here you have the writing. And Costello's vision of himself as a celebrity with an agent offering Breslin some advice. "It sounds colorful." It makes for one of the first portraits, and one of the great portraits, created by reporters who were called The New Journalists. Breslin and the others were simply hungry, hungry for fame, and they knew how to earn that fame by telling the truth in compelling, insightful, wonderful prose.

### THE LAST GALLO LIVING AT 51 PRESIDENT ST.

The last Gallo living at 51 President Street is the grandmother, Mrs. Big Mama Nunziata, who is 77 and never scared easily before and sees no reason why she should start backing off now. She lives alone in a bare, four-room apartment on the second floor of the empty three-story building which once housed the Gallos, and their armed gang. . . . Mrs. Big Mama Nunziata would spit at a forest fire. She has seven children, 28 grandchildren and 22 great grandchildren, but she lives at 51 President Street, where all the trouble is, because three of the grandchildren, Joey, Larry and Albert Gallo, need the help, not the rest of the family . . .

There was this Sunday morning a while back when somebody in Brooklyn deliberately set off loaded rifles and two members of the Profaci gang, the Gallo rivals, were badly hurt. One of them was Carmine Persico. Since Persico had once tried to garrot Larry Gallo, the police, acting on a wild hunch, went looking for Larry.

They busted into 51 President Street, and for their troubles ran into Mama Nunziata, who was in a mood to fence with them. "Larry?" she said. "He watches the televeesh with me all night."

"Mama," one of the detectives said, "the guy who tried to strangle Larry got shot pretty bad and we want to ask him about it."

"Oh," Mama Nunziata said. "Is this boy, is he all right?"

"He's not dead, but he's hurt pretty bad."

Her eyes opened wide. "Oh, he's not dead," she said. "So tell me, this boy. Is he a good boy or is a bad boy?"

"Bad," the detective said. "Very bad."

Mama smiled in triumph. "Then it's better off he dies." That ended the interview.

Later, when Larry came back to 51 President Street, Mama Nunziata sat quietly in the apartment and kept looking at him.

"What's the matter, Larry," she said, "you can't shoot straight?"

From this column, a bestseller was born and published in 1969: *The Gang That Couldn't Shoot Straight.* The book is filled with humor, and as it is from a time before the Sopranos came into living rooms and slurred many Italian Americans and delighted many others with the Mob's crude speech and cheap crime, it can be forgiven today for its weaknesses and praised for its humor. It became a movie in 1971. It made lots of money. It featured a young actor named Robert De Niro.

The fame and the piles of money—for a writer from Queens—that the movie would earn Breslin in the years right after the book came out would cause nothing but grief for the editors that came later in his life. Famous. Flush. Aggrieved. Breslin would repeatedly launch one of his crusades against stability at home and at work. But through it all he would follow Mama Nunziata's advice and stick to one thing:

"This Valachi," she was saying, "what does he do? He's with a Genowaysee for 30 years and all of a sudden he stool pigeons . . .

"Look," she said, the hands out in front of her now, "what do these people want? Do they want to be a gangster, a thief and a stool pigeon all at the same time? That's no good.

"You got to stick to one thing."

And of course came the Lion, mascot for a time of the Gallo gang, and perhaps more famous in the movie than De Niro or even the star,

Jerry Orbach. Off screen, in what could feel ironic, Orbach would be friends with Crazy Joe Gallo, the Mafia clown prince whose lion it had been, and Orbach was with him, celebrating with champagne at the Copacabana nightclub the evening before Gallo's forty-third birthday on April 7, 1972, when Gallo would be gunned down around 4:30 A.M. inside Umberto's, a red sauce Italian clam joint on the corner of Mulberry Street in Manhattan's Little Italy. The Gallo party was about to dig into second helpings of scungilli, shrimp and pasta, according to the *New York Post*, when the four assassins burst in and opened fire. Gallo had tried for his gun. Too late. He stumbled out the front door and died.

This was the Mob in all its ruthlessness. These were not the gangsters of Runyon, who were warmhearted and could be made to sing in a musical and who welcomed Runyon to their tables, in effect to become their Homer and make them heroic.

"Don't go near Tenth Avenue," Breslin quoted Runyon as being warned when he returned to New York after covering the baseball season. "They got a lot of killers there."

" 'Where on Tenth Avenue,' he said.

"If there are killers, he reasoned, then that means there are also a lot of crap games and, even better, loose dolls. When he got to the corner of Tenth Avenue and 47th Street, he took one look at the guys standing around and wishing mightily for trouble, and at once he felt at home."

The Mob, in all its history, had never been warmhearted. Its assassinations, extortion and bombings, and preying on honest Italian American shopkeepers were well known from its earliest days. But now they were becoming ugly celebrities and soon they would have John Gotti, perhaps the ugliest of all.

> [Sammy the Bull] Gravano and Johnny Gambino went to the boss, John Gotti, who conducted thuggery out of two social clubs, each with the same dreary brick fronts . . . They are an indictment of the film and news businesses that, without understanding, have made Gotti and all about him so deliciously sinister. When the whole thing consists of dreary little people in preposterous storefronts, dungeons really.

Breslin does not write about them often, but when he does, this is the shift in tone from his writing about the labor racketeer, Tony Pro, and the Prime Minister, Frank Costello.

> Gravano, who is trying to trade his stories for his life, testifies that he and Gotti sat in a clubroom and thought they were God and a murder was ordered and then they went to dinner.

This version is informed not just by the facts, but by his wife, another honest, gifted Italian American who had to live in the shadow of Mob stigma, something Breslin mentions in his writing. He would rarely find humor in gangsters later in his career, though his deft touch could still make you smile—as it does in his 2008 book *The Good Rat*, which chronicles the crimes of two cops who were Mob hit men with badges. As a reviewer noticed, he wrote operatically, but he captured the repugnance of these men.

> He became but the first of eight murders that Burt Kaplan admits to perpetrating along with Gaspipe Casso and the two detectives Eppolito and Caracappa. That there could be more than only eight is at least possible. You get tired of confessing to all these killings and just stop. Anyway, who wants to hear about another in a long line of bad guys shot in the back of the head?

Breslin's earlier comedic version of the Gallos descends from Runyon, and he captured through Big Mama Nunziata the buffoonery of this deadly world:

> "It used to be crazy here. They had the lion. Ooohhh, what a big head he had. He ate $5 worth of steak every day. We got him out on the leash walking down Umberto's, and this fellow comes up from the docks and he says, 'What a big head that dog got.'
>
> "I say to him, 'Dog? That's no dog. What's the matter with you? That's a lion.' You should have seen him run back to the docks . . .
>
> "Then Joey had the panel truck and he put the lion in the back all cops stop him one day . . .
>
> "Joey says, 'Please don't open the back of the truck. It's very bad.'
>
> "You know how nosey those cops are. This one goes right to the back and opens the doors to the truck. So here's the lion, with the big head, and the cop he yells and starts to run. Joey got to grab the lion before the lion chases the cop."

# THE FIRST PLANE TO DALLAS

The president had been shot, according to an ABC Radio bulletin at 12:36 central standard time. At 12:38, CBS became the first national TV network to report the news.

Breslin, according to Dick Wald and Jim Bellows in their book *The World of Jimmy Breslin*, knew from the start this was his story. "When President Kennedy was killed, Breslin was on the first jet from New York to Dallas."

The assassination occurred at 12:30 central time. By 12:33 the assassin, Lee Harvey Oswald, had walked out of the Texas School Book Depository, apparently less than a minute before the area around the building was locked down. By 1:00 CST the president was declared dead. By 2:00 the vice president had left Parkland Hospital. When the body of the man who had been president of the United States joined him aboard Air Force One, along with the woman who had been First Lady, Jacqueline Kennedy, LBJ was sworn in as president. It was 2:38. Jacqueline Kennedy was still wearing the bloodied pink suit she had on when the convertible presidential limousine sped away from the book depository, and she was heard by others in the car to say: "I have his brains in my hands."

The media confusion of the first hours—dead, reported dead, unofficially reported dead, priests tell a 32-year-old Dan Rather of CBS he is dead, Walter Cronkite considers what language to use, reports of Oswald's arrest, reports on the murder of Officer Tippit at 1:15 P.M. CST by Oswald—all of this confusion had subsided by the time Breslin arrived at Love Field in Dallas. By the next day, at a press conference, he was able to "pepper," gently, the doctors who worked on Kennedy with questions that would only make sense when his account "A Death in Emergency Room One" appeared in the *Trib* in the Sunday, November 24, editions.

"Essentially he was a storyteller," Richard Kluger wrote in his magisterial work, *The Paper*, which chronicled the life of the *Trib* and its important impact on democracy from the era of Horace Greeley, founder of the *New York Tribune*, and James Gordon Bennett, founder of the *Herald*, to the era of Breslin and Tom Wolfe.

> His usefulness to the paper was well illustrated by the work he did following the assassination of John F. Kennedy. While other reporters were concentrating on the fallen President's assassin, theories about his involvement in a plot . . . Breslin busied himself interviewing the surgeon who had tried to save Kennedy's life, the priest who had administered last rites, and the funeral director who provided the best bronze casket in his stock.

Breslin "gently but thoroughly" questioned the doctor, 34-year-old Malcolm Perry, and used his answers in reconstructing the loss of hope, the stoicism of the First Lady, and the final efforts to save what was left of a man under the harsh surgical lights.

The long piece Breslin filed is held up as one of the great examples of modern journalistic storytelling.

> DALLAS—The call bothered Malcolm Perry. "Dr. Tom Shires, STAT," the girl's voice said over the page in the doctor's cafeteria at

Parkland Memorial Hospital. The "STAT" meant emergency. Nobody ever called Tom Shires, the hospital's chief resident in surgery, for an emergency. And Shires, Perry's superior, was out of town for the day. Malcolm Perry looked at the salmon croquettes on the plate in front of him. Then he put down his fork and went over to a telephone.

"This is Dr. Perry taking Dr. Shires' page," he said.

"President Kennedy has been shot. STAT," the operator said. "They are bringing him into the emergency room now."

Perry hung up and walked quickly out of the cafeteria and down a flight of stairs and pushed through a brown door and a nurse pointed to Emergency Room One, and Dr. Perry walked into it . . .

Perry called for a scalpel. He was going to start a tracheotomy . . . The incision had to be made below the bullet wound . . .

[H]e started the tracheotomy. There was no anesthesia. John Kennedy could feel nothing now. The wound in the back of the head told Dr. Perry that the president never knew a thing about it when he was shot, either . . .

Just as he finished the tracheotomy, Malcolm Perry looked up and Dr. Kemp Clark, chief neurosurgeon in residency at Parkland, came in through the door. Clark was looking at the president of the United States. Then he looked at Malcolm Perry and the look told Malcolm Perry something he already knew. There was no way to save the patient.

"Would you like to leave, ma'am?" Kemp Clark said to Jacqueline Kennedy. "We can make you more comfortable outside."

Just the lips moved. "No," Jacqueline Kennedy said . . .

The IBM clock on the wall said it was 1 P.M. The date was November 22, 1963.

Three policemen were moving down the hall outside Emergency Room One now, and they were calling to everybody to get out of the way. But this was not needed, because everybody stepped out of the way automatically when they saw the priest who was behind the police. His name was the Reverend Oscar Huber, a small 70-year-old man who was walking quickly.

Malcolm Perry turned to leave the room as Father Huber came in . . .

Everything that was inside that room now belonged to Jacqueline Kennedy and Father Oscar Huber and the things in which they believe.

Father Huber pulled the white sheet down so he could anoint the forehead of John Fitzgerald Kennedy. Jacqueline Kennedy was standing beside the priest. Now this old priest held up his right hand and he began the chant that Roman Catholic priests have said over their dead for centuries.

"*Si vivis, ego te absolvo a peccatis tuis. In nomine Patris et Filii et Spiritus Sancti, amen.*"

The prayer said, "If you are living, I absolve you from your sins. In the name of the Father and of the Son and of the Holy Ghost, amen." . . .

"Eternal rest grant unto him, O Lord," Father Huber said.

"And let perpetual light shine upon him," Jacqueline Kennedy answered. She did not cry . . .

When he was finished praying, Father Huber turned and took her hand. "I am shocked," he said.

"Thank you for taking care of the president," Jacqueline Kennedy said.

"I am convinced that his soul had not left his body," Father Huber said. "This was a valid last sacrament."

"Thank you," she said.

Then he left. He had been eating lunch at his rectory at Holy Trinity Church when he heard the news.

Breslin was still in New York City, perhaps on his way out of the 41st Street offices of the paper. Perhaps not quite yet. Only minutes had passed since the first news had reached him.

He was not there. But if you read the short story he wrote—and really that is what it is—then you were. You were there and you knew more about the death of John F. Kennedy at Parkland Hospital than you would have learned from reams of reporting by the wire services and newspapers, and hours and hours of radio and television commentary. It was, in fact, the only thing you needed to read sixty years later. Your heart aches. You understood the crime. You understood the victim's condition and that you were in the victim's family: America was wounded, critically if not mortally. The criminal, in this and all of Breslin's reports from Dallas, is hardly worth a mention.

"A Death in Emerrgency Room One" has been criticized, Kluger writes, for getting certain facts wrong even as Breslin strove for "an attempt at clinical accuracy."

The story contained errors, he points out. The correct names of surgical procedures, the title of the chairman of the department of surgery (Breslin had characterized him as the chief resident) and the operator's words were among them. Yet, rereading the story, Kluger said Dr. Perry thought "the major focus is correct" and the mistakes "to be expected in such circumstances."

Complainants about Breslin's work have a number of times asserted that he sacrificed, as Kluger also says, accuracy for emotional impact. But when the dart hits the bullseye, as it does here, both accuracy and emotion are served equally in the creation of a story that brought you truth, which is not a hard and fast thing to be conveyed simply in a collection of well-organized facts. His is an honest form of storytelling, not one of deceit or sloppiness. At the time Breslin wrote it, how he wrote it also was seen as something new, something revolutionary, a form of reconstruction designed to put the reader there, with the author, in the scene of the tragedy.

Praise for his work often includes the critical judgment that his prose resembles that of Hemingway in its short, seemingly simple sentences that build through their very compression a compelling story.

If you were to read Hemingway's journalism for the *Toronto Star* you would see that is often the case in these pieces, which like Breslin's are far shorter than all but the shortest Hemingway story:

> During the late friction with Germany a certain number of Torontonians of military age showed their desire to assist in the conduct of the war by emigrating to the States to give their all to laboring in munition plants . . . they now desire to return to Canada and gain fifteen percent on their United States money.
>
> Through a desire to aid these morally courageous souls who supplied the sinews of war we have prepared a few hints on "How to Be Popular Although a Slacker." . . .
>
> The first difficulty to be surmounted will be the C.E.F. [Canadian Expeditionary Force] overseas badge. This is easily handled, however. If anyone asks you why you do not wear your button, reply haughtily: "I do not care to advertise my military service."

In another piece of his journalism on valor, "War Medals for Sale," the author would walk from medal and coin shop to pawn shop to secondhand shop to capture "the market price" of valor by asking how much a medal could be sold for. No grand statements necessary. From the *Toronto Star*, December 8, 1923:

> The reporter got, in succession, a price on his coat, another offer of seventy cents on his watch, and a handsome offer of 40 cents for his cigarette case. But no one wanted to buy or sell medals . . . You could sell your old military puttees. But you couldn't find a buyer for a 1914 Star. So the market price of valor remained undetermined.

The reporter-to-reporter comparison might be a better comparison than one that puts Breslin's journalism beside Hemingway's later novels or nonfiction.

But if there is a book by Breslin that could be compared in simple elegance and precise detail to Hemingway's work of nonfiction—say, *Death in the Afternoon*—it might be that first book, *Sunny Jim*. The account of the life of this legendary horse trainer, Jim Fitzsimmons, is simple in its prose and emotionally complex in its grasp of a man and his stables and jockeys and his work, which could be summed up for Fitzsimmons in the way Breslin would later sum up his own work: you won a big race on Saturday, you went to work the next day not looking backward for one minute at that fame which could not beat tomorrow's horse.

"Breslin deals in emotions the way some columnists deal in issues," said Jim Bellows, the last editor of the *Trib*, and Dick Wald, its last managing editor, in the book of Breslin's columns they composed together. "They are the stuff of his writing and his articles gain or lose an audience by how well the public can identify with his private responses to the world . . . He has a particular aptitude, though, for dealing in tragedy, pathos, and sorrow . . . he does his work with an odd mixture of restraint and emotionalism that manages to capture the mood of sorrow in its varying shades . . . He became so wrapped up in it that, after filing 'A Death in Emergency Room One,' he went out, re-did all the research that he had gathered in the first place, and tried to file the story again. When he finished covering the Kennedy funeral in Washington he was unable to talk to anyone for several hours."

They composed that book in a graveyard of a city room. It was all that was left to compose that day in 1966, after the reporters and editors were gone, their fifth-floor desks empty, the presses on two and three silent, the trucks no longer belching out of the first-floor loading bays. They sat in the newsroom to compose this book on the very last day of the paper's life. They had to do so, because Breslin had taken a publisher's money and failed to deliver a book. In this case the publisher agreed to accept a compilation in exchange for the money advanced.

The book organized by Bellows and Wald compiles a very good sampling of the work of this talent that Bellows and his editors nurtured.

If "Emergency Room One," published November 24, 1963, is a textbook example of The New Journalism and all the truth its personalized storytelling could enable through careful reporting and a reconstruction of events—not by ignoring the facts or creating the facts, but by breaking through the strictures of the past—"The Gravedigger," published November 26, 1963, the day after JFK was buried, is the iconic example of what set a great reporter apart from what Breslin derisively and a bit unfairly called "the scribblers," or even the best reporters for the then most assuredly astringent *New York Times*.

It is the example of Breslin's brilliance taught in schools. It is a story most often taught in encouraging the young to look for that which is difficult. If the teacher is too vigorous, there is the risk of failing to teach that the first job is to satisfy the reader or viewer's simple interests: Who won the game? What was the score? Or in the case of the funeral of John Fitzgerald Kennedy, what did the larger picture look like?

"The Gravedigger" only works if it is set against those factual accounts. The loser's locker room is only poignant if the account butts up against a story that begins with the score. The true power of the column as journalism is not in its simple and poignant beauty, which is fine, but in the way it served as a counterpoint to the reporting of the main events that were unfolding as the United States prepared to bury a president. The column, seen in this light, is not so much what made

Breslin special as it is what made the newspaper he worked for special. That is easy to lose sight of today, when we are talking about artifacts.

It is a little unfair to the reader to give these short excerpts of this particular column. So if you haven't read it twice, look it up.

IT'S AN HONOR

> Clifton Pollard was pretty sure he was going to be working on Sunday, so when he woke up at 9 A.M., in his three-room apartment on Corcoran Street, he put on khaki overalls before going into the kitchen for breakfast. His wife, Hettie, made bacon and eggs for him. Pollard was in the middle of eating them when he received the phone call he had been expecting. It was from Mazo Kawalchik, who is the foreman of the gravediggers at Arlington National Cemetery, which is where Pollard works for a living. "Polly, could you please be here by 11 o'clock this morning?" Kawalchik asked. "I guess you know what it's for." Pollard did. He hung up the phone, finished breakfast, and left his apartment so he could spend Sunday digging a grave for John Fitzgerald Kennedy.

It ends like this:

> Clifton Pollard wasn't at the funeral. He was over behind the hill, digging graves for $3.01 an hour in another section of the cemetery. He didn't know who the graves were for. He was just digging them and then covering them with boards. "They'll be used," he said. "We just don't know when. I tried to go over to see the grave," he said. "But it was so crowded a soldier told me I couldn't get through. So I just stayed here and worked, sir. But I'll get over there later a little bit. Just sort of look around and see how it is, you know. Like I told you, it's an honor."

And on the way to the ending, Breslin makes a few more points, which would tell you what he considered most important about the events at the side of the grave Clifton Pollard had dug:

> Yesterday morning, at 11:15, Jacqueline Kennedy started toward the grave. . . .
>
> Everybody watched her while she walked. She is the mother of two fatherless children and she was walking into the history . . . Even though they had killed her husband and his blood ran onto her lap while he died, she could walk through the streets and to his grave and help us all while she walked. . . .
>
> Then it was over and black limousines rushed under the cemetery trees and out onto the boulevard toward the White House. "What time is it?" a man standing on the hill was asked. He looked at his watch. "Twenty minutes past three," he said.
>
> Clifton Pollard wasn't at the funeral. He was over behind the hill.

There is one other piece to this trilogy of reports Breslin sent back to his reader in New York from this, the funeral for a hatless, Roman Catholic, Irish president. It is a piece published on November 25, 1963, the day JFK was buried in the grave Clifton Pollard had dug, and a day before "The Gravedigger" appeared, that consciously or not in its concluding paragraphs can be felt as a harbinger.

> But now you noticed the soldiers. You saw the ones standing so stiffly around the coffin, and the others moving slowly and clicking their heels while the bayonets sparkled. And then everything came over you, and you stood in the rotunda of the Capitol Building of the United States of America and looked at a coffin that held the body of a President whose head had been blown off by a gun fired by one of his own people and now you fell apart inside and there was this terrible sense of confusion and inability to understand what was going on. And there were tears;

> of course there were tears, there have been tears for three days now; and then you started talking out loud.
>
> "Oh, Christ, what are we doing here?" It was a prayer, not a blasphemy.

At this point the newspaper found it necessary to guide the reader by inserting a cross headline, "Art of Hating," before the column continued:

> Dallas. You started to think about Dallas. In Dallas they sat and told you that a Communist shot the President of the United States. They sat and told you that, while everybody in the town with any brains knew that John Fitzgerald Kennedy, the President of the United States, was shot because this is a country that has let the art of hating grow so strong that now we kill our Presidents because of it.
>
> And Dallas does not own hate. Dallas is a collective word and it means Birmingham and Tuscaloosa and, yes, Scarsdale and Bay Ridge and the Bronx, too. Dallas means everyplace where people in this nation stand off with their smugness and their paychecks and their cute little remarks, and run their lives on the basis of hate. Everybody has a piece of this murder. Everybody who ever stood off and said, "that Jew bastard," and everybody who ever said, "I don't want niggers near me" is part of this murder.

These three pieces, taken together, certainly give you three elements of Breslin's powerful sense of craft: the immediate "STAT" of "Emergency Room One," the poignant sound of the backhoe in "It's an Honor" and the harsh and sweeping indictment that closes "Everybody's Crime."

A fourth element of these final pages of Camelot, and one that under pressure or in haste, or under the presumption of good taste, could have been ignored, is in the minutiae that take place away from the black bunting, the crepe, the horse-drawn caisson. It is the final act of noticing you can often see in his work. He stays to observe when everyone has in one way or another moved on. This fourth piece was published on November 27, 1963. It is the best kind of closed-room crime reporting.

> Within five minutes after the assassination was confirmed Friday afternoon, the public information officer for a Senate subcommittee sat dazed in his office and when the phone on his desk rang he picked it up automatically.
>
> The caller was a lobbyist for an important industry.
>
> "It's terrible," the one with the Senate subcommittee said.
>
> "Yes it is," the lobbyist said. "Now tell me something. We would like to know what effect Kennedy's death is going to have on this investigation of our industry that you've been planning. What are the implications."

This column, "The Smooth Transfer of Power," is shining and hard as a pure white diamond.

> Evelyn Lincoln, Kennedy's private secretary, knew enough to get into her office Saturday night and clean out her desks and files . . . She was getting out of the way before the first of the hungry people started piling into her office.
>
> This is what you found here after you finally looked around at what had happened after the longest weekend you had ever spent: a weekend you want to forget. . . .
>
> There was a transition here. A swift one, too.
>
> This does not mean the transition of power from a dead president to his successor. . . . and the other important people who run this country . . . these things that went on were far beneath them and were unnoticed.

But some of the little people, the ones who use politics as a way to make a living, were brutal.

Breslin, when his work on "Emergency Room One" was over, could not speak for several hours, according to Bellows.

When he finished all his work in Washington, Breslin went home to Queens, walked into a bar named Pep McGuire's, and did not come out for two or three days, according to Breslin. Pep McGuire's was at the center of Breslin's mythical universe, and there he now found solace. Alcohol, which would continue to fuel him for years into the future, had already lost the warm golden glow of a sunny morning in a mug and an elbow and an ashtray not on a desk in the *Long Island Press* newsroom but on a warm wooden corner of a bar, polished by rags, spilled drinks and elbows.

Now its mystical properties deadened pain, creating a darkness inside him as bleak as the city and the nation outside the bar.

"I went into Pep's bar and I never came out. You just drank the sickness right out of your system; the bleary day." He told the interviewer this on the 50th anniversary of JFK's assassination.

As for the work itself, he said, like Sunny Jim, he had not looked back on it. He did not read it again. Not "The Gravedigger," not the other columns from the simultaneously grieving and scheming Capitol. "What for," he told me, to whom he more expansively once said, "Let's reminisce about tomorrow."

He had to earn a living.

# YOU! YOU! YOU! YOU!

1964 saw Breslin writing three columns a week and one on Sunday. Marvin the Torch and Fat Thomas, the characters he was creating by hyper-realizing the lives of his friends, shared the space with the guilty and their lawyers stalking the halls of the criminal courts, the nomination by Breslin of Breslin's wife Rosemary Dattolico for the first woman president—first Italian Woman president—pickpockets practicing their seasonal trade, Jimmy Hoffa and his Teamsters, bookies, widows, the Kennedy Library, drug dealers, and a vacancy at the top of the Mob.

This was the pace of fame. Three columns a week. A feature on Sunday. The pace was driven by immediacy. The natural immediacy of news; the immediacy of the present tense. *Tell me what is happening. Now.* This was what drove Breslin. All of him. All the time. Now. It earned Breslin bylines on the front page of the *Herald Tribune* as well as his usual placement on the split front page, meaning the front of the second section of the paper. It would soon earn him the princely sum of $125,000 a year. He couldn't keep track of his expenses; he somehow was always late on his bills. He continued to collect his stories in bars and courts and on street corners. He continued to model them on his friends, shape them around his enemies and steal them from his family's store of experience.

The year began with a vacancy at the top of a Mob family.

> Among serious problems which must be faced in the upcoming year is the one which has fallen on the gangsters of our city, who are a part of the regular Brooklyn organization. Just as the New Year's holiday began, their boss, Joe Magliocco, dead of a heart attack, was buried in a rather quiet funeral at East Islip, L.I. Joe was the second Brooklyn leader in a row to die of natural causes, Joe Profaci passing on to his own reward a year ago. This two-in-a-row is most certainly an all-time record, for gangsters seem to die most frequently of marksmanship, and not heart attacks.

Now, Magliocco was a 300-pound gangster whose redeeming quality might have been his prodigious appetite and his skill as a cook. He had been killing, extorting, and threatening from the day he arrived from Sicily. He had been through the Castellammarese War of 1931. He had been at the Mob conferences in Cleveland in 1928 and Appalachia in 1957. He forced restaurants to take his table linens. He forced bars to buy from his liquor company. He did well enough in crime to own a six-acre waterfront Long Island estate. Recently, he took over the Profaci crime family when his brother-in-law Joseph Profaci died of liver cancer a year earlier during the still ongoing Gallo-Profaci wars that featured bombings, shootings, the kidnapping of Magliocco and, of course, a lion.

Magliocco himself was able to die on December 28, 1963, and not sooner, because—when summoned before his accusers after his conspiracy with Joe "Bananas" Bonanno to kill Tommy Lucchese and Carlo Gambino and take over the National Crime Syndicate failed when another ambitious mobster ratted them out to the intended targets—he was deemed in such ill health he was spared the normal penalty of death.

These were serious criminals. And the late 1950s and early 1960s were a good and bloody time on the streets of New York—though largely not anywhere that mattered, like Manhattan. And so, at this time in newspapering in America, Breslin could still write about the Mob with tongue slightly in cheek. And he was writing about them, it seems, with an eye toward what would become his next book.

By the time he wrote this column, the Gallos of 51 President Street and the larger and better armed Profaci faction had reached a detente.

> The only trouble Larry [Gallo] faces is an indictment in Brooklyn. A grand jury, after looking over all the evidence, came up with the startling conclusion that Gallo and his people had conspired to kill all of the Profaci people and take over their legal and illegal businesses.
>
> But the charge that the Gallos wanted to kill all the Profacis is open to serious debate. A good gunsmith could wreck this bill of particulars. The Gallos, it seems, had a habit of placing .32 automatic cartridges into .32 caliber revolvers. The automatic cartridges are copper plated and can louse up a gun, it seems.
>
> "It is just another indication that the Gallos do not work cleanly," a gunsmith said last night. "If they want to kill everybody they have to stop being so frivolous with their weapons. They also have to learn how to shoot straight."

And there it is: the same theme we found in "The Last Gallo Living at 51 President St." two months and ten days earlier. The gang that couldn't shoot straight and their lion were well on their way to success in fiction and in film. Breslin's approach to crime, as his approach to the Vietnam War, would change over time. Though he would never entirely give up the colorful characters, they would become largely fictionalized and there would be the darker humor embodied in Un Occhio, a godfather headquartered in a dusty candy store with empty shelves and his voracious wolf.

A little over two decades later, by July of 1987, he is using his humor this way:

> The other morning in federal court, I watched Salvatore Mazzurco, a stumpy little man, receive a huge sentence for being a Mafia drug dealer. Aside from spending the rest of his life in jail, he has to pay reparations to a rehabilitation fund.
>
> Right away, I was irritated that I could not apply for special reparations. Mazzurco and the ones like him have cost me fortunes of money and hours of pleasure that cannot be calculated. . . .
>
> Once, writing stories about bad boys was a big industry, and I probably was going to be one of the richest writers the world has known because I could write about bad boys with some humor.
>
> When I first started a newspaper column, I had perhaps 150 street characters, from Jiggs and Ruby to Fat Thomas and the late great Peppy. . . .
>
> In 1969, I wrote a book, *The Gang That Couldn't Shoot Straight*, and it was a best-seller and then a movie. I had publishers and producers actually sitting at my kitchen table waiting for the next humorous book about the mob.

The column, which appeared under the headline "It's a Crime the Way the Mafia Does Business," used Breslin's humor in a remembrance of halcyon days, but spelled out why no humor remained.

> These men like Mazzurco were everywhere selling heroin, particularly in the poor neighborhoods. As I have no way to make a man who sells heroin to children into a comic figure, I did not write another humorous book about gangsters.
>
> You cannot count the money I had to pass up. I also lost an entire area from my newspaper column. . . . In a city where there were under

> 500 murders in 1965 . . . there now were more than 2,000 killings a year. Drugs were everywhere, Attica rioting, and now there was almost no way to find a smile in crime.
>
> In the last 12 years, I have been able to write about only one Mafioso, Un Occhio, and I made it plain he was involved in dope.

Breslin, as you can tell from the last sentence, always affirmed Un Occhio was real, but no gangster or heroin dealer on Pleasant Avenue, where Un Occhio held court, would support his claim. Many were asked. When Breslin himself was asked by a questioner from Pleasant Avenue, early one morning in 1992, he shouted into the phone "HE'S REAL. GOOD. BYE." He could not afford to lose the last comedic gangster.

> And so the other morning, I was in court watching Mazzurco from Caffee Licata walk into jail forever. . . .
>
> If this had been the old days, and Mazzurco had been in there for some legitimate crime, gambling or loan sharking, I would have had the column done in two hours. Instead, it took me seven hours. And nobody's laughing, especially me.

We had, in New York, by 1987, come very far from Damon Runyon.

Breslin wrote thirteen more columns in January, fifteen in February and at least eleven in March. When you pull these yellow clippings from the morgue, with their red stamp markings "TRIBUNE 1964" and the hastily pen-drawn circles around the bylines, you get a good sense that even as great as the writer might have been, the newspaper would be in the trash can, and the clipping of the column folded sharply over and over again, and then slid into a fat brown envelope holding many other clippings and stamped "BRESLIN, JIMMY" which was pushed down into a drawer in one of the rows and rows of file drawers in "the morgue," as the newspaper libraries used to be called. Breslin always knew this. In a sense, he kept writing novels and nonfiction books to outlive that drawer. In his opening pages to *Damon Runyon*:

> And now, here in this old building in Austin, Texas, just because I was leaning on the drawer . . . I decided to pull it open. . . . and inside the envelope is packed with clippings . . . I finger a Runyon clipping with a red date stamp on it, September 4, 1931.
>
> Now the envelope moves as if it is breathing, and from the clip there comes a rough voice.

From the present drawer of clips that rough voice is Breslin's. "What's doin'?" "Beautiful!" "Good Bye." "Breslin."

In one of these drawers we find an interesting set of clippings that were tucked away just before the year 1964 began. They are dated December 11, December 12, December 13, and December 15. They concern the kidnapping of Frank Sinatra, Jr.

The kid was 19 and following in his father's footsteps. Sitting in a room at the Harrah's Casino at Lake Tahoe a little while before he was to go on with Tommy Dorsey's orchestra. Sinatra, a singer, of course—and his roommate, 26-year-old trumpet player John Foss, who would soon be the only witness to the crime, answered a knock on the door.

It was December 8, less than three weeks after the Kennedy assassination. Thanksgiving, glum, had passed. Christmas was still two weeks away. The year that could not get any worse just did.

Now the front pages were again filled with national tragedy. The Kennedy Camelot and the Sinatra cosmos, intersecting. Kidnappings don't often end well, despite the seriousness of the FBI's pursuit. Here you get an idea of both the scope of Breslin's talent and the relentless pace of the news, and the relentless pressure on a star who played with the grace and speed and muscle memory of a pro basketball player, but in a season that never ended.

This is where Breslin's reporting begins. He is sitting in the San Francisco airport:

> The end never was any good in a kidnaping case. And, now, as you sit in an air terminal and wait for a plane to go to Lake Tahoe, you wonder what it is going to be like for Frank Sinatra Jr. It is almost two days now since he was taken away . . . And as you sit here, you remember what an old guy told you about kidnaping cases when they became more than a day old. . . .
>
> "These things get settled fast or it is a mess," he said. "Once you go over 18 hours with a thing like this, you got big trouble. On the second day, you got murder."

The old guy, who Breslin chooses not to name, was working a kidnapping case when he made his statement. A few days later, the three-year-old who had been lifted from the porch where the old guy stood would be found dead by the side of a Long Island parkway.

It is old school noir, you could say, Breslin the shoe leather police reporter, hands in his trench coat, cigarette burning, tie undone, putting himself on the porch at the scene of a prior kidnapping, on his way to another. He sets the stage for a grim outcome.

It's a West Coast kidnapping for an East Coast newspaper. One that occurred when it was already December 9 in New York, so Breslin is writing what amounts to a second-day story, when it appears in the editions of December 11. By the time he gets to the scene, plenty of shoe leather had already been laid down. But he would write vivid crime stories that captured your imagination and that is what he did that cut through hundreds of dark headlines and acres and acres of reporting from indifferent to excellent, and what is interesting is that in their own, admittedly grittier, way, they mirrored his approach to the Kennedy assassination. Then too he arrived well after the presidential press corps, and the local and regional press corps, and delivered what was really needed. A voice.

His first effort on Sinatra Jr. was pretty good for an airport lounge, but in the end, a little bit of an average day.

You are fingering the beads of a rosary of days that can lead to a bad ending. Then he comes to his last paragraph, and you are fingering the beads to a darkening time.

> These are the kind of things kidnapings bring out. Now we have another one. Another month like the one in which we just came through and the only way to live will be with a .38 stuffed into the front of your belt.

Then he is there. It is the next day. And the crime writer and storyteller hit his stride. Now we again see why the *Trib* took him off sports almost as soon as he got there and they had serialized his Mets book. The editors there, they needed *aaanNnnnything, anything* to keep shaking up the joint and they had found genius.

The first piece after he arrived opens in a way by now familiar:

> George C. Jones had his black windbreaker zipped up and the car windows closed when he started his 2 A.M. tour.

* * *

> Clifton Pollard was pretty sure he was going to be working on Sunday, so when he woke up at 9 A.M., in his three-room apartment on Corcoran Street, he put on khaki overalls before going into the kitchen for breakfast.

It seems simple. It seems matter of fact.

But if you asked his editors, they would tell you he was never on time. If you asked Tom Wolfe, he was a pile of bowling balls wreathed in smoke. If you were to ask his sons—the twins were around nine at the time—they would tell you, for them, it could be torture. If you were to ask him as he handed you a page, he would tell you, "It's no good. Fix it." Meanwhile he was already crumpling into a ball what could have been the next page of simple, matter-of-fact sentences. If they were good enough.

"In the winter, J.B. used to walk at three in the afternoon. It was getting dark. To Rockaway. And walked from OneSixteen to OneForty-Nine (that's how 149th and 116th are said properly in Queens and elsewhere in New York) and back in the rain in the dreary, freezing weather. He used to study the shore break," said Kevin Breslin, who could surf. "He was walking and working. He would talk to himself, and now I realize that he must've been writing the lines . . . and that's when he was doing the book also and the column.

"He did this incessantly. Wake up at dawn. Write. Write. Write. Then we'd have to come as prisoners in the car to the beach. It was brutal all the way. Down Woodhaven Boulevard, Cross Bay Boulevard, over the bridge into Rockaway and my mother would sit in the car." Kevin talks sometimes like his father's typewriter.

Breslin was a man who whatever his reverie, needed and wanted to have his family beside him while he worked, even if he sometimes had a very hard time saying what was going on.

"I know J.B.'s life was chaotic, but it was also family-centered," says Kevin, and not apologetically.

Now we see Breslin the family man in Los Angeles writing about this kidnapping that the defense attorneys would soon attempt to turn into a circus by starting to whisper, then saying aloud in court, that Sinatra Jr. had staged it to get publicity. This would keep up through the trial. And like all ugly whispers, it would stay in the air around Sinatra for a very long time.

Just as with Son of Sam, when the murderous lunatic struck close to home and Breslin felt empathy and fear, you can feel his feelings for the Sinatra family.

> The temperature was 47 degrees, cold for Los Angeles. . . . Bel Air is a place with narrow roads which wind around hills and run past some of the most expensive homes in the nation. Jones wears a cop's uniform, but he isn't a real cop.
>
> He drove slowly, and he was on Roscomare Road at 2:55 when he thought he heard somebody call him as he drove past . . . Jones looked out the window and saw somebody walking in the middle of the road . . .
>
> This kid walking toward him, in an overcoat, T-shirt, shoes but no socks, was Frank Sinatra Jr., and now the worry was taken out of a kidnaping case because the victim was safe. . . .
>
> The kidnaping came to an end with the young Sinatra hiding in the trunk of George Jones' patrol car so newsmen wouldn't grab him. Jones drove up to the door of Mrs. Nancy Sinatra's home at 7000 Nimes Road and got out and rang the bell. Nancy Sinatra answered.
>
> "I got your son here in the trunk," Mr. Jones said.
>
> Nancy Sinatra gasped. Then Jones realized what he had said. "I mean he's all right," he shouted.

Breslin touches on the doubts cast on Sinatra by newsmen and the whisperers. And then he comes back.

> But everything like this went away in the afternoon when Frank Sinatra Jr., with his mother holding him by one arm and his 16-year-old sister Tina, by the other, walked through the sunshine down the steep driveway . . . and one look at this kid walking toward you told it all.
>
> He had a dark gray overcoat and a white shirt open at the throat. His head was stuck into the collar of the coat and when he looked up you could see that he was crying a little bit and he was shaking a little

bit and that he was nothing more than a boy who had just had a scare thrown into him, the likes of which he will never forget. The kind of scare no man knows how to handle.

This, then, is what Breslin brings to a story. It is not a human touch. Nor is it humanizing events. Nor is it a 60,000-foot edition of humanity. It is people. Living their lives. With you. At a very painful time.

Next he will show us something, again like Kennedy, again like Sam, but not in the rote way editors pull one of their five tricks from their sleeve to spark a slow July day by frying an egg on the sidewalk and putting that picture on the cover. He is repeating his themes and motifs in much the way any novelist would. The columns from November and the columns in December are part of the same story. They are parts of a whole, told as newspapers must tell stories. He is serializing the novel of the city and the nation.

He will show us the manhunt for three men who will turn out to be incompetent enough, even for criminals, to be called amateurs. He will do it in a way that earns him some room on a front page crowded with the Defense Department budget, the federal education budget, a sex probe in the Senate, and a state liquor investigation. The victim is safe. New headlines.

A kidnaper is a man who must be caught and he is always caught . . .

He is as definitive and declarative as he was in his opening column with its grim foreshadowing. This time of course, he will turn out to be right. But today's job is to get you there.

It all came down to the straight-faced men in business suits who kept coming out of the brown wooden door marked "Employee's Entrance" at one end of the two story FBI building on Sixth St. . . .

> They were from all over . . . They were headed for all the places on which the Sinatra kidnaping centered yesterday.

By now the doubts and rumors of a hoax are back, and back forcefully. The situation is not helped by the fact that there are no leaks from local police to clear them up—the FBI has locked them out of the case. Nor helped by the fact that the FBI was renowned for not talking unless it suited the FBI. In this case it did not. So Breslin dwells on the rumors and then gets himself out before it's too late.

> Because if this is a kidnaping, you have played games with somebody else's nightmare. So all you do is sit here and report as best you can.

It's artful. And it will have to do. Because we are writing running commentary. And today the commentary just has to get you to come back to tomorrow's paper, when maybe there will be a score, and something definitive to write about. But the commentary is immediate, as it would be filing from a press box inning by inning, all of it getting handed to the desk editor to read and roll up to squeeze into a heavy clear plastic carrier tube with a leather flap at the top that is snapped closed. And now a door to the pneumatic pipe is opened and this torpedo filled with words is set in the pipe and with a pop and a *shwoosh* it is sucked in and launched down to the composing room to be set in type.

> Last night lights were on in the building on Sixth St. and work on a serious kidnaping case continued. And it is a serious case. No matter what actually happened during Sinatra's 53-hour disappearance, a major crime has been committed.

On Page Six, where that sentence appeared, there was also an item on the upcoming presidential campaign. Already in the works. The score was in. *Mrs. Kennedy will have no role in the campaign,* the reporter wrote.

The end, when it comes, in his column of December 15, is what makes Breslin's reporting a textbook for anyone writing nonfiction crime against a deadline.

We begin by arriving with the suspects in two cars at the FBI offices on Sixth Street in Los Angeles.

> The first car into the parking lot was a two-tone blue Plymouth and when it stopped the kid who was sitting between the two men in the front seat started to reach down to the floor to pick up the container of milk between his feet.
>
> "I want to bring this with me," he said.
>
> "Just leave it there," the man on his right said. The man said it coldly and something happened to the kid's face and he looked up to see the crowd around the car and his eyes widened to show fear and now Barry Keenan, 28 years old, was beginning to understand that these two men with him, these tall men with gray hair and lined faces who had been so quiet, were going to take him to some people who someday might put him away forever for the kidnaping of Frank Sinatra Jr. . . .
>
> The two men took Joseph Amaler by the wrists as he came out of the second car . . . and now other FBI agents got around and they all started walking Barry Keenan and Joseph Amaler . . . Then half way between this parking lot and the entrance to this two-story modern building, Keenan turned and looked as he walked . . . and his eyes followed the yellow taxi cab . . . Then Keenan's head turned and he looked at the black panel truck that was headed the other way. . . . He was doing exactly what they all do . . . when they are under arrest for a thing that they know is big. They see what they are leaving . . . because somewhere inside them is a fear that they will never see these things again.

This is how it ends, Breslin was saying once again. You stand alone. It is the existential underpinning. The prose, the detail, was all stuff he had to collect painstakingly from those who were in each of the places: near or in the cars, near or on the walk . . . and it continues . . . the kind of reporting that is aimed at getting to the truth. And it really does read a little like one of those West Coast crime novels that San Francisco and Los Angeles are noted for. Beautiful!

Then we are at a money-on-the-table FBI press conference.

> The brown walnut desk was covered with money which was in stamped wrappers and Simon (Bill Simon, FBI Agent in Charge, Los Angeles field office) and Casper (Joseph Casper, Assistant Director, FBI) stood behind the desk and looked at it. This is $167,927, gentlemen, they said . . .

And then Breslin gives the reader a grace note.

> "Put a little expression into your face," somebody said.
>
> "That's a lot of money." Casper didn't change his face. He had come to this town because it was a kidnaping and a kidnaping is a kind of thing the FBI does not feel one should be animated about.

It is the kind of moment that could occur at this kind of press conference. Perhaps it was a kneeling photographer's suggestion, made as the reporters looked over his head at the money.

It is easy to hear the "Rat-a-Tat" of the two fat fingers on the keys, moving hard and fast as Gene Krupa on his drums, according to his editor, Stan Fischler, who worked in the same office as Breslin during an intermission at the *Journal-American*.

Then to court.

> Right after this, Keenan and Amaler were taken out of the building and put into cars and driven downtown to a fifth-floor room in the United States Courthouse, which had fluorescent lights and dark vinyl flooring . . .

If you had worked for the editors Breslin worked for and did not come back with the lighting or the type of floor, they would send you back. He didn't need to be told, of course.

> Amaler was scared. He is a 6-1, 175 pounder, with dark blond hair that is streaked with lemon from being in the sun continually . . . he lists his occupation as a diver for abalone, a shellfish which runs in the waters around here. . . .
>
> Keenan came different now. He is 5'11" and weighs 135. That's awfully thin. Why is he so thin, you wondered. . . . There was no fear in this kid now. He looked straight at you and would have kept it up forever . . . and then he slumped in the chair. The slump told you to go to hell.

That is who kidnapped Frank Sinatra, Jr. The choice of one *p* in *kidnaping* that he is using is not some personal one on Breslin's part. It is a paper's way not to waste space when the hot metal was set into lines of type that were set into columns laid down in trays on heavy metal carts on wheels in the noisy-with-metal-and-men room where the newspaper was composed. Each character took up space on paper. This newsprint, the giant rolls of it, were a large part of the overhead of printing a newspaper. This parsimony can be seen in the choice not to use a period after abbreviations, such as *Blvd* or *Ave*, to shun commas where possible, or in the choice to use numerals and not spell out numbers larger than the number ten.

That courtroom scene had plenty of detail, but when Breslin leaves the court, the column takes an important turn.

We are with another family. Not where it ended. That happened already, a couple of days earlier.

> To find out how Keenan could kidnap and wind up in jail all you had to do yesterday morning was get into the middle of the street in front of the Hall of Justice and call a cab and tell the driver to take you to 4326 Oakwood.

What you find there, this time, is neither dramatic nor poignant. It is banal. Keenan's father is a stockbroker who lives in a $60,000 house with his second wife of 21 years and their three daughters.

> "What does he do for a living?"
>
> "Well, he was a salesman," his father says. "I haven't kept up with this because he left here when he was married."
>
> "And he's still married?"
>
> "No, they broke up about three years ago." . . .
>
> He looked at his wife for help in remembering the name of the girl his son had married.
>
> "She was a nice little girl," the wife says. "But too young to be married. I just know there is some mistake. Why, he was going to stay with us this weekend. He called on Friday and said he would try to be up before the weekend with his father's Christmas present."

Breslin makes no judgment. It is, for Breslin and for you, not where the crime ends, but where the story ends. Back, through the fog, to somewhere near where the kidnapping began.

What Breslin did over the course of four columns was not so much show off his uniqueness. That was in the delivery. As for the work itself, it's not showy work at all. But it is the kind of storytelling that left him open to the charge that he went beyond the facts, or reported things he could not have seen as though he had seen them and not just learned them in his version of the New Journalism. For the moment, let's leave that aside. What he did was make the *Trib* unique, and that was his job. He did it by telling the truth, in details, and in places that others forgot. It is not the same thing as an anchor telling you things that another person saw and telling you, "I saw them." That is lying and making oneself bigger. Bigger than the story. Breslin knew it was telling the story that made you. Save that kind of "I" for polishing a bar.

What the critics will single out for their snipes at this time in his career is something else entirely, but before they can do it, Breslin must give them ammunition, which he does by taking us for a ride. Fast. Careering. In a bright red Fire Department of the City of New York vehicle. A Chief's car. We are on our way to something, down the streets of Brownsville. The Christmas lights are strung across Pitkin Avenue. And we are there. This is something reporters do, ride with firefighters. No one is shooting at you, usually. No one dislikes you, usually. And most of the time you watch people be heroic and not get anything but tired. It's serious work, though. And the risks to a firefighter can be great. And it is also, for Breslin, a break from crime reporting. For even though fires and why they are burning is serious, no one can deny the fun of the riding in a column with the deep basso horns and the 36,000 pounds of chrome and brass and red behind you.

> For a little bit, when the red Dodge turned the corner and came out onto Pitkin Avenue, there was this crazy thought about the Christmas lights. The lights were strung out over the street and they were burning in the cold dusk . . . But it was strange to see them here. This was a Saturday, and on a Saturday on Pitkin Avenue in Brownsville, Brooklyn, nothing

> is supposed to go on. The lights must work automatically, you thought. Nobody in Brownsville would turn on lights on a Saturday.
>
> Then the car straightened out and the driver pressed the siren button and began to gun the car down a little lane in the middle of the packed street and now all you could do was hope that this guy driving, whoever he was . . . was going to get everybody through alive.
>
> . . . You hoped he wouldn't stall because there was no stopping this car you were in on a dime. Behind this chief's car a big brute of a Ward-La France hook-and-ladder was rolling at a speed which could not be stopped easily. . . .
>
> This was the fourth time in the last hour that the 120 Truck Company, the world's busiest firemen, had turned out to answer an alarm. And these runs down Pitkin Avenue now were starting to wear out your nerves. . . .
>
> The signal had come in at 4:32 P.M. Everybody had been sitting in the kitchen in the back of the old firehouse, trying for the third straight time to have a cup of coffee, when the bell rang in the box on the wall.
>
> It was a luncheonette this time. . . . It looked like nothing at all, except that you knew how many men working in this 120 Truck Company had wound up in the hospital . . .

You. You. You. You. You. Five times in the first ten paragraphs.

It's a pretty gripping story. And there is no doubt that this use of the second person in its telling puts you right there. That's a reason we have the second person. It puts *you* in the story. It is immediate. It is from your perspective. It is not removed as a third-person narrator would be, or open to the accusation of self-centeredness, like some stories that revolve around an "I" and can put the author at the center of the story's universe. That is a reason why journalists like Tom Wolfe and Breslin used it. *The New Yorker*, in its somewhat long-winded and pompous argument with how Wolfe or Breslin chose to write, decided to parody Breslin *and* sideswipe Wolfe:

> For a moment, there was this crazy thought about how Sunday used to settle you down to a slow pace while you made your way through the fat gray wilderness of the Newspapers. Which could take you all day, but you didn't care. You didn't care a bit. But now you're reading the new *Herald Tribune* and there's a helluva difference.
>
> You care. You care a whole lot. You know that now there's a guy sitting behind a desk at the *Trib* who cares, a guy who must feel the heartbeat of this city and maybe of the whole world . . . You've just turned with a tremendous sort of urgency in your fingers to Jimmy Breslin, and in a moment you're one with this one buzzing the traffic on Pitkin Avenue . . . You're suddenly right in the middle of life. . . .

That's how "Jimmy Bennett Doesn't Work Here Anymore" begins.

You You You. And again, five more times. Eight times "you" in two paragraphs. Two possessive "yours," three contracted "you ares," and one more contraction: "you've."

You don't even need to be a *New Yorker* subscriber to get the point. And you certainly don't have to race down Pitkin. It continues. Somewhat tedious. Somewhat pretentious.

> Right here you stop the speed because it's Sunday morning and that's no time for such excitement, particularly involving you. You turn the page . . . and here you find a story written by a guy by the name of Tom Wolfe. You remember a writer name of Tom Wolfe . . . you know right off this isn't the same Tom Wolfe. This Tom Wolfe writes: "You know how it is in New York. You are walking across the street. . . ." Which makes you wonder if some guy somewhere in this mass of experimental fragments called the *Sunday Herald Tribune* may possibly be able to write something in the third person . . . Or even in the first person if he's got to be obtrusive about it. . . . And you wonder if other writers on the staff might start to write like you did when you were a college sophomore . . .

The story has a clever headline too. "Jimmy Bennett Doesn't Work Here Anymore," referring the crossword-loving reader back to 1835 and James Gordon Bennett, founder, publisher and editor of the *Herald*.

The writer—who has an old New Yorker name, J.Q. Purcell—isn't ready to quit for a long time still. But here is the gist of what he is attempting very slowly to say: He hopes for "an important sort of person, one who stays off the street," which is to say, a person who works exactly like Mr. Purcell. And by now you wonder if anyone will read this piece of his to the end.

Breslin apparently did.

> The other day I received a letter from my old friend Sarah Phillips, who I have not seen in 27 years and as I read her cheery words it causes me to think back to the time when I was 8 years old and accompanied my great aunt to the drawing room . . .
>
> The above is about the way a magazine called the *New Yorker* starts all of its stories. I may be a little off because I have not read the magazine enough to get that purposely dry, Old English style . . . But I read that magazine when it came out the other day. It has devoted two pages to a parody of a writer named Jimmy Breslin. I looked at the name of the person who did the parody . . . the name has got to be phony because I never heard of any J.Q. Purcell and neither has anybody else.

Breslin went around to his literary agent, Sterling Lord, and to a lawyer and to several of his friends who dissuaded him from killing Purcell and dumping the writer's body in a body of water.

Joey Bracato, the bartender, had the final say: "What I can't figure out is why they would take a shot at you in the *New York Enquirer*."

Another reason fire trucks are important to Breslin, beyond the sad fact that Brownsville was burning, and beyond the poetry of motion, was his favorite arsonist who needed to get away before the trucks and patrol cars arrived.

That arsonist was Marvin the Torch and because most businesses aren't going to make it to a third year, his services were in demand.

Marvin the Torch first appeared on April 30, 1964, in the *Herald Tribune*. In this early column, Marvin the Torch is promising a custard stand owner, whose business was on the wrong side of an amusement park, that he would make his problem go away. Marvin, Breslin noted, had had a couple of drinks, and that made him feel charitable:

> Marvin the Torch never could keep his hands off somebody else's business, particularly if the business was losing money. Now this is accepted behavior in Marvin's profession, which is arson. But he has a bad habit of getting into places where he shouldn't be and promising too many favors. This is where all his trouble starts. . .
>
> The custard stand was just an old boarded-up place and it was an insult to bring Marvin the Torch anywhere near it. Marvin the Torch is a man who has burned in the best industries. But here he was, stuck with another favor, so he picked up the gas cans and went to work. As long as he was at it, Marvin decided to put a little spectacle into the job. Marvin the Torch wanted to try to make the roof blow straight up into the air without bending the nails in it. This would have been all right, except Marvin the Torch's fire caught a good south wind and the wind carried the fire straight over the amusement park and before the day was over, Marvin the Torch's favor job on the custard stand had also belted out most of a million-and-a-half-dollar amusement park.

Breslin grounds Marvin's crime on a solid understanding of how arson is done as well as a strong sense of irony:

> Now, arson is a three-man job. Two men pour, then one of the pourers comes out and becomes the blanket man. He holds an old car blanket

and throws it over anyone coming out whose clothes are on fire. The driver counts the gas cans to make sure none is missing. In short, people don't pay you if they find gas cans in the ruins of your accidental fire.

Marvin, a person who some insisted couldn't exist, did. Gloria Steinem, feminist trailblazer and fan of Breslin, explains both a difference between a Purcell and a Breslin and puts to rest any doubt about Marvin when she discusses these things in an interview:

"He was always street smart. Street smart means that you can inform and excite and invite readers from the street up. An awful lot of writers start from the academy down which doesn't work so well. He never did. He always had this nose for incredible characters. I remember being astounded that there really was a 'Marvin the Torch.'"

# THE BARD OF QUEENS BOULEVARD

"He ate at some of the great dinner tables of the country, but he hated legitimate people and loved thieves."

That is how Jimmy Breslin would describe Damon Runyon early in his book on that writer. It was clear he also was writing about himself.

"I am here," he wrote in his 1991 book *Damon Runyon*, explaining what he was doing standing at the file drawers in Austin, Texas, "because more than anybody else I've ever heard of, he beat the New York newspaper business. Beat it to a pulp. And his life gave off a reflection of more than three decades of the city of New York, and it has almost become the official record of the times."

Writing that resembled his became known as Runyonesque. Breslin, by those who saw easy similarities and not the distinctions, was known as the Damon Runyon of Queens Boulevard.

That is wrong. What they had in common was that both men beat the newspaper business to a pulp. And Breslin chronicled more than five decades of the city of New York. What set them apart was the cadence of their prose, the intent of the writing, and the world as seen through their characters' eyes. Breslin was unique.

Breslin was the Bard of Queens Boulevard.

His characters were not Runyonesque. They were Breslinesque.

"I grew up being afraid of my feelings and suddenly my brain finds a way to make them my main strength," Breslin wrote in his book *I Want to Thank My Brain for Remembering Me.*

"I replaced my feelings with what I felt were the feelings of others, and that changed with each thing I went to, so I was about sixty-seven different people in my life."

One of those people was Marvin the Torch. Others included Klein the Lawyer; Un Occhio, the Mob boss; and Fat Thomas. Their mischief and misfortune was real: too many wives, arson gone wrong, too many bad bets among them. They may have been spun around the armatures of real people but it was this thing that Breslin has noted resided in his brain—his mind—that brought each of them to life. Allowed them to tell the truth. Allowed the reader to feel not represented *by* a newspaper but represented *in* a newspaper, and not simply in the grotesquerie of dark inked headlines. They inhabited him. He inhabited them. He did this not only with his characters, but with the many whose identities were not cloaked in hyperrealism. Breslin's paper's ink might rub off on your fingers, but the people came alive in your face.

To capture those feelings through the eyes of his characters as their lives evolved and do it in the City Column format that Breslin wrote in—around 1,000 words—and in the vehicle in which those words appeared—daily newspapers printed on cheap newsprint and tossed away after one day's discussion or bent elbow argument—required clarity in characterization and vividness. Sometimes with his characters, especially Fat Thomas, Breslin could define the arc of a life across intervals that were sometimes spaced weeks and months apart. Like a poet singing as he walks across Greece, Breslin lets the story unfold, and reshapes it along the way.

This is not a cheap journalism trick. This is in the tradition of oral history as now told by an itinerant poet of newsprint. It was also the way Breslin's character columns were retold by readers across the city. "Hey, did you read Breslin today?" And in a sense, that too is part of the genre, the City Column, as Jimmy Breslin reinvented it. AJB (after Jimmy Breslin), it becomes adopted by other newspaper and sports columnists in New York, Philadelphia, Boston, elsewhere; this becomes the way a story is told with a narrator who was often present as a character himself. It draws, as Breslin notes, from great columnists and writers BJB (before Jimmy Breslin), but it is an authentic, new voice, and new style.

"Sing to me, oh Muse, of Marvin the Torch, setting fire on those distant shores . . . of the twists and turns of Fat Thomas and the many griefs he suffered . . ."

Breslin's mock heroic characters first stood not on some Attic shore, but on the cracked sidewalks of his early childhood home.

In this way Breslin's characters aren't romantic characters, though there is a certain romance in reading about them. Breslin learned from Runyon, but he wrote for a post-Runyonesque world. And when he wrote about Runyon, who was certifiably his idol, he was in fact writing about himself. He studied Runyon and the foundation he had laid, then went beyond him without taking a single thing away from him.

"While there are still plenty of thugs around who seem lovable at first, it all winds up with them selling drugs to kids. . . . the money all comes from selling crack to thirteen year-olds, and I don't know how to make that bright and funny."

And he didn't try. He drew his often wry humor, and the joy and often hopeful attitude that many of his characters contained, from an understanding of the Athens of a nation's low-rise urban world:

Queens. He didn't paint them in the bright lights of Manhattan's Great White Way—Broadway. Breslin painted his people in the neighborhoods—the towns—of Queens and in its criminal courts, and its bars and its restaurants and the grand offices of the borough president that lined the 7.2 miles of Queens Boulevard. His characters and the stories drawn from their lives often served as a respite for the reader from the crime and violence by haters, drug lords, Caucasians stuck in the past, ugly mobsters and from civil unrest, war and cheap politicians who stole dimes from parking meters; the stuff, in other words, that filled the front pages of newspapers.

For all their mishaps, Breslin's people often had a charitable view of the world. They put human in the human condition. Breslin used them to provide clarity even as they provided relief from the kinds of things he often had to write about in his column. And when he wrote in his compelling way about those crises and tragedies for too many days and weeks in a row, he, in his pain—or his editors, in their occasional wisdom—called for a story from Klein or Fats or Marvin or Mutchie, who was a bartender.

This was Breslin's World Without End, where the longest voyage was 32.39 miles on the A train from 207th Street in the Inwood section of Manhattan to Land's End in Far Rockaway, Queens. His Queens was home to around 1.5 million people who lived in everything from houses on stilts in a tidal Appalachia in Jamaica Bay called Broad Channel to the vertical slums of dangerous housing projects. It was a reporter's delight: the clubhouse politics of a corrupt democratic party, a police force in residence most of whose members came from out of town, a couple of airports with plenty of cargo to choose from, and the Mafia and Irish mobsters. The rest of the country, for Klein the Lawyer, Marvin the Torch, Mutchie and largely even Fat Thomas, who occasionally accompanied Breslin abroad—to Washington, D.C., or the South—was *terra incognita.*

Of course, from the start, except for the enlightened, no one in New York's chattering classes or the Washington Beltway punditorium believed these robust characters existed.

Foremost among these was Rosenthal of *The Times.*

Abe Rosenthal was considered a vulture by some of the writers in residence at Bleeck's according to published accounts. And according to his obituaries he was a tyrant, monomaniacal and given to fits.

But this bow tie-wearing little man also gets credit for turning the Gray Lady's gray columns into something a little less gray and with a larger world view. The paper even in the 1960s had the resources and the stated intent to cover all that was important. By the time Rosenthal rose to run it, the paper had all the young talent at hand to straddle technological change. Of course Rosenthal, who presided over great events and great change, was described by some as perhaps the greatest editor that paper had seen. But that accolade tended to be given by some of those who worked for him. Breslin did not like him at all.

"We are almost mortal enemies," Breslin wrote in his introspective book on his brain. "At one time he was editor of *The Times* newspaper and I wrote columns for a paper called the *Herald Tribune* about life in a large saloon on Queens Blvd . . . But since it was in Queens, nobody knew anything about it. Every time I mentioned it, people thought it wasn't true. Mostly this was because of insane jealousy. Rosenthal announced that I was making everything up. He showed up one night."

The night Rosenthal showed up in one of Breslin's Queens' haunts, Jimmy Burke, who later would become famous for holding up the Lufthansa Freight Terminal for close to $9 million, was there.

> Fat Thomas was roaring at the bar. He was six-three and weighed 415 pounds. . . . He had 51 arrests for bookmaking. . . . Now Fat Thomas was real, alive and barging around Pep McGuire's . . . Seeing this, Rosenthal said, "It's all true!" He wound up with so much whiskey in him that he threw himself at a huge blonde Lufthansa stewardess. He buried his head in her chest.
>
> "Abe, she wants to throw you in an oven," Fat Thomas said.
>
> "I know, I can't help it," Rosenthal said.

Free of Rosenthal, Breslin and Fat Thomas could get on with The New Journalism, which included telling stories, true stories, based on real people.

Rosenthal himself later went on to write a column.

One time, Breslin read it and thought it an embarrassment. So he called Rosenthal's paper and left a message asking how he could have ever stood at a bar with Breslin and "pretended to be an equal."

Breslin had at this time in his life an almost Falstaffian persona, combining wisdom with humor and beer. He also had an ability to turn a slight into an unforgivable injury. But in the case of Rosenthal, the day some 25 years later when Breslin saw Rosenthal in a wheelchair after triple bypass surgery as he himself was being released from convalescence after brain surgery—that day he felt warmly toward Rosenthal, he said.

"The guy once caused newsrooms to quiver and presidents to wonder how they could fend off his anger and appeal to his vanity and humor. Now he was waving good-bye from a wheelchair. If he couldn't do the wave, people would be waving goodbye to him. I had a warm feeling about him. If illness was the reason for this, then it was wrong. I should have liked the guy all along on his brains alone."

In the arc of Breslin's amusement, bemusement, anger and forgiveness of Rosenthal we are seeing Breslin polishing his greatest character of all: himself. For a good Catholic like Breslin, a near death experience was certainly a very good time to forgive, having yourself just asked for the same.

No less than Klein, with his wives and payments; Fat Thomas with his bad bets and bad debts; Marvin The Torch, who finally found a woman to marry him (he knew she was the one when she accepted that the placard with numbers he held across his chest in a couple of his pictures was actually a license plate); there was Breslin himself. Breslin with his neighbors, noise, and children, always with no money or the threat of no money or a creditor on the phone. Breslin was his own greatest character, by turns dark or light, a many-faceted character who was inhabited by James Earle Breslin, the abandoned boy, and whose heart never turned away from the goal of turning the inarticulate into the understandable.

So when Fats mocked Rosenthal, there was Breslin: dark haired, impish smile, sparkling eyes, chubby, with a glass of the golden nectar in his hand doing what a great journalist or a truly smart criminal does best: he was stealing with his eyes, stealing with both hands. Happy in his kingdom, the abandoned boy now was both jester and prince, boon companion and shrewd observer. It was "Beautiful," as he liked to say, and he was at this moment "J.B. Number One."

Sometimes, in his pettiness, there was no crime too small:

### THE SIGN IN THE YARD

The wife of a new neighbor from up on the corner came down and walked up to my wife and started acting nice, which must have exhausted her.

This woman is one of the people I have to live with. Four years ago, in the true style of an amateur, I "moved out a bit." I moved onto a block with a lot of other people who live side by side in houses. Now, people are all right. Get them alone and they're pretty good. But put five of them together and they start conforming and after that all they are is trouble. Put 16 families on the same block, the way it is on mine, and they are not people any more. They are enemies. . . . .

"I haven't gotten a chance to see you since the baby," the new one said. "How nice. This is, uh, your. . . ?"

She knew the number, she knows everything. She knew my take-home pay by the end of the first week she was on the block.

"Fifth," my wife said.

"How wonderful," she said. "And did you plan this one?"

"Oh, yes," my wife said sweetly, "why, everybody I know plans their fifth baby."

THE WOMAN got mad and walked away. Which was great. I was going to say something to her that she could tell her husband for me, but I didn't have the time. I had to stay on Walter, from the Dazzle Sign Painting Co., who was on my lawn and acting like a coward.

"Put it up, Walter," I told him.

"Not in the daylight," Walter said.

"An argument is an argument, but if you do this it lets everybody know that you're crazy," my wife says. My wife ran inside the house. She is the former Rosemary Dattolico and she is very Italian. She likes knives on black nights, not big posters in broad daylight.

"Let's go, Walter," I said, and Walter, from the Dazzle Sign Painting Co., put in both the stakes and tacked the sign on and when he was finished, right there on the lawn was the most beautiful sign you ever saw.

IT WAS ABOUT three feet high and five feet wide and it was in three bright colors and it read real good. On the top, in two lines of big red upper case letters, the sign said:

SORRY TO MAKE YOU LOOK AT THIS BECAUSE I KNOW HOW TIRED YOU PEOPLE GET MOVING YOUR LIPS WHEN YOU READ.

> Underneath this, in smaller, but still real big blue letters, was a line which said, "PEOPLE I'M NOT TALKING TO THIS YEAR."
>
> The line was centered. Right under it, in neat columns, like a service honor roll, was the name of everybody who lives on my block.

Good on you, James Earle Breslin, you're a good man.

In reality, you had to get *this* close and squint to see the words on the actual sign that was put up but that factually accurate description would lose the truth, and the humor that could only be found in Breslin's imagined in-your-face retort to his neighbors.

Who doesn't from time to time hate their neighbors? Who wouldn't enjoy imagining putting up a sign like that? Breslin made that sign for you.

While Breslin's truth, like his characters, came off the streets of his childhood, his prose came out of good grammar, careful choices, and common sense in putting together each column. It came out of the bars and of his years scratching out words and counting them as if they were money. They came out of a personality that was fundamentally that of a criminal because James Earle Breslin, "J.B. Number One," was the ultimate reporter—a traitor who would betray a friend for a thousand words. When Breslin wrote this column, it was October 1964. It was a year in which many of his characters were very busy. So was James Breslin. And what made these particular columns such a joy, if not to write, but to put in the newspaper, was their context. America was wrestling with ignorance and ugliness. Race. Poverty. Poor Education. Crimes as big as these. There was strife. Violence. And far away but coming soon: a war in the heat of a country whose name would soon become well known: Vietnam.

> "Nobody ever had a sign like this," Walter said. "Nobody. I paint 'Fire Sale' and 'Prices Slashed' and for gin mills I do 'Under New

Management' or 'Sunday Cocktail Hour' but I never in my life done a sign like this."

"Beautiful," I said. I stood back and admired it.

FOR A YEAR NOW, my wife has been hissing at the neighbors, "He's writing a novel about the block and you're in it because he hid a tape recorder under your kitchen table." But this sign of mine beat any book . . .

"I think you're sick," Walter said.

"No, I'm not, I just hate those people."

Everyday life. One of the things that was also essential to write about.

Who doesn't from time to time hate their neighbors? "Beautiful."

# RIOTS, RACE & THE ONE PERCENT

Any nostalgia you might have had for the 1960s begins to break up after you read Breslin's columns on the assassination of John F. Kennedy. When you read the work that comes in the four years that follow, it is gone. Instead, vividly, Breslin shows you the great price of attempting to wrench a society from the complacent ignorance of the status quo.

Looking back at these great battles more than sixty years later, when our society is again riven and violent, it is easy now to understand the Latin, even if yours is as rusted as a door hinge to your adolescence: *status quo ante bellum.*

But Breslin was writing these things as they happened. It was a time when it appeared the status quo was going to change and despite the death of Kennedy and his sail-snapping Camelot, America might, if not mature, at least move forward.

On July 2, 1964, Lyndon Baines Johnson, the 36th president of the United States, signed into law the Civil Rights Act.

On July 18, there were riots in Harlem.

There is an easy first thought of irony in this. But we can put that away. Coincidence is more like it.

There had been riots before in Harlem, and they most often started because of the way a police officer in a foreign land attempted to impose himself. Shooting, arrest, it didn't really matter. Because in Harlem everyone knows what is behind this: an inequality in income, in opportunity, in education and in justice. Fear by whites. Breslin had written about these in May.

The legislation was all right and would do a great deal of good and lay part of a foundation so strong that no one could foresee a crack. But on Thursday, July 18, two days after James Powell, 15 and Black, was shot three times by off-duty police lieutenant Thomas Gilligan, who was white, the shooting, the police response to the shooting and a growing divide in the community over whether violence was a better approach than nonviolence in seeking change, all were on the table as partial explanations as summer seemed to boil over. None were the cause.

"I'm a Tom and I'm prepared to be a Tom when I can stop women and children from being shot down in the streets," one great leader, Bayard Rustin, told a crowd. He was advocating for calm.

"We Want Malcolm X. We Want Malcolm X. We Want Malcolm." The words come out with smiles from the bright, unworn faces of the young, seen on newsreels advocating for something more.

"The days of the sit-in, the lie-in, the crawl-in, the beg-in is outdated," said Malcolm X.

The incident itself, looking back, had some similarities with an incident on February 4, 1999, when police fired 41 shots at 22-year-old Amadou Diallo. Stopped near his building, he ran for a doorway. He then went for his wallet. They went for their guns, thinking he had one. Nineteen shots, the medical examiner found, had struck the Guinean immigrant.

In this 1964 case, Powell raised his right hand as he stepped out of a hallway where he had chased a white superintendent who had hosed down other Black students sitting on *his* steps, *his* stoop. Some said the superintendent had hurled the obvious epithets. He would clean up these dirty "N—s." Some said Powell had a knife—he had brought two with him from the Bronx, one of his friends said, when he came down for a summer program at the Robert F. Wagner school. Others said Powell had raised his hand in defense when Gilligan pointed his revolver and thrust his gold shield at him.

The only knife that came into it was about eight feet away, where one was found in the street, according to reports from the time.

Downtown, a hot summer and riots had been anticipated at City Hall and at the offices of news organizations.

In May, Breslin moved to Harlem. He told his Editor-in-Chief, Jim Bellows, in a memo that he would use small words to capture big concepts. Bellows prints the memo in his autobiography:

> Tomorrow night I intend to move into somebody's apartment in Harlem . . . What I intend to do there is simple. Build five parts and build them on anything of this sort: small facts . . .
>
> The entire story is based on one idea: These are people. They are bewildered, uncared about and angry. They have a right to anger because white people would prefer to speak to them in great generalities and do nothing about the housing or the type of food they have to eat because of the salaries they make . . .

The result were five columns couched as "Reporter's Notebooks," which was a genre that newspapers used when the editors wanted to suggest that what you were getting was the raw scribble from the scene, untouched by rewriters in the main office, which of course was rarely the case, though in fact Breslin's work usually came in pretty close to how he filed it.

The series was introduced this way:

"There is poverty in Harlem, and violence and hatred, and there are marriages too, and humor and friendliness, and, most of all, there are people, 450,000 of them. . . . Today on the brink of a long hot summer that raises fears . . . Breslin begins a five-part inspection of Harlem and its people."

This tells you who the audience was. Part of that audience rode commuter trains on an elevated track across One Two Five Street before it *chh chhed* and clacked and rattled through Spanish Harlem and then dove down below Park Avenue. You could see into tenement windows through torn curtains if you looked out of yours as the train pulled out of the station and headed downtown. A glimpse, at least, of a southeast portion of Harlem. If you stepped out onto the platform and looked east, you were looking out at a main artery of Harlem. In daylight there was everything from records to buy to dentists to see to bars where you could also add a little hope to your day by giving some change to the numbers man.

Breslin's five notebooks from Harlem were written toward the end of May.

Thirteen months earlier, Martin Luther King's "Letter from Birmingham Jail" had been published in his newspaper, laid out beginning on the front page.

"For years now, I have heard the word 'Wait!'" King wrote. "This 'Wait' has almost always meant 'Never.'"

Perhaps the act of publishing said something about a shift in editorial consciousness at the *Herald Tribune*, but if you left Harlem, you still couldn't get a cab to take you back home.

The columns are important. They were important when they were written, because this kind of simple exposition that Breslin used was mostly reserved for the foreign desk for frontline accounts from war zones and the like. They are important now as pebbles tossed midstream in a series of events unfolding from 1919, 1935, 1943, 1964, 1965, 1967 through at least May 2020. Riots. Riots. Riots. Riots. Riots. Protests.

The notebooks began with Hope: a marriage between a Marine, Carroll Taylor, 24, and a young woman, Sandra Hopkins, at Salem Methodist Church. But the notebook page turns and it is clear that it is Hope against History.

"I was just understanding how you figure out your life or your future or whatever it is on a day like this when you happen to be colored," Breslin asked.

"I don't want to know about that now," Taylor said.

This is Notebook Number One. It goes from Hope to History to Firepower.

> Across the street are the buildings where the police believe the young kids who claim they are going to kill white people this summer sat on steps and stare at police cars.

The column ends with one of those couplets that neatly summarize the fact that news reporters are best at predicting the past.

> "Riot," the bartender was saying in Maxie's. "Who's got time for that? People have to go to work every day. Doesn't anybody know that?"

Notebook Two, Notebook Three, Notebook Four expand on each of the themes he had laid out in his memo to Jim Bellows. Money is one:

> "Money," a three your old says as she holds out two pennies in her hand. Her mother is being dispossessed at this time. The child runs to the store on her own and uses her money to buy little wax bottles filled

with sweet fluid. Soda, Breslin says. Her mother gives her a nickel more. She is preoccupied.

Police is another: the fight between a Black soldier and a cop in 1935, the arrest of a shoplifter by police and how an unfounded rumor of the youth's death turned into shops destroyed in 1943, and now this, James Powell. Breslin is not a historian or a conscience.

He neither blames the cops nor justifies their actions, nor does he say, he just shows: They are the only officials anyone sees on the streets. His coda:

"A mockery . . . of all the big thinking and big show and big money that this town is supposed to have," he says in Notebook Four.

He is there as his reader's witness. He is there to remind us.

There is one other thing that sticks out when you read these columns: Breslin was accompanied by a man with a gun. By now he is on his way to making serious money, the kind news reporters called "TV money." The kind that just ten years later would be the equivalent of more than $600,000 depending on how you compounded the growth. Like a foreign correspondent on network TV wearing a flak jacket and a helmet and accompanied by the armed ex-soldiers detailed to them, the man with the gun is there, Breslin says, because 21 years after the last riot in Harlem, someone was concerned about a white man walking around Harlem.

When the riots happen, Breslin comes back to Harlem. He is driven up, as he cannot drive. He will never learn.

"We grew up with all this, always racing to a fire or a murder or something. Always. Always something terrible," Kevin Breslin said.

"Like the riots in Harlem, we had to drop him off close by. My mother is driving and leaving him there. He just got out. And like, he would just leave. We'd just drive away. We (James and I) were nine or ten at the time. We were in our pajamas."

What he writes about Harlem is what is captured in the headline to the July 20 column that appeared on the front page: "Fear and Hate—Sputtering Fuse."

> The shirtless children ran through the gutters and played with the broken glass and the dull brass cartridge shells from the riot of the night before.
>
> The flat sky was an open oven door and its heat made people spill out of the tenements and onto the stoops . . .

The cadence eerily reminds you of Sam, and his dark, terrible note. Sam did, in that note, capture the pain of the city though in his case it was a canvas for his madness. Here it sets a scene.

> The cops were everywhere, four and five of them on a street corner, wearing white steel helmets and the people of Harlem watched them and hated them yesterday afternoon.
>
> "When I see a white cop, I can't help myself, I just can't stand looking at one of them," Livingston Wingate was saying.

Wingate was a lawyer for Harlem Youth Opportunities Unlimited (HARYOU) and Breslin took his statement as a harbinger of the night to come.

> When people of position talk the way he did the trouble is bad. And yesterday afternoon, while everybody in Harlem waited for the sun to go down and night to cloak the streets and make moving around easier, you wondered just how bad it would become.

Breslin shifts the scene, puts himself in the car in which he was driven to Harlem as it pulls to the curb to make way for fire trucks on 129th Street. And then he gets to the heart of the matter:

> Right away, somebody moved off the stoop, a kid with a shaved head and a gold polo shirt.

The "kid" whose age Breslin puts at 19, goes from stoop to stoop collecting some other youths.

> He said something to them and they looked at the car . . . Then he came walking back . . . and when you stared back at him, his eyelids came down and made his eyes narrow. "What are you looking at you big fat white bastard?" he said. "Oh, come on, it's too hot for this nonsense," we told him. "We're goin' to show you what's nonsense," he said. "We're going to stick some nonsense right into your fat white belly."

A firefighter with an axe comes up. The kids ignore him. This is Harlem. "'What the hell are you doing here?'" the fireman said to Breslin. "'Don't you listen to the Newspapers? . . . They were stoning us last night . . . you don't know what it was like here. They were trying to kill us. Get out of here if you got any brains.'"

There was no fire. The trucks pull away. "'Hey, fat white bastard,' the shaved head called out. 'Why don't you stay around here till these trucks leave?'"

The trucks left, the kids surrounded the car, and one tried to get in the back door. It was moving too fast. But the next time Breslin is driven to a riot in 1991 there was to be no such luck.

In the case of the 1964 Harlem riot, the column goes on and makes all the expected points about civil rights and garbage cans from roof tops; about sinful history and a Black arm throwing something; about publicity and rabble-rousing.

The Harlem riots were not an isolated event. Nor were the riots that erupted in other cities the next year and in the following years the only fissures. Hardly. There was heat and violence and ignorance across the nation. There were plenty of states which had many ugly, openly hate filled places. It was on this map of the United States that the great, memorialized events took place.

There was on August 9, 1964, what Breslin called "the second funeral" for Andrew Goodman, the civil rights worker who on the night of June 21 had been shot and killed with a racist's .38 caliber handgun—one likely drawn from a the holster of a Sheriff's deputy—and then buried, possibly still alive, in a 100-foot-long, 25-foot-high red clay wall along with his fellow Freedom Summer activists, Michael Schwerner and James Chaney, in Philadelphia, Mississippi.

> Chaney was a n— and they are easy to kill. Goodman and Schwerner were Jew n— lovers from New York, and you were, of course, supposed to kill people like this.

Breslin captured the twisted Klan logic. The logic of the State of Mississippi that would be the decision not to prosecute after the alleged killers were identified and the bodies dug out seven weeks after they were interred was something else again. The state's only prosecution came much later. The guilty verdict: For manslaughter. Not murder. It came 41 years to the day that the three young men were killed.

The federal prosecution by the Justice Department's Civil Rights Division was ferocious and it would come swiftly. It would be led by a man named John Doar, a Republican, who was already known as the face of the government's civil rights efforts. He rode across Alabama with the Freedom Riders in 1961. He and a federal marshal led the squad that escorted James Meredith into the University of Mississippi in 1962. Before those doors were opened, and they were not opened wide, a governor had been leaning against them to keep them closed since the day Meredith first applied, and a student and citizen militia fired on the National Guard accompanying Doar, Meredith and the marshal. The army had to be called in and there were two civilians dead and at least 166 National Guard and 48 Army soldiers wounded or injured.

In 1965 Doar, as an Assistant Attorney General and a statement of Lyndon Johnson's determination, walked from Selma to Montgomery with the thousands of freedom marchers who, after two thwarted efforts, succeeded in arriving on their third march. This week, he was already supervising an FBI investigation into the murders. Soon he would begin doing what he would become known for, meticulously building a case. In 1967, he managed to get convictions against 7 of the men involved in the crimes. Those included a Sheriff's deputy and the state head of the Klan.

But today, on August 9, Breslin was at the Ethical Culture Society on Central Park West. The widow of Schwerner and the mothers of Goodman and Chaney held hands. A student, Ralph Engelman, who was a part of the voter registration drive, spoke, Breslin said.

> "Andy risked not only death, but also dying in vain. How fast the public forgets this is a question."

The Goodman nanny, a Black woman, wept. "I raised him. I nursed him. They go and kill him."

"We Shall Overcome" was sung as the mourners exited. The police stood straight and the chauffeurs were somber, Breslin said, and "all of 64th Street" seemed to be crying. And then the procession headed to Mt. Judah Cemetery in Cypress Hills, Queens. And when it was over, there was Breslin. Again alone.

> It was much easier burying Andy Goodman in Queens yesterday afternoon than it was burying him at night in Philadelphia, Miss.

Then gravedigger William Weatroski came up and stuck a red wooden stick into the dirt at the head of the mound. A small black plastic sign was on the stick. "Andrew Goodman," it said.

Weatroski took a red bandana from his hip pocket and began wiping his face with it.

"What's that?"

"Nothing. I was just talking to myself. I was just wondering how long the name on the sign is going to last."

The staying longer than anyone else. The noting of detail. The tying of the opening themes together in a deft noting of the ease of burial, this time. The talking to the gravedigger. These are all familiar elements by now, already part of journalism's professional curriculum after the legend-building Kennedy column. This is how to cover a crime and its aftermath and capture with simplicity what it means and what will endure.

This time he shows you how to incorporate what already had become known as "The Gravedigger" into a story with a sweep even larger than the murder of a president, who after all, whatever he embodied, was just one man, embodying hope. These three young men represented a nation's reluctance to face a foundational crime, one that without being faced makes hope impossible. In order to tell it in this column he uses the gravedigger. It isn't the rote repetition of a journeyman, it is, in this case, used as a motif. Everything before it is strictly necessary, plain, matter of fact, and takes you there.

He will use the sweat and hard work that goes into this technique now in column after column as he serializes over the course of columns and years the struggle, the failures and the successes in trying to confront this crime dividing a nation.

Soon enough, there was the Nation of Islam and the violence it wrought, as this was another group who wanted the privilege of living separately and didn't want any disagreement.

And there was Breslin, on February 28, 1965 attending their annual convention in the Chicago Coliseum which he viewed as an ugly sideshow with Elijah Muhammad of Chicago a pitchman for violence.

> He lives in a sand-blasted $15,000 house and he slumped between bodyguards in the backseat of a new Cadillac limousine. But he wants more than just money. He wants his people to be violent. And he has turned the Black Muslims into the Mafia of the Negro people. . . .
>
> He is an old pale-faced, ignorant little burglar . . . but somehow he is able to put violence into the ugly shaved heads who surround him . . .

Breslin points out the attendance of this the most important annual gathering was just a couple of thousand, and they did find the energy to drag a dissenter from his seats and beat him, because they did not like a speech he gave in a park.

This fierce beating came a week after Malcolm X at 39 was murdered on Sunday, February 21, in Harlem's Audubon Ballroom—gunned down by followers of Elijah Muhammad's violent Black nationalists. The column appeared on Thursday, February 24.

> The Unity Funeral Home is a two-story white brick building with a green canopy going out to the curb of Eighth Ave. in Harlem between 126th and 127th Sts. The sidewalk in front is white from crushed rocksalt. The Inez Beauty Lounge is on the left. The Nina bar is on the right.
>
> They hold the wake of Malcolm X in this setting. It will last until Saturday morning. Then he will be buried.

> The body of Al Hajj Malik Shabazz, Malcolm X's full name when he died, or Malcolm Little, as he was born, or Big Red, as he was known on 125th St., was in a small green carpeted chapel in the rear of the second floor of the funeral home last night.

Almost everything else about the case will be a matter of controversy and documentaries and drawers and drawers and bags and files of police and FBI evidence and the testimony of many. But when Elijah Muhammad stepped onto the stage in midafternoon, there was only one thing that was important to him: he had told his followers in the movement that he was not going to be killed in revenge—Allah would see to that, Breslin reports. Malcolm was killed for the essential crimes of having a mind open to evolving beliefs and the reckless audacity to point out the hypocrisy of a political leader—Elijah Muhammad—and his numerous affairs.

The shopworn cheapness of this little burglar, as Breslin characterized him, would be a theme echoed by Breslin in his later depictions of the political catastrophe of Nixon. There, once again, John Doar, Republican, plays an important role. After much wrangling, arm-twisting and an understandable concern over making the right choice by Chairman of the House Judiciary Committee, the New Jersey Democrat Peter Rodino, he is appointed its chief counsel. Doar would fill two essential needs: a bipartisan definition of the investigation and a strong prosecutorial mind.

He would lead with a quiet passion the methodical gathering, cross indexing and preparing of all the evidence in a case that became known popularly as Watergate. By the time of Nixon, Doar already had plenty of experience with the idea that the law of the land did not apply, some thought, when a sense of privilege of race or class was a motive for cheap crimes, and plenty of confidence that meticulous work documented on index cards in different colors could bring it all back down to the idea that was America.

In March 1965 there was Selma. TV and radio captured the sweep and significance and historic moment of the five days of marching from Selma to Montgomery with leaders like Martin Luther King, Ralph Bunche, and leading another chapter in a movement, Philip Randolph, the union organizer of the Pullman Porters who were all Black and all underpaid and unrepresented railroad workers. They were accompanied by federal generals and their troops and helicopters as well as FBI agents and US marshals in their suits with their Justice Department authority.

Breslin wrote more than a dozen columns on Civil Rights in between the murder of Malcolm X in February and St. Patrick's Day on March 17. He had been in Harlem, Chicago and in Selma. In a number of these columns, written in Alabama and when he returned to New York, he captured with simplicity and in his detailed, matter of fact way, a few of the underlying reasons for the march and the underlying qualities of the marchers and the opposing forces of a state's history endorsed by a backward governor who flew a Confederate flag above that of the United States on his statehouse. Breslin did not give the northern, liberal state in which he lived a pass either.

A column that appeared soon after on March 25 had this headline over it:

ALABAMA NEGRO SCHOOL:

COAL STOVES, COLD KIDS

> A shack in a dirt field behind the school serves for a bathroom. There is a small coal bin on the side of the school. A tin basin, used by the students for carrying coal inside to the pot-bellied stoves, is on the

> ground next to the bin. A long-handled axe stands beside the building. The students gather wood at lunchtime and chop it for the fires inside.
>
> . . . The principal, John Bowen, who also teaches the fifth and sixth grades, stood outside the school yesterday.
>
> . . . "Well," he said. "I work for the county school system. You shouldn't work for a person, then give him bad publicity. But I have to say to you can't learn in this school. There's no way to learn here. It's just impossible."

The column had opened by setting the scene beside the march route, Route 80, in Lowndes County, Alabama. It describes the public school for 80 students as a once yellow building, with all the glass windowpanes gone and a roof that flaps in the winter wind.

> In the winter, the wind comes strong and blows parts of the roof away and the students sit in class under the cold sky.

A boy repaired one of the benches the students sat on. A metal sign covered a hole in the floor. One of the brightest students would leave the school in a couple of years to join her father, who was a sharecropper in the fields. The column is a meticulous demonstration of what "separate but equal" meant to the governor of Alabama, George Wallace. School books from 1939. Kids with torn pants, a student whose ambition was to wait on tables. Shoes with no laces. No lunch at lunch time. One boy eats his white bread with hot sauce on his way to school in the morning. This is a long column. And it goes on in this painfully detailed way for the readers of the *Trib.*

> The lunch period ended and Bowen said goodby and went back into school with these little children who are brought up as semi-human beings.

And the visitor drives off. Down the highway where the state troopers sang, "The n—s are coming," as the marchers marched for putting things like this school into the past, Breslin says, in thousands now, in Montgomery, where "the great Tony Bennett" is present to entertain the marchers. The day before the state legislature had passed a resolution condemning the ministers who joined the marchers.

> And the Governor of the State of Alabama, of the United States of America, which in 1965 has the Rolen School as part of its great educational system, sits in his office and says he is not going to give in to this mob rule of Communists.
>
> The people here must be seen to be believed.

Breslin writes more columns, capturing the casual racism of a State Senator commenting as the marchers sing and come by the statehouse. "Tell you one thing," this lawmaker is quoted as saying, "Taint anybody can't equal n—s for keeping time to music."

And then Breslin, and his friend, Fat Thomas the bookmaker, stage a Retreat From Selma, which Fat Thomas, at the moment retired and weighing 485 pounds—he has been as slender as 415 and has had an avoirdupois as substantial as 495 according to Breslin over the years—has checked into the Jefferson Davis Hotel, and is now, after breaking furniture and failing to change anything else, he is checking out.

In a tour of the town, Fat Thomas, whose name on numerous rap sheets is listed as Thomas Rand, had observed:

> "All they do is sell guns down here.
>
> "A guy goes into the store orders a pound of baloney, a 100 rounds of ammunition, and a loaf of Wonder Bread."

Abused in Selma, insulted in Montgomery, where one person called out "You fat beatnik" and where a shoeshine stand owner ordered his shoeshine boy not to polish the shoes of this "white trash," Fat Thomas, at the airport took out a little book he had been keeping during his stay. Bookmakers, when they were not carrying flash paper, often carried one of these little notebooks.

> He started calling every place that had abused him. He told them all the same thing. "Go out and buy yourself a Dalmatian dog so he can bark when he smells the smoke . . . Because your joint is going to have an accidental fire in the middle of the night very soon."
>
> Then Fat Thomas hung up, drank his beer and got on the plane for New York, which is where he and everybody else belongs.

Fat Thomas, whose existence a short man with a big ego, Abe Rosenthal of *The Times*, had doubted, went home to people like Marvin the Torch who specialized in accidental fires and who Gloria Steinem had attested was very real.

Steinem, who started *Ms.* and who found Ronnie Eldridge instrumental in setting up the *Ms.* Foundation, would share a number of adventures with Breslin in the years to come. Some of them were with an amazing group of writers at *New York,* and some of them in what can only be called "The Wilderness of Mailer," their quixotic 1969 bid for city office in New York—with her as press secretary and Breslin in the City Council president slot and Mailer of course on the top of the ballot as the mayoral candidate—on the secessionist ticket that promised to bring statehood to New York City, bring decision making down to the neighborhood level, and give a city-state the political clout that it warranted as an economic engine for America. The whole thing was set up not to win, but to make a point. At least for Breslin and Steinem. Mailer started to take it seriously.

But first there was Selma, and later there was the beginning of Bobby Kennedy's campaign, and then there would be the assassination of Martin Luther King and then the assassination of Bobby. But now he had left Selma and was back home in New York, a city not immune from a pernicious form of racism and a less visible form of segregation. These columns he wrote after returning from Selma were perhaps the trickiest to manage in the diction and length of a column as they tried to combine poverty, race, and apathy and weave it all in the context of what seemed to matter most, when in the meantime these troubles remained unresolved. And do it all without abstraction.

He had been home from Selma just a few days when the first of these columns appeared, on St. Patrick's Day.

It was a very important day in New York when the city's Irish Catholic Americans would parade up Fifth Avenue following a green stripe painted down its center that passes by St. Patrick's Cathedral, "The Powerhouse" of the faith. Francis Cardinal Spellman would be standing in front of its wide open grand doors to give the faithful his blessing.

In 1965, St. Patrick's Day, which is celebrated on March 17 in Manhattan, came two days after President Lyndon Baines Johnson gave his historic "We Shall Overcome" speech, which used language of the Civil Rights movement and urged the passage of the Voting Rights Act:

"At times history and fate meet at a single time in a single place to shape a turning point in man's unending search for freedom," Johnson said before the Joint Session of Congress. "So it was at Lexington and

Concord. So it was a century ago at Appomattox. So it was last week in Selma, Alabama.

"There, long-suffering men and women peacefully protested the denial of their rights as Americans. Many were brutally assaulted. One good man, a man of God, was killed."

The Reverend James Reeb was killed on March 11, and the presidential aide Dick Goodwin was already thinking about the speech he would craft for Johnson.

Breslin wrote, "So many of these deaths in the civil rights movements have been wasted because they came when people were interested in other things. But the Rev. James J. Reeb did it right. He was white, not black, and he went out while everybody was looking."

Johnson said, "There is no Negro problem. There is no Southern problem. There is no Northern problem. There is only an American problem. And we are met here tonight as Americans—not as Democrats or Republicans—we are met here as Americans to solve that problem . . .

"But even if we pass this bill, the battle will not be over. What happened in Selma is part of a far larger movement which reaches into every section and State of America. It is the effort of American Negroes to secure for themselves the full blessings of American life.

"Their cause must be our cause too. Because it is not just Negroes, but really it is all of us, who must overcome the crippling legacy of bigotry and injustice.

"And we shall overcome."

Breslin wrote:

> No, the City of New York is not Selma. Don't ever accuse this joint of being a small town. We're too sophisticated for that. We don't pull off big messy civil rights murders. We kill people differently. We maneuver

them around and box them in and then we let them sit and die as human beings a little bit at a time, day after day on the streets. Then we let time do the rest . . . Then we sit in trains and read the Newspapers about Selma. . . .

There is a simple thing which can be done about this. A very simple thing. Stand up like a man. New York ought to try this just to see how it feels. . . . Stand up and see what it's like to be a man . . . and give some kid a chance . . . The President of the United States stood up on Monday night and it was a sight you are never going to forget. But right now, on St. Patrick's Day, when there usually is a green stripe running up Fifth Ave., the City of New York sits with a stripe down its back. The stripe looks just a little bit yellow today.

# BOBBY

The gun this time was an Iver-Johnson .22 caliber Cadet. The Cadet was an ugly little thing with a worn wood grip and a dull scratched gunmetal frame. It had been bought second-hand. It held eight bullets in its cylinder and proved once and for all what every hitman knew: you didn't need the stopping power that gun magazines illustrate with gelatin tests showing penetration and expansion; you didn't need anything except to get close enough to put one in right behind the ear. From there fragments of the skull and the bullet do what is needed. In this case that was to the cortex, cerebellum and brainstem.

That is what a man named Sirhan Sirhan, 24, did. He did it on June 5, 1968, after stepping from behind an ice machine in the kitchen of the Ambassador Hotel just after midnight on June 5. And that was the beginning of the end of another dream. This time it had been embodied in this boyish, toothy man with 10 children born since his marriage to Ethel Skakel in 1950 and one last one, Rory, on the way. He now lay dying on the floor. His hand had just reached out to shake the hand of Juan Romero. The busboy Romero now crouched down over Robert Francis Kennedy, the Senator who had just won the California Democratic primary and seemed destined for the White House. There was no need for reconstruction when it happened. Breslin was in Los Angeles and a witness this time:

> He was shaking hands with the kitchen workers who leaned across trays and cups and saucers and bins of ice cubes. Shaking hands with them and looking at them with those deep-set blue eyes . . . and I guess he never saw the guy with the gun.
>
> The gun did not make a very loud noise. Four or five quick, flat sounds and Kennedy disappears . . . and here is the guy with the gun.
>
> People run from him through the kitchen . . . and Bill Barry grabs the guy and Roosevelt Grier pounds on him . . .
>
> Robert Kennedy is on his back. His lips are open in pain. He has a sad look on his face.

The dying became death about 26 hours later at 1:44 A.M. Pacific Standard Time, according to news accounts. He was age 42, even younger than his brother, who at 46 had been president of the United States when he was killed in Dallas on November 22, 1963, with a 6.5 millimeter Mannlicher-Carcano bullet from the Western Cartridge Company, according to an account from the Warren Commission which investigated the president's assassination.

The Kennedys, Malcolm X, Martin Luther King:

Each of these deaths has introduced myths and theories and by now there are many narratives, often revised, often conflicted, often captured in movies and books.

But that is not really what matters, is it.

What matters is what changes.

In this case, by the time 12 hours later when the body was placed aboard an Air Force jet provided by the White House for a flight from Los Angeles to New York where it would lie in state at St. Patrick's

Cathedral, the nation was racked with grief, filled with anger, and as it had been already riven and now had lost its hope: its national dream now had become a national nightmare.

The Kennedy family's political leadership during this tumult would now fall to the fourth son of patriarch Joseph Kennedy, Ted Kennedy, the Senator for Massachusetts. Just a little over a year later he would bring new tragedy into the life of the family, and that of a young woman, drowned when she could not extricate herself from the car he borrowed from his mother and drove off the bridge at Chappaquiddick. And what had felt like a rising tide of liberal, equitable politics soon ended with Lyndon Johnson at the high water mark.

The plane itself was piloted by the same Air Force major, Warren Smith, who had commanded the flight that carried home the body of Bobby's brother what seemed like such a short time ago.

Aboard, according to Carl Pelleck, a correspondent for the *New York Post,* were three widowed women:

"On the plane were three women widowed by assassins' bullets: Mrs. Ethel Kennedy, the Senator's widow, expecting their 11th child; Mrs. John F. Kennedy, widow of the Senator's brother, cut down in his third presidential year, and Mrs. Martin Luther King, whose husband, the civil rights leader and Nobel Prize winner, was killed two months ago."

When it landed at LaGuardia it was 8 P.M. in New York. Terence Cardinal Cooke, another patriarch, one who commanded millions of Roman Catholics, many of them Irish, would bless it, and hold a private service for the family.

Every detail of what came next was meticulously planned: from the 5:30 A.M. opening onto Fifth Avenue and to the public of the cathedral's grand bronze doors to their closing well after 10 P.M. Friday night when the last public mourner had mourned. A funeral mass, ticketed by the Kennedys, would come the next morning at ten, and then the funeral train to Washington. Something not seen before. It was all, as everything public except sometimes death, for the Kennedys, carefully organized and scripted. They were a family all right, but they were a political machine. Bobby and Jackie, in grief, with love, and with ruthless efficiency had spent the past four and a half years taking the reality of JFK's presidency and Joe Kennedy's dynastic ambitions and using it as a foundation for the Kennedy mythology.

"I was in charge of St. Patrick's that night when they brought the body and we set up all these different vigils," said Ronnie Eldridge. Ronnie had first met Jimmy Breslin through Bobby. "People coming in and standing there after the family left. It was an incredible night. Unbelievable. And the next day putting the funeral list together and all that, they made so many lists. They blew out all the copy machines of the Pan Am building."

Breslin himself had been on the campaign trail with Bobby Kennedy for months. Others were writing those gray columns that are inevitable with political coverage of this kind. They call it a horse race. But it's a very long track, often muddy, sometimes dusty, and the race itself between political parties or party factions in the case of a primary is more exciting to insiders than the rest of us who simply want to know what Eugene McCarthy, the poet, and Bobby Kennedy, the benighted, stand for. What colors the winning jockey will wear.

Of course Breslin brought something that could be called a winning ticket. He knew who he was writing for. You. He brought his touch. And with that he brought hope. It is what he had been doing since the *Trib.* And the horse race writers, as they would be known only in political circles, are not actually good horse race writers because those actually write more like Breslin. They did not put you there, at the rail, where you can smell the horse, and feel the jockey's silks. They did what they had been doing since before Breslin got to the *Trib*. Dulling it up. Middlebrowing it.

On March 25, Breslin writes from Stockton, California:

> At Stockton, rusted pickup trucks sat in the dust in front of the shacks that lined the road from the airport. . . . Only the tinted glass front window of the new building in town, the Bank of America, broke the monotony of one-story poverty. . . .
>
> Kennedy gave the speech he was to give throughout the weekend. He said the nation is troubled and divided. He said the deaths and maiming of brave young men in Vietnam are indecent.

It is a beautiful column, and it goes on to capture the heckling and the jeers and lack of police protection when he stepped off a plane in Los Angeles where the mayor did not like Bobby Kennedy. But already it has captured in a way the others could not the entire Kennedy platform of racial equality, social equality, economic equality and an end to foreign aggression.

This was an important day in a young campaign. Kennedy had announced just a few days earlier, on March 16. He had come that Saturday to the Senate Caucus room where his older brother had announced his own candidacy from Delano, California, where on March 10 he had met with Cesar Chavez of the Farm Workers at the end of his 25-day hunger strike.

A few days later, in a column that appeared on March 27, Breslin captured something else. Youth. Imagination. The things that Bobby Kennedy could touch in a way that even his brother Jack could not.

> For a politician she looked very good. She did have braces on her teeth and her high school uniform, a navy blue blazer, was a little rumpled. Otherwise she was fine.
>
> She said her name was Chris Harrington and that she was 15 years old and that she had been in politics for a week now and she liked it very much.
>
> She sat at a desk in the doorway to Robert Kennedy's campaign headquarters on Wilshire Blvd. and she took phone calls from people who want to do volunteer work on the campaign. When the phone on her desk rang, she squirmed in the chair, reached out an grabbed the phone in the middle of the first ring.

This was the seventh, and last hopeful column of at least eight that he wrote in the thirteen days since his first appeared on Friday, March 15.

Breslin's coverage had begun in the back seat of a car in New York City, Ronnie Eldridge recalled.

"One day I'm in the car with [Bobby Kennedy] and we're driving someplace and he says I forgot I have to go back to the Carlisle. There's a reporter who's going to Vietnam tomorrow and he wants to talk to me and so they send me into the lobby to find Jimmy Breslin.

"And there's Jimmy Breslin standing in the lobby waiting for the senator. So he came back into the car and the two of us were in the backseat and they had a whole discussion on Vietnam because they had an argument because Kennedy hadn't yet come to oppose it. So that's how I met Jimmy," said Ronnie, then a Kennedy protégé. Later, looking back on 35 years married to Breslin she summed it up, "We had good times."

Now here he is on the funeral train, warning people crowding around it to get back, and Eldridge recalls they all held their hands over their hearts and "there wasn't a space between here and Washington that there weren't people standing there with their hands over their hearts." It falls to Breslin to explain why:

> The railroad train carrying the body of Robert Francis Kennedy left Pennsylvania Station in New York City after a long, hot, ornate and lovely mass at St. Patrick's Cathedral. The coffin was put in the last car of the 21-car train. Then 1,500 people shuffled through the passageways and got on the train.
>
> The train swayed and slid down the platform and went into a tunnel under the Hudson River. It came up in the weeds and marshes of New Jersey, and it was here that it started. It was here, on the roads running through the weeds, and in junk yards and factories alongside the tracks, that the funeral of Robert Francis Kennedy took place.
>
> The rest of it was a ritual which could be afforded and put together only by very rich people who also are important. But the people on the sides of the railroad tracks, so many of them Negros, so many of them openly weeping, were different. The ceremony at St. Patrick's and the ceremony at Arlington, were very small and insignificant next to the shimmering dignity of human beings crying for another.
>
> At Newark, the platforms were packed with the people Robert Kennedy had fallen in love with. I don't know what it was like at the start with him. But I know what it was like at the end, when he talked for two days about finishing his last campaign in Watts. He couldn't wait to get to Watts, where he felt he belonged. And he came to Watts in a convertible; he had to ride in convertibles because his brother was killed in a convertible. And he came with his eyes flashing and his hands reaching . . . Robert Kennedy was committed to these people in a way that probably no other white man has ever been, and now they stood on the platforms and wept while the train carrying the body of an Irishman they trusted went past them.

Sirhan Sirhan, a Palestinian Christian, a Jordanian citizen, born in Jerusalem but by age 12 an adolescent living in America, as he would for the rest of his life, most of which was spent in prison, thought he was killing a man who was helping to send bomber planes to Israel to inflict harm on the Palestinians.

But as the funeral train progressed, Breslin notes, one mourner on one of many crowded platforms was seen to land on the tracks in front of a speeding diesel headed in another direction, now a blur of yellow spit off the bow of the train. This important detail is counterpoised against his vivid portrayal of what the assassin had failed to kill: the Kennedy spirit. That attention to a simple detail is what makes Breslin special. He uses it both as a bridge and to add richness to what comes next.

> And now, right next to you, very young, very composed, very handsome, very open, here he is.
>
> "Hello, I'm Joe Kennedy. Thanks for coming."
>
> He shakes hands with a firm grip.
>
> Joe Kennedy is 15. He is a student at Milton. He is one of the 10 children whose father has just been murdered and is in a coffin in the back of the train.
>
> His mother is a widow at 40 and she is pregnant.
>
> And Joe Kennedy is going through every car of this 21-car railroad train, the funeral train, so he can shake hands and thank all the people for coming to help bury his father. . . .
>
> "Hello, I'm Joe Kennedy." Murder my uncle. Murder my father. But I am a Kennedy and I come with my head up and my eyes looking right at you and I do this because a Kennedy must go on.
>
> The train had just hit the people. It had hit them like a warning from the gods . . . Stay away, your family lives with death.
>
> And the answer to it was: "Hello, I'm Joe Kennedy, thanks for coming."

# WE'LL NEVER BE YOUNG AGAIN

By now the presses of the *Herald Tribune* had long been silenced. Labor strife had killed it and with it the camaraderie of Bleeck's barroom.

"We were all ambitious and we were too young to have the jobs we had. You know, I was the managing editor when I was 37," Dick Wald said. "Jimmy was writing a column that had a fixed spot. . . . [Dave] Laventhol wouldn't wind up being the City Editor of a major metropolitan paper for another ten years, anywhere else.

"When [Whitney] bought it, he decided that it was a great newspaper and it was what he wanted, but he needed a different kind of paper," Wald said. "He made the management decision to make it an essential read because of what it was, not because of the news that it brought in." And this was the foundation on which what became known as The New Journalism was laid.

"They gave us power . . . and Whitney put the stamp of approval on it. The other thing was we just enjoyed what we did. Everybody there would sit around after the paper was up. Uh, we'd probably go to Bleeck's for a drink except Tom Wolfe. He didn't drink much."

But the romance of journalism isn't always so great when you are unemployed, or the child of an unemployed news reporter.

"I remember my mother saying, 'Your father's out of a job,'" Kevin Breslin recalled. "I somehow remember in the back of my mind thinking, 'This is bad.'

"You start thinking of what my grandma used to say, you know, 'you're going to the poor house.'

"I think we just assumed everything would be OK and not have to lose our house or something.

"I wasn't shell-shocked because when I was nine, J.B. was going through a little bit of a tough time and I had my trumpet repossessed and I was asked to leave the school music band, which ruined my career in music." Kevin has a funny half smile as he says this. "This was just before the Mets book.

"But when the next one closed down [the *World Journal Tribune*] I remember thinking 'this is a strange business.' But the *Herald Tribune* all I remember is that it seemed like the place my father worked. I loved the cafeteria . . . I remember the unique smell . . . I think it was the cafeteria smell that wafted through the entire newspaper, that inside the smell of ink, oh yeah, and cigarettes."

Before the presses made their final run and it was a final last call for the *Trib* at Bleeck's bar, there were many columns and many nights. In the amber light refracted off the damp bar, Breslin sat with Walt Kelly, who was supposed to make Pogo cartoons and not drink according to doctors, and with Wald and Jim Bellows, Dick Schaap and others. Through a glass of gold and a wreath of smoke, Wald recalled, Breslin would mutter "what a crappy column" he had written even as he was thinking about the next one and dreaming about the novel he was already plotting out. Rent receipts, utility bills, the milkman; these things mattered little. He usually did not think of them at all.

His agent of many years, Sterling Lord, recalled the one time he did. Rosemary Breslin had called him:

"'Look, Sterling.' I guess I've been working for a year or so with Jimmy. 'We got a problem here because Jimmy has run up bills at five or six different companies here. And I need help in eliminating the problem.'

"So I had a suggestion and she took it. And I was able to eliminate the debt problem in about a year. So he's all clean now. And the next day he came in the office and he said, 'Sterling, is there any way you can reinstate one of those bills?' He said it was always interesting fighting with those guys over the phone. See that's what he missed, the fighting. But I couldn't do it. There's no way I could start it again."

Between the day John F. Kennedy was buried and "The Gravedigger" appeared in the papers and the day Bobby Kennedy was killed and Breslin was there—in his memory, sitting on the assassin's legs as he was wrestled down (though in other accounts memory may have played its tricks)—he had written well over 750 features and columns for the New York newspapers he called home. In one year, the number was greater than 174 pieces.

He had interviewed the mobster Dutch Schultz's killer, who called him on his first day out of jail and asked Breslin to meet him at the Port Authority to talk. He had flown to London as Churchill lay dying: "he dies in an attached house on a very common street, with only a detective walking up and down in front of his door." He had gone to Dover to the Park Inn pub to seek a man who took soldiers off the beaches at Dunkirk. "You know, it wasn't exactly simple," said the man, who couldn't remember the date of "something that children will be memorizing in school a 100 years from now." But the man offered an idea: "Well, why don't you come inside and chat a bit. I hope I can remember enough for you." Breslin captured the pageantry of the Knight of the Garter's funeral, his coffin on a gun carriage from 1880 pulled along by sailors hauling white ropes. And then he found the people to whom Churchill mattered most, those who were under the bombs.

> "And 'e was around that mornin'," one woman said, recalling when Peggy Anderson's 15 year old was killed by one. . . . " 'e come up to Peggy Anderson and 'e says 'Where's your husband' and she says 'Trainin' in the army . . . and 'e says 'You 'ave to stand fast down 'ere. And then 'e shook 'is fist and said 'e was going to fix these goddam Nazis . . . and then 'e left and 'e was crying like a little kid in school when 'e walked away. 'E was crying for Peggy Anderson's daughter and if 'e could do that for 'er then we can go out and cry for 'im today."

Breslin had captured the ugliness of Sen. Joe McCarthy when he wrote about the righteousness of a man's restoration to his job eight years after he was flayed in Washington hearings. Firemen, bookies, horse betters, racketeers, Teamsters, Mob bosses and widows and riots; the dead and the dying. Day in, day out he smoked Pall Mall cigarettes, he typed, he drank, he made notes, he smoked, he typed and the papers and the public were better for it. If you did the rough math, Breslin at times appeared in daily papers and Sunday supplements more than three times a week. Whether in his home precincts of New York, or the highlands of Da Nang, or the damp serenity of Hyde Park he brought something, almost all the time, to you: he put you there. You were with Frank Sinatra's son walking out to the press after his kidnapping, shouldering union laborers finishing up at the World's Fair, gazing at Tony Provenzano standing alone before the bench, counting time already, imagining Little Tommy blessing himself "Jesus, Mary and Joseph," as machine guns and bombs and dynamite are discussed with the "Men Of the IRA" and the boy stands on a chair to peer down into a British prison yard.

As the senator's personal bodyguard, ex-FBI agent Bill Barry, leapt into the fray—brave, but too late for Kennedy—Breslin captured the scrum that included Los Angeles Rams defensive lineman

Rosey Grier, retired now after a tendon torn in his last season, who wrested the gun from Sirhan Sirhan's hand as it appeared pointed at the writer George Plimpton. He captured the shouts of "We want him alive. We want him alive," from the powerhouse California politician Jesse Unruh who jumped on a table as the crowd shouted, "Kill him, kill him," and writer Pete Hamill, who would go home and weep, threw a punch.

The chaos of the scrum, the solidarity of good soldiers in Vietnam with rioters in the US, the sadness and the steady absorption of the pain of the world, no wonder it was chaos at home where bills were unpaid, milkmen were threatened, children walked on eggshells, his wife conferred with his agent to find the money, and the ghosts of the house his father walked out of permeated the soul of this writer—whose smile could be cherubic when the face wasn't twisted into a bellowing rage—even as his family lived in a much finer house, with, so far as is known, only one possible alcoholic—the writer himself.

The chaos and antics and the love also at home were described best by Kevin Breslin:

"He was boisterous. 'Fuck this and fuck that and I'm going to sleep in a funking hotel. [but] He had a whole different side to him and in the kitchen, [he would say] and watch this little boy . . . 'Dad loves Mommy,' thank God you know, because joint was wild. She was him; he was her. It's like, it didn't matter that the world's caving in. They were like a team."

And the Breslins, in 1965, were another family in Queens sending a man to Vietnam.

"It must have been dangerous because when he shipped out, every night, we would have to pray. My mother would have my brother James, my sister Rosemary and me on the floor praying on our knees to make sure he was okay. He was there for four or five months," Kevin Breslin said. And in Forest Hills, as in so many homes, prayers flew East.

But first, the impresario dressed for war. "We had to go to the army navy store," Kevin said. "He was buying like a flak jacket with all the pockets. A military belt with the canteen green shirts, green pants. I remember he's trying it on. He paraded around the bedroom. And he had a canteen and the old buckle military belt with a hidden back where he could put money. You'd think it's a comedy. He's getting dressed to go to Vietnam. We didn't know what Vietnam was except it was a war." Breslin found out soon enough what that meant.

"Yeah, it was July, it was some fucking place. Mostly the dirt. When I found you could put your face in the dirt and still breathe it was a good spot. I don't know what they teach in basic training camp, when I'm fucked bad, I know what to do. 'How deep in the dirt can you put your filthy head?'" In 1965, a good many of the other faces in the dirt were Black.

> By Jimmy Breslin
> *Herald Tribune* News service
> SAIGON, Aug. 16—The radios sit on bunks and on boxes in the mess halls and out in the field they are on top of the sandbags. Every hour the music stops and the News begins: "rioting in a section of Los Angeles."
> And the Negro soldiers stand and listen. And they talk. They talk with uniforms over their Black skins.

The column continued. It simply captured the debate and discussion of what was on the mind of these American soldiers in the summer of

Watts, where the riots had started as so many things seem to with a police car stop, then of course came the rumor—the cops had kicked a pregnant woman—and then from August 11 and for another five days, rioting of a kind that claimed thirty-four lives, according to published reports, of a kind that had the government send in 14,000 National Guard soldiers.

> "They ask you why you're here when you can't be straight at home," a tall one, smoking a cigar said. "Why shouldn't they!" the other one said. "How can you come over here and say to the people, 'We going to liberate you,' when you got go out in the streets and riot to liberate yourself at home."

His face was in the dirt. But his head was not in the sand. There were many good war correspondents in Vietnam by that year, some so good that it would have been hard to show up in July and with all the talent in the world catch up by August with Malcolm Browne of the Associated Press, David Halberstam of *The Times*, Peter Arnett, and Neil Sheehan with their depth of knowledge of the war, the soldiering, the politics and the nuances of policy. Breslin did something simple and clear. He told the story of what events in life at home meant to the soldiers here. One soldier reminded his colleagues of Lemuel Penn, the Lieutenant Colonel home from camp in Georgia and shot by the Ku Klux Klan. "They got us over here defendin' Georgia. Next thing you know they'll have us fighting for South Africa." The Vietnamese, who were our allies themselves, did not get a pass on racism. Breslin closes this trenchant column by capturing something that remained true well after the war was over—the Vietnamese too wanted little to do with Black Americans.

But Breslin's best war reporting came when he got home. From Travis Air Force Base, he captured the cost of war in a country thousands of miles away. The headline summarized the topic nicely: "Wounded, Dead in War Arrive Nightly at Travis." The subhead captured the rest: "Unloading of Vietnam Casualties From Big Jets Becoming Routine." Breslin takes you inside the big, windowless transport, first noting the squadron of nuclear armed B-52s parked nearby. Inside, where the nurses are getting twenty-seven casualties—twelve ambulatory and one psychiatric, the rest on litters, ready to come home.

It is warm, the broken bodies are covered only in sheets, but now, with the Northern California air very cool at dusk, "They came out, one after another, with casts and with bloodstains on their sheets, and the nurse's tanned hands pulled olive drab blankets over their broken bodies and she talked quietly and looked into the face of each of them. Then he would be gone and the medics would place another piece of the war in Vietnam at her feet. And she would bend over and reach for the blankets." It's graphic, it's detailed with blood seeping from casts, colostomy bags, legs that can't bear the touch of the blanket. It's not the defeat of Gallipoli, but is the same scene as when the troop ships returned to the piers in Australia.

"'I have a colostomy. I'm 25 and I have a colostomy. I was going to marry a girl. She's in Pennsylvania. If I ever heal up I can marry her.'"

The next night's plane, someone whispers as the column closes, will only be carrying coffins.

And in 1967, when the war is at its height, he captures another fact of this war: "Friendly Napalm Changes Return Address on a Soldier's Letter." The soldier had been there two months. Breslin is shown the letter. The soldier's father allows: "The letter. You can keep the letter if you do one thing for us." "Yes?" "Put in the paper that he was a very good son for us."

What was most important about going to war, for Jimmy Breslin, was that it opened his eyes to the cost of war, and opened his heart to the question of whether this war was our country's to fight. But he didn't opine, he just continued to write simple war stories. The kind you can find at certain Air Force bases during any American War. The kind that Meyer Berger wrote in *The New York Times* on October 27, 1947:

"The first war dead from Europe came home yesterday. The harbor was steeped in Sabbath stillness as they came in on the morning tide in 6,248 coffins in the hold of the transport *Joseph V. Connolly*."

Breslin went home to Queens, New York. Despondent, he could not write.

The journalist Lawrence O'Donnell, writing about the White House following the assassination of another Kennedy, Bobby's brother, JFK, in his book *Playing with Fire: The 1968 Election and the Transformation of American Politics*, best states what Breslin must have been feeling:

"There was a moment in the White House late that day that captured what everyone in the Kennedy circle was feeling. Mary McGrory, a columnist close to the Kennedys, said through her tears, 'We'll never laugh again.' Daniel Patrick Moynihan, then an assistant secretary of labor, said, 'Heavens, Mary, we'll laugh again. It's just that we will never be young again.'"

Vietnam was in the past. So was Bobby, whose views had evolved from those of a young man once actively involved in the architecture of his brother's Southeast Asia plans, to one now dovish and vocally opposed to President Lyndon B. Johnson's plans. Bobby was dead. The Bobby America needed—created in a large part by sympathetic reporters, who knew and chose to downplay or ignore the ruthless determination that Bobby had exhibited in the past and had exhibited in his calculated bid for the party nomination—would not sit in the West Wing. The funeral train had arrived in Washington. The solemnity had begun. Breslin was there. As it was with the war dead, who Berger heard a sailor murmur "came home too late," and point out to another sailor that the signs welcoming the troops home or congratulating on a job well done were painted over or faded, now it was with the hope for peace and unity and a future that Bobby seemed to promise to the young woman who scooted over to grab the telephone on the first ring. It had faded away.

# POST HASTE

The correspondence from Executive Editor Paul Sann to Publisher Dorothy Schiff is poignant in the matter-of-fact way it captures Breslin's despondency. It was unearthed by Howie Sann from his father's files and the Dorothy Schiff Papers at the New York Public Library and shared with us.

June 14, 1968

DOLLY: Breslin, sad to say, is in a deep depression now. Hasn't written since Monday's column and says he can't. He's taking next week as one of the 4 unpaid vacation weeks he has coming. I sense, talking to him, that there's no way around it; he's just plain choked up and says he never would have written a line on the RFK tragedy except that I kept on him.

...

The memo, neatly typed on the cheap and now yellowed copy paper, of course goes on to the mundane but all-important matter of money. Because the *Post*, like its staff, was no stranger to having not quite enough money to go around. Though the paper now made money, Schiff, like the man who would later purchase her paper, Rupert Murdoch, was heard to say, knew that you didn't sweep money, even pennies, toward the door. "They're my pennies," the media baron said.

"On the matter of pay, I would suggest that we let the checks go through for the two columns Bres missed this week—and let him owe us two—but take him off payroll for next week. Is this okay?"

"Told Paul OK" is handwritten on her copy.

Society born and bred, Dolly Schiff, a debutante, a socialite, and a Republican by station had now become the owner of the paper and an active Democrat and New Dealer. In 1939 she had bought majority ownership of the *Post*, the oldest continuously published daily newspaper in America. It had been founded by Alexander Hamilton in 1801, and now Schiff, who at first named herself Treasurer and Vice President, would soon become the first woman newspaper publisher in New York. Her second husband, who she had awarded the title Publisher, had stepped aside. Her third husband would get the title Editor, but in 1942 Schiff would take the title of Publisher for herself.

Under Schiff the *Post* was a crusading, pro-union, staunchly liberal paper that took on big names in its exposés and still kept the paper sexy and breezy. She ran the paper with a firm hand, a sharp eye on costs and "closely supervised editorial policy," according to *The New York Times*. When she sold the paper to Rupert Murdoch in 1976 he of course promised to change nothing, then made a 180-degree turn with regard to power, the powerful, social welfare, and reform.

One of the veteran photographers, Louie Liotta, explained on the way to a photo shoot in a tenement apartment of a disenfranchised Black family in Brooklyn, one of whose members had committed a violent crime: "It's the same picture, just a different caption." If you were to have heard the enthusiasm and optimism the paper's hard-edged tabloid veterans voiced upon the sale to the 49-year-old Australian, you would know two things: reporters consistently best predict the past and Rupert Murdoch ought to have on his tombstone, "I won't change anything."

Breslin in 1967 was sure he belonged at the paper. He and his agent, Sterling Lord, had begun discussions even while Jock Whitney was still involved in publishing the short-lived successor to the *Trib,* the *World Journal Tribune.*

In a *New York Post* Office Memorandum that he wrote addressed to "Mrs. Schiff" after Breslin called him and began his wooing, Paul Sann said, "Sterling said Bres called me because he has reason to believe the ship is sinking and I am the only editor he wants to work for in the town. I said I loved Bres too . . ."

But it's always about the money. And much future correspondence between Schiff and Sann regarding Breslin would be to that point: first rights, New York rights, syndication rights, editing rights, vacation rights. The correspondence goes on for pages and pages.

In the manner of Breslin himself, Sann in a memo dated December 6, 1967, invokes Fat Thomas.

> DS: Mr. Breslin's delayed in Sicily but his real authorized spokesman, Fat Thomas, told me last night that he's pushing hard on his book [*The Gang That Couldn't Shoot Straight*] so that he can start the column again by March 1. Fat said Bres means to have us for his NY outlet and "don't want dem bums on the *News*." Fat could be right but I'll get the star himself when he gets home.
>
> The book is a novel built around the Gallo-Profaci wars in Brooklyn. Bres went to Sicily for the Mafia trial for background on the playful Walyos.

By February of 1968 the deal to get him there was done. But Breslin's love of the paper would be short-lived. Five months after Bobby Kennedy's death, the *enfant terrible* behavior that plagued his editors and colleagues throughout his career showed up.

It began on November 6.

Breslin had returned, by all accounts deeply wounded by the death of Bobby, to writing. On November 5 he covered the election-eve arrival of Richard Nixon at Kennedy Airport, the motorcade, the final campaign rally and the election night atmosphere at the Waldorf as the returns came in. There was a lot to cover and Breslin had a lot to say. The column came in long.

Paul Sann, whose tenure as Executive Editor lasted thirty years, had trimmed the column for space. Sann and Schiff—and she said this in a memo—believed one of the virtues of a column was to be able to tell all that needed to be told in the allotted space (except, of course, when in their wisdom it was okay to let the column run as long as they saw fit.)

Here is how Breslin repaid Sann: "Breslin called me at home at 6:30 last night in a towering rage fueled with liquor." He told Sann the trims had cost him valuable lines and if this continued, he would not be writing for the *Post*. He told Sann that if he was not good enough to write to the bottom, he would "start on the *Daily News* on Monday."

Breslin threatened to go to "dem bums" at the competing paper even though he would be breaking his contract. He told Sann the paper could sue. Somehow the discussion turned to the point of where the column was displayed in the paper. Sann, perhaps foolishly, suggested that another placement could result in a shorter column.

"I never finished my sentence. My friend hung up. I don't know whether in the gray dawn, Jimmy will decide to favor us with some prose."

He did.

Some of this correspondence is captured in a piece Howie Sann wrote for the *Columbia Journalism Review*. It should be noted that the piece, published September 8, 2017, was longer than the editors saw fit. It was trimmed. Howie Sann was still unhappy about that, he said, in a conversation that took place nearly six years later.

In the immediate aftermath of the Kennedy coverage, there had been from Sann and Schiff concern, compassion, and the idea that Breslin's coverage of the campaign from start to tragedy could have been worthy of a Pulitzer Prize. But after the Nixon column Breslin began nursing the start of a vendetta against Sann, Schiff, and the paper that continued through 1975, when he proclaimed that the *Post* was "the worst paper in the world."

In the end, wounded and angry, he would stay a little over eleven months. He wrote just over 104 columns: It was, at least, a little bit longer than the "cup of coffee" Tom Wolfe recalled having spent at a couple of the places he had worked before the *Trib*. But for Breslin, it was a shorter stint than his journeyman sports career at the *Journal-American*, which was his "prison" for a year and a quarter beginning in 1959. That stint was one where his sportswriting was evolving, and where he demonstrated his strengths when he committed a five-part series on the growth of bowling into a billion-dollar business once automatic pinspotters replaced the tedium of a pin boy's day.

But the months at the *Post* were a critical time for Breslin.

They had begun to unfold well enough.

On February 26, 1968, Paul Sann, after months of negotiation, had received from Breslin's agent, Sterling Lord, the deal memo that would bind him to the paper. Breslin had written brilliantly and beautifully before the death of Bobby. After the death of Bobby he had written some columns beautifully, some less so, like a player riding out a contract. And his output was smaller.

Before Bobby, there had been MLK. In the April 10, 1964, edition, he wrote:

> The woman stood up and closed her eyes and started to sing.
>
> She sang yesterday in the Ebenezer Baptist Church, over the casket of Martin Luther King, Jr., sang to his children one of who was too young for it and concentrated on a lollypop, sang to Coretta King, who listened with her eyes closed, sang to everybody who was in the church to bury a man who died trying to help.
>
> And then it was gone and they were wheeling the casket up a side aisle. They wheeled it past Charles Evers, who was doubled over and weeping, and Robert Kennedy, who came down a row to be next to him. Martin Luther King Jr., shot in the twilight in Memphis, Tenn. Charles Evers had a brother, Medgar, who was shot in the back in the night in Mississippi. Robert Kennedy's brother, John was shot from behind in the daylight in Texas. And further up the aisle was the sister of Malcolm X who was shot on a Sunday afternoon in New York.
>
> The casket came out into the crowd waiting in the sun. It was hitched behind two mules. The mules started up the street away from the red brick church and 200,000 people, maybe 300,000; the Atlanta newspaper said half a million; walked with the casket and the mules. They walked under a high sun and the men took off their jackets and the women were singing softly and it would have been beautiful, except all of us have been here before.
>
> There have been marches and funerals forever in the last five years and everything was supposed to change and nothing has changed. The Black man in this country is still a n— and his children are the children of a n— and the Congress of the U.S. has to fight with itself to pass a civil rights bill that isn't worth drawing up in the first place when you see what really is needed. . . .

It is a beautifully crafted column and a very hard column to quote. And it is an even harder column to read in full.

> John Doar was talking . . . while he walked in the sun yesterday. Once, John Doar put up his life in Southern towns as a Justice Dept. civil rights man. Last year, the Civil Rights Division became a domestic troop deployment agency and John Doar quit. And yesterday he walked behind his old friend Martin Luther King . . .
>
> "You think of the dead on a day like today," he was saying. . . . "Herbert Lee, he was the first in my time. Summer of '61 in Liberty, Miss. There was another one they killed in that town. I think his name was Louis Allen. Then you had the Rev. Reeb in Selma. Schwerner, Goodman and Chaney in Philadelphia, Miss., Medgar Evers, Mrs. Liuzzo, so many of them dead. And we've gotten nowhere."

On April 4, Breslin had been with the Rev. King and he wrote about his last hours, in Memphis.

"He couldn't find his tie," the column began. It continues with the Rev. Ralph Abernathy pointing out, "Martin, why don't you look on that chair."

"'Oh,' said the Nobel Peace prize winner Martin Luther King, Jr.; who like any of us was ready to blame anyone else for misplacing or taking his tie."

The men in room 306 discuss dinner. They want soul food and wonder if another man's 31-year-old wife is too young to know how to cook it.

It begins like this as a matter-of-fact column, filled with the commonplace: of walking onto a narrow balcony; of seeing the Cadillac, black, supplied by a funeral director and waiting to take King around.

There is Jesse Jackson. There is Andrew Young. Names that also have never gone away. And there is a thicket. And it was from there the shot came this time:

> He was 39 and for 14 years he had been trying to keep a country from falling apart and now he had been killed by one shot from a rifle. . . .
>
> It was 6 P.M. on Thursday, April 4, 1968. The Rev. Martin Luther King, Nobel prize winner, lay in front of an open green door, with the cheap silver numbers 306 nailed to the door. The door was to a $12 a night double room in a place called the Lorraine Hotel in Memphis, Tenn. . . .
>
> He was 39 and he had a Nobel Peace prize and he spent his life trying to help, but very few listened.

The next day, April 5, there was fear, there were flames, and there were riots in Washington. Breslin was now there and he reported on this. And on the 9th, of course, he was in Atlanta for the funeral.

This writing on race, on riots, on civil rights and on hatred, by now extended back to the assassination of John F. Kennedy and the 1964 Harlem Riots, and it continues through the months before he arrived at the *Post.* If you want to consider Breslin's state of mind when he arrived at Sann's door, think of him as a young man who had more than four years immersed in and consumed by one of the most violent periods in a nation's history.

During the year before—at a time after the *Trib*, and during and after the life of its short-lived successor *World Journal Tribune*—Breslin's syndicated work appeared in various newspapers. During this time there was Newark. July 14, 1967. A riot. Armed conflict. Tanks in the streets. Twenty-six, at least, dead.

> It started with kids running in the dusk with garbage cans and bricks and throwing them through store windows and reaching through the smashed glass and grabbing anything and running away. . . .
>
> And now at 4 o'clock this morning the city of Newark started to come apart. . . .

It began with the tempo and simplicity of his Harlem riot coverage. But that seemed so long ago now, a time when riots were confined. Here, a city was plunged immediately afterward into decades of darkness: flight by whites, neglect by politicians and years and years of increasing violence, crime, and gang rule on the streets. Newark became a place where FBI agents from the field office there went to lunch in pairs.

In Detroit, just about two weeks later, his column ran under the headline "Guardsmen Shoot, People Loot."

> DETROIT—There is no sanity. A National Guardsman in an apartment on the first floor fires his M-1 up the dumbwaiter shaft and a Guardsman up on the top floor fires down the shaft. . . .
>
> On a street called Linwood an armored personnel carrier comes out of the blackness and into the glow of a burning building. One street light is left on the block. The Guardsmen don't like lights around them on the streets. They fire from inside the carrier at the street light.

It was urban warfare. Only in that regard and one other was it different from what could have been written in Vietnam. The other difference was that here troops were shooting at US citizens and the citizens were shooting too. Looters were shot. A fireman was shot right between the eyes. He left a child, Breslin reported.

On February 19, 1969, Breslin's final column for the *Post* would appear. That same Wednesday, the front page of *The New York Times* had laid out above the fold a report on six wounded in an Arab attack on an El Al flight in Zurich. On the bottom in a narrow column the paper reported Mario Procaccino would run for mayor. And an important item ran with a picture across three columns on the lower right: "Radcliffe to Consider a Full Merger With Harvard."

In a narrow little ad, in the style of a two-line personal, in type much smaller than that in even the boxed news index it was placed under, was this: "You are on your own. I am giving up my newspaper column. —Jimmy Breslin." The ad had been addressed to Robert J. Allen, one of Jimmy's characters.

What actually prompted the rift? There were a multitude of possible factors. Could it really have been a trim of a column that ran long in order to fit a box that the paper's editors had determined would "always" run under a two-column-width piece? Desolation? Breslin's placement in the paper? He later would claim his work was buried back by "the girdle ads." Was it the fact that with the January 1969 publication of *The Gang That Couldn't Shoot Straight* to critical acclaim, bestseller sales numbers, and a movie with MGM soon on the way, he had become "awash" in money? This last idea would be reminiscent of his first conversation with Jock Whitney before he joined the paper, when he told America's richest man that he could not afford him. Whitney had paid him $20,000 to start and $200 a week in expenses, according to the author Richard Kluger, an income that rapidly grew to surpass $125,000 per year.

Did the fact that Breslin saw himself as a novelist, and was now freed by his new-found wealth from the constraints of daily journalism, play a big part? Was the bellowing and quitting simply Breslin covering up the fact that with creditors at bay, and money in the bank with the promise of more on the way, he could turn to his true calling? The

Novel. The themes of money, lack of money, ambition, failed ambition, genius, curly haired dreamer, betrayal, lifelong grudges, vitriol and revenge, and perceived slights would continue to appear throughout his career. And they would become more pronounced. To quote Joe Flaherty, who would soon observe Breslin closely during the course of writing *Managing Mailer*, his book on the Mailer-Breslin 1969 New York City political campaign:

"Breslin's life . . . is starred in, written, produced, directed, and most important, publicized by Jimmy Breslin."

And that in one neat sentence probably sums up as well as anyone can J.B. Number One.

After Bobby there were at least sixty-two more columns before the final column that ran on February 19.

Those columns included good ones that contained dark humor—"A Farewell to Bumpy (Johnson)"—and good ones that spoke of courage—"Lindsay in Harlem."

# BUMPY'S FAREWELL

"A Farewell to Bumpy" is a wonderful look at a Black gangster who went head to head with the white gangsters of the Mafia—who had backed down from no one since he was a boy, and who went on to take over a good part of Harlem's heroin trade.

> Ellsworth Johnson, who was known as Bumpy in the Black sections of every city in the country, is dead of a heart attack at 63.

It begins as an obituary should; an obituary of a man who wanted to own the heroin business. It notes he had a temper. "And on these occasions he was more dangerous than an infantry platoon."

And then Breslin takes us back to where Bumpy as a boy got run out of Charleston, South Carolina, because he didn't talk properly to white people when he delivered their newspapers. He came to Harlem, Breslin notes, and panhandled, while nurturing his fierce determination that when he was old enough to work, no white man was going to put a broom in his hand.

By the time he died, he had lived a life that "made him the only Black man in the country to get what he wanted when he sat down with the Mafia."

The column quickly puts you in the room with Bumpy, as if Breslin, who like his hero Damon Runyon could eat at the best tables in the country but preferred the company of criminals and thieves, was there with him.

> There was a morning a month ago when Bumpy was eating hash for breakfast in the Stage Delicatessen on Seventh Ave. and listening to a man tell of his troubles with a shylock.
>
> "Just don't pay him any more," Bumpy said.
>
> "But the Italians would be comin' after me," the man said.
>
> "Well, you just tell them that you left the money over to Bumpy's and if they want it, they come and get it."
>
> "Tell them that?" the man said.
>
> "Just that," Bumpy said. "And that'll be the end of it."

Pretty much everything you need to know about the power Bumpy Johnson had accumulated on the streets. And the setting, better than any movie set, captures how Bumpy enjoyed spending his power: at ease in one of the best delicatessens in the world.

Anecdote piles on anecdote, you learn more about Bumpy Johnson, his rise to power, his hard fists and soft hands in just a few hundred words.

> Bumpy had a head that broke a thousand nightsticks. He came up when Dutch Schultz and Owney Madden ran Harlem. He was in and out of jails. Alcohol, numbers, gambling. [And yet] . . . "In 20 years with this man, we never once had a fight in the house," his wife said yesterday. "He left everything bothering him at the door."

We learn that Bumpy was the best chess player in Harlem, that he went to school to learn to mix chemicals for a pest control business he owned. That he was halfway, when he died, through studying the ideals of Greek culture: the concept of *paideia*, which explicated the ideal way to educate a person to become a good citizen.

And we learn of Bumpy's prized possession:

*Courtesy: Louis Schiro*

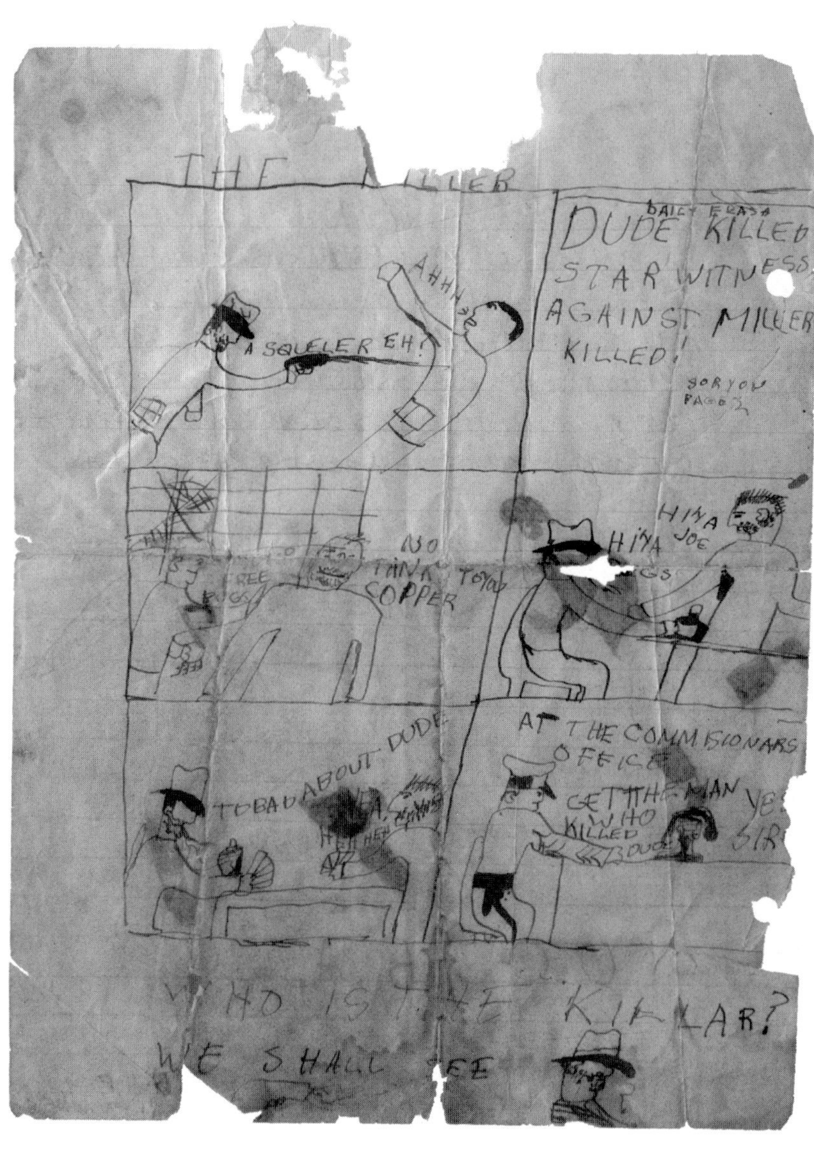


A page from Breslin's first newspaper, *The Flash*. A star witness's murder is the big story under the headline "Dude Killed." *Courtesy: Ronnie Eldridge and Jimmy Breslin*

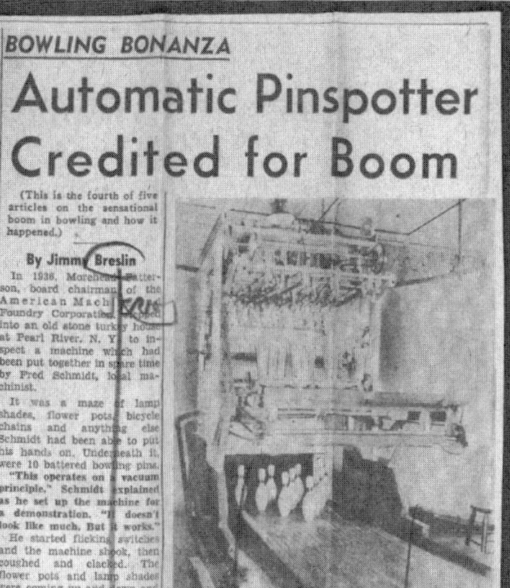

BOWLING BONANZA

## Automatic Pinspotter Credited for Boom

(This is the fourth of five articles on the sensational boom in bowling and how it happened.)

By Jimmy Breslin

In 1938, Morehead Patterson, board chairman of the American Machine and Foundry Corporation, stepped into an old stone turkey house at Pearl River, N. Y. to inspect a machine which had been put together in spare time by Fred Schmidt, local machinist.

It was a maze of lamp shades, flower pots, bicycle chains and anything else Schmidt had been able to put his hands on. Underneath it, were 10 battered bowling pins.

**"This operates on a vacuum principle," Schmidt explained as he set up the machine for a demonstration. "It doesn't look like much. But it works."**

He started flicking switches and the machine shook, then coughed and clacked. The flower pots and lamp shades were coming up and down and the pins were moving with them. When the demonstration was finished, the pins were standing.

**DIDN'T LOOK LIKE MUCH**

It didn't look like much, as Schmidt said. But it worked and Patterson turned around and said quietly, "I don't think you belong to your envelope factory anymore. You better come down to New York with me. I think we'll have to do some business together."

This was the start, the first slow, sure step, of bowling on its path to becoming the huge billion dollar business of being one of the nation's major entertainment sports.

For without the automatic pinspotter, now as common as carpet in a bowling alley, the sport never could have grown. The pinspotter has eliminated the pinboys and they were the difference between a small, hard-to-operate sport and a business today in which people invest fortunes.

**NEEDED AUTOMATICS**

**"The sport meant nothing without automatic pinspotters," Lloyd Ludwig was saying in his financial district office. Ludwig is head of the American International Bowling Corporation, which operates alleys on a chain basis. "We have stock issues for our company and by March we'll have 35 centers in operation. It would be out of the question with pinboys.**

**"It's simple. The pinboy ran the business. A 15-year-old high school kid could tell you when to open and close your place. When he came to work, you could open. When he left to go home and sleep so he could go to school the next day you had to close your place. It was either him or some older guy who would hang around and swallow wine and then you'd be better off with nobody."**

**INSTALLED IN 1950**

It took 14 years before the pinspotter could be perfected for use. After years of tinkering and trying to produce one at a workable price, AMF installed two machines in May of 1950 at Lou Feibel's Lanes in Teaneck, N. J. The next year a complete set of pinspotters were in action at a place in Mt. Clemens, Mich.

The way was clear now for bowling to become big business and in 1950, Schmidt was in a group which opened the 50-lane Bowlero in Clifton, N. J. It was the nation's first big bowling center and it made a tremendous hit.

Instead of a bar, you had a cocktail lounge. Instead of benches there were plush theatre seats. Glass and chrome and ventilation replaced the old smoke and wood.

Today, million-dollar bowling buildings dot the nation. With the cost pegged at 50 cents a game for bowlers, the sport has become an integral part of modern American living—an era where participation in a sport has become more important than the old fashioned business of sitting in a seat and watching an athletic event.

In the New York area 100 gleaming centers have been erected in the last 10 years and the trend is to build more, rather than stay put.

**"Look at this," Emil Lence said. He was standing in his Woodhaven Lanes, which are less than six months old, and watching the crowd bowl.**

**"I promoted fights. I thought that was sports," he said. "I didn't know what bowling was. But I knew what a good fight was. Then I got into one bowling deal. Now I'm in three and I don't know when I'm going to stop. This is too ig a thing. We go 24 hours a day and sometimes I wonder if we have enough room."**

NEXT: Leagues, the backbone of bowling.

LONG, LONG AGO . . . Here is the automatic pinspotter in its earliest days.

## JIMMY BRESLIN

### Room at the Top

Among serious problems which must be faced in the upcoming year is the one which has fallen on the gangsters of our city, who are a part of the regular Brooklyn organization. Just as the New Year's holiday began, their boss, Joe Magliocco, dead of a heart attack, was buried in a rather quiet funeral at East Islip, L. I. Joe was the second Brooklyn leader in a row to die of natural causes, Joe Profaci passing on to his own reward a year ago. This two-in-a-row is most certainly an all-time record, for gangsters seem to die most frequently of marksmanship, not heart conditions.

Magliocco's funeral was disappointing. There were only two flower cars and six limousines. This is a long way from the hundred or so limousines which followed such as Frankie Yale to the cemetery, and set a style we have come to expect from our racketeers. It also would seem to indicate that Jessica Mitford is widely read in that set. More likely, however, is a natural shyness towards publicity, since Joe Valachi, the national stoolpigeon, and Sidney Slater, our local stoolpigeon, told everything they could imagine about organized crime during the last year.

With Magliocco gone, there is a big job open for some ambitious gangster. Since all gangsters are ambitious, there could be a family squabble over the job. This would bring about the usual increase in the number of missing persons.

Clockwise, from top left: Early Breslin. He writes about sports, in this case bowling, for the *Journal-American*; Writing about the mob with a sense of humor; Breslin's first known byline, age 18, for the *Long Island Press*.

## The Face on the Barroom Wall!

### TV Sets Off Squabbles, But Patrons Love It

By JIMMY BRESLIN

*"Sorry Mac, you gotta make room for him so he can see the television screen . . . he's a regular here and I mean, after all, I gotta take care of him."*

*"It ain't bright enough . . . brighten it up it's too dark. And don't ring the cash register . . . it makes everything go waving around."*

*"What time is the game on?"*

*"Game! We're getting the fights tonight."*

*"Fights! . . . Game! . . . With Milton Berle on you guys want that stuff?"*

*"I ain't been home one night this week. I better buy one of these things and stay home at night or my old lady'll divorce me . . . and take the kids with her!"*

*"Put on the news, I haven't read a paper today . . . I like to follow this world affairs stuff pretty close."*

. . .

That is about what you hear on an average night in a Long Island tavern. It's 1949 taproom conversation . . . television style.

Perhaps no where else has television made itself felt more than in that little neon-lit harbor from the cares of the world down at the corner of your Long Island street.

Now don't get the wrong idea. The amber fluid still flows. It will probably take more than television to change that. In

(Continued on Page 39)

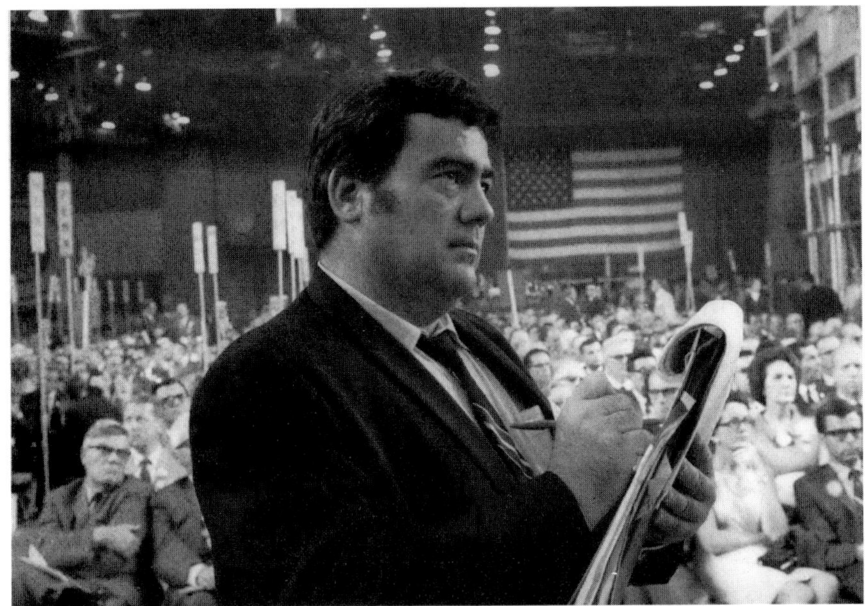

Jimmy Breslin at the 1968 Democratic Convention, International Amphitheater, Chicago. He witnessed behavior by police toward demonstrators that led him to coin the phrase "police riot." *Courtesy: Zuma Press, Inc. / Alamy*

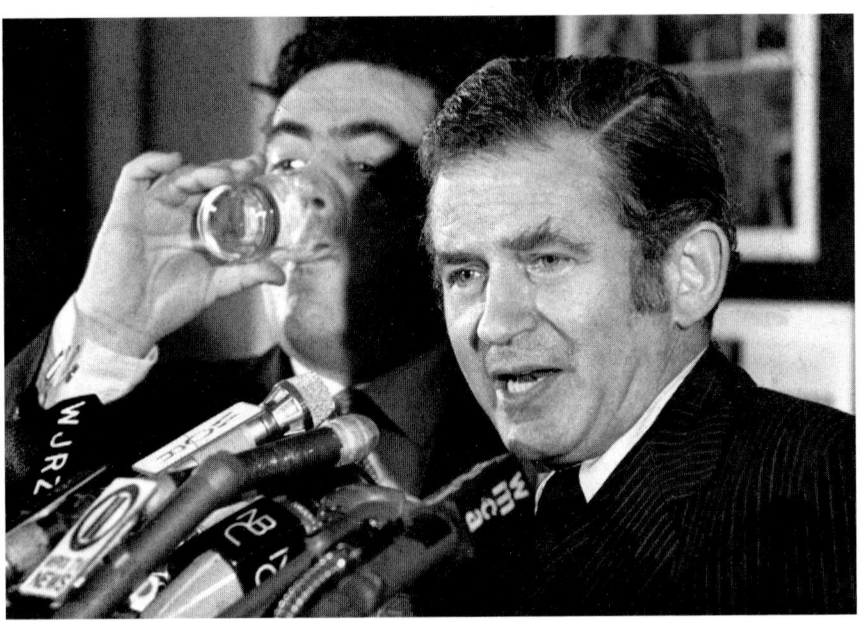


Norman Mailer announces his candidacy for mayor of New York City, with Jimmy Breslin running for city council president, 1969. *Courtesy: CSU Archives / Everett Collection*

MAILER-BRESLIN

AND

THE 51st STATE

DEMOCRATIC PRIMARY, JUNE 17th.

Jimmy Breslin and Norman Mailer's 1969 run for office was a political "campaign of ideas." They did not set out to win the positions of president of the City Council and mayor of New York. They set out to call attention to the sorry state of New York City politics and propose radical change: make New York City the 51st state and put its taxpayer dollars to work—for its residents. *Courtesy: Michael Gross*

Jimmy Breslin and his wife, Rosemary Breslin née Dattolico. 1974. *Courtesy: Susan Wood*

Breslin walking with attorney and politician Paul O'Dwyer and other New York politicians including Bob Abrams and Mario Biaggi (date unknown).

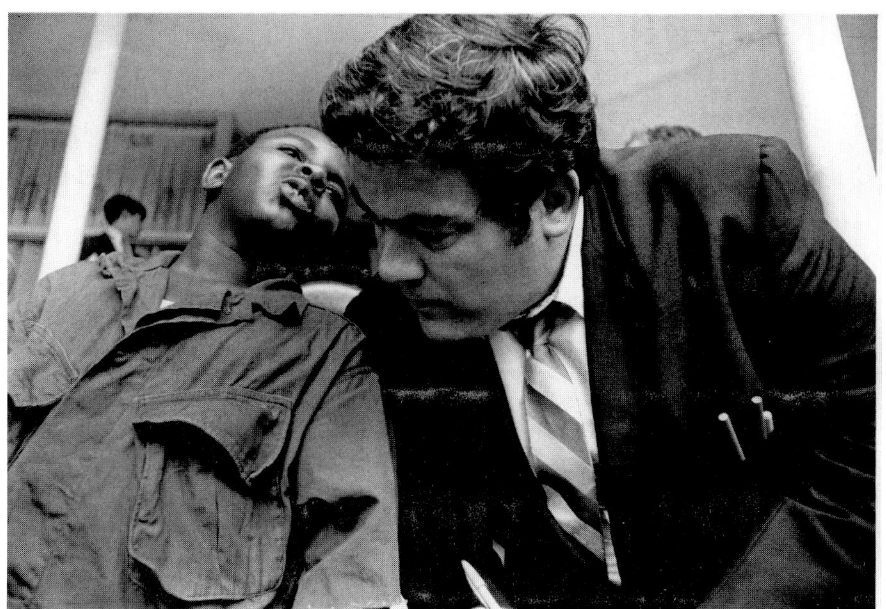

How to listen. *Courtesy: Keystone Press / Alamy Stock Photo*

Watergate special prosecutors Richard Ben-Veniste and Jill Wine-Volner talk with reporter Jimmy Breslin on their way to U.S. District Court in January 1975. *Courtesy: Danita Delimont / Alamy*

June 6–14, 1976, New York State Democratic delegates meeting at the Statler-Hilton Hotel, New York City: Jimmy Carter's press secretary, Jody Powell (left) talking to Jimmy Breslin after a news conference held by Governor Carter. The leaders of the New York Democratic Party endorsed Carter at the press conference. *Courtesy: Keystone Press / Alamy*

“Two tough guys from Queens,” *Daily News* Metropolitan Editor Dick Oliver with Breslin at Oliver’s 60th birthday party. *Courtesy: Kate McGrath*

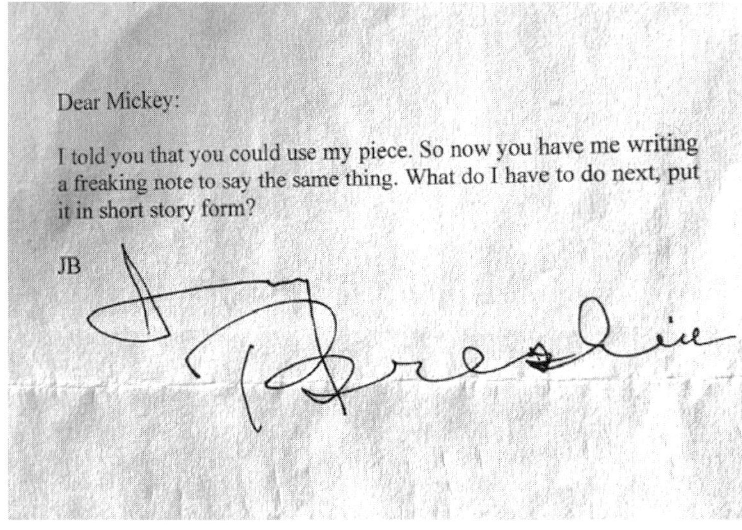

Dear Mickey:

I told you that you could use my piece. So now you have me writing a freaking note to say the same thing. What do I have to do next, put it in short story form?

JB

Breslin’s note to Michael “Mickey” Brennan granting permission to use Breslin’s essay in his landmark book *They Must Fall: Muhammad Ali and the Men He Fought*. *Courtesy: Michael Brennan*

Jimmy Breslin street sign unveiled, May 30, 1987, on the corner of 42nd St. and Third Ave. *The Daily News* was just down the block at 220 East 42nd. Sign was put up by New York City worker Keith Joyner who, according to *Spectrum News*' Bob Hardt, told reporters present that Breslin was a "for real guy." *Courtesy: Alamy*

New York Governor Andrew Cuomo, preparing to speak "as the elected representative of the Cuomo family" at Jimmy Breslin's funeral service at Church of the Blessed Sacrament in Manhattan, March 22, 2017. *Courtesy: Charles Eckert*

Ronnie Eldridge exchanging hugs following her husband's funeral service. *Courtesy: Charles Eckert*

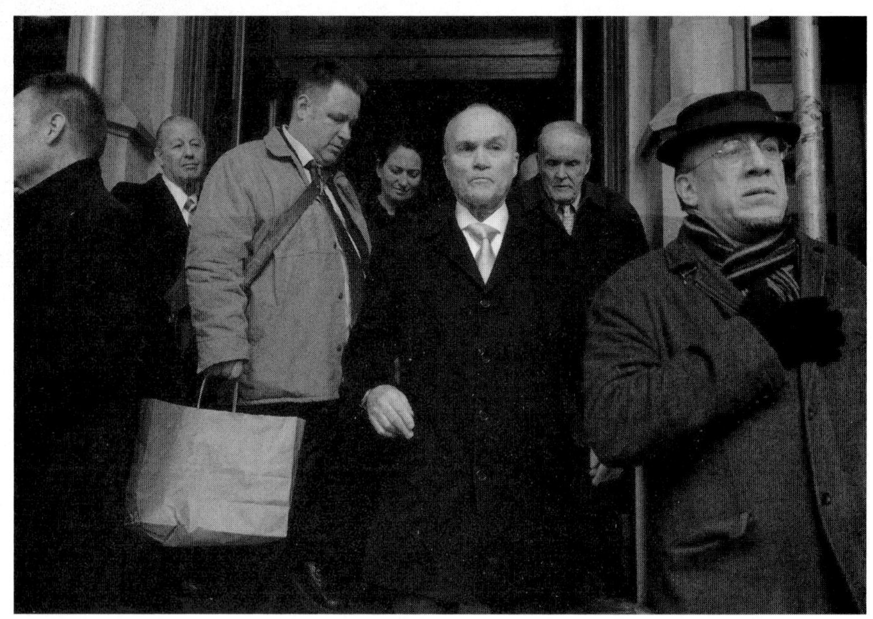

Police Commissioner Raymond Kelly, exiting Breslin's funeral service. *Courtesy: Charles Eckert*

Left to right: Hap Hairston, City Editor *New York Newsday*; author, as Police Bureau Chief *New York Newsday*; reporter Curtis Taylor; and Barbara Strauch, a *New York Newsday* editor. *Courtesy:* New York Newsday

Left to right: Columnist Murray Kempton; Andrew Maloney, US Attorney for Eastern District of New York; the author as City Editor *New York Newsday*; and Jimmy Breslin. At Murray Kempton's 75th birthday celebration. *Courtesy*: New York Newsday

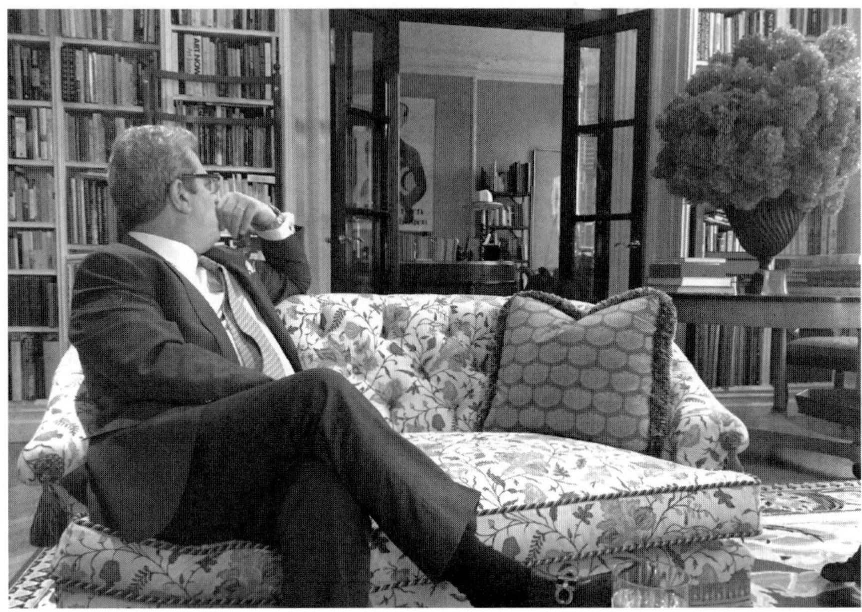

Admiring Tom Wolfe's hat while waiting to interview Wolfe at his impeccable New York City apartment. *Courtesy: Ted Gerstein*

Author interviews Jimmy Breslin and Ronnie Eldridge in 2015 at their Manhattan apartment. *Courtesy: Ted Gerstein*

Kevin and James Breslin discuss growing up Breslin. *Courtesy: Ted Gerstein*

Jimmy Breslin in Costello's Bar, any morning 1986. Full frame of cover image. With him is Fred Percudani known to the clientele as Subway Fred, the world's rudest bartender. *Courtesy: Michael Brennan*

> His prized possession was a typed-up three-act play and a sheaf of poems he had written. One of his poems was about Alcatraz:
>
> Fools in high places should not dwell
> For they make life a living hell
> And leave behind when they pass
> A monument like Alcatraz

We are now far beyond the abilities of the best obituary writer. We are inside the life and mind of a person whom Breslin had spent a lot of time understanding. The kind of person Breslin the writer would call early in the morning when he needed something for a column.

And then, at the close, we discover that this had been an intensely personal voyage.

> He always had his own way of explaining who he was. There was one day when a young girl came to Harlem to teach and she was nervous about it, and Bumpy, as a favor to somebody, went over to her.
>
> "Don't you think about anything, you'll like it fine here," he said. "Now you're here for the Head Start program. Great program. All these things started under President Kennedy. And I served under President Kennedy."
>
> "You did?" the teacher said. "Where?"
>
> "I served in Alcatraz," Bumpy Johnson said.

The teacher was Breslin's sister, Deirdre. The somebody was Breslin.

Michael Daly, who heard the story from Jimmy Breslin himself, says it went like this:

"Do you know who I am?" Bumpy asked, addressing Deirdre's class.

"Yes, Mr. Johnson," the class replied.

And Deirdre Breslin now had the best behaved class of students in Harlem.

And that is Breslin's farewell to Bumpy.

# LINDSAY IN HARLEM

John V. Lindsay, tall, charismatic and with an aristocratic bearing that belied just how little money he had in his bank accounts, was the Mayor of New York at this time. Since January 1, 1966, he had served as the city's first Republican Mayor since Fiorello La Guardia. A wonderful book—*The Cost of Good Intentions*— shows us how hard he and others involved in New York's liberal experiment tried, who the brilliant young people he surrounded himself with were, and why by the time of Mayor Edward Koch it all had turned out the way it did.

After the death of Bobby Kennedy, to Breslin, he was a remaining hope. It was July 2, 1968:

> The temperature in the streets of Harlem had just gone under 100 for the first time all day, and the smells came out of the basements and the tenement hallways and the garbage cans alongside the stoops. . . . It is here, in the Harlems of New York . . . that John Lindsay puts up his body, and he was standing at the curb of 137th Street, dressed in a polo shirt, unpressed slacks and brown loafers. He was looking at the open hallway and broken windows of a deserted tenement.
>
> A gray haired woman pulled at his arm.
>
> Lindsay pulled his arm away and declined to go look at this building's basement. He had seen enough of these in the past months. He heard the woman say that what came out of that basement was killing her block and he made sure his staff took a note.

This mayor, Breslin notes, had prevented violence twice, personally, in just the past couple of months. Once, a Housing Police officer had shot a youth in Williamsburg, Brooklyn. A protest meeting was being held. "It was not going to be a marching protest," Breslin writes. Lindsay showed up unannounced. "To give justice when it has not been given to you," Lindsay told the angry crowd, "is greatness."

> This is the third summer that Lindsay goes onto the streets of New York to try and prevent violence. One man walking is an insane way for a city to conduct business. And Lindsay knows the great danger. But in the end, in July, in 100 degree heat it is the only thing that can be done.

When you looked at Lindsay looking up at the faces in the wide open tenement windows, Breslin says, you were looking at the only major politician in America "who can do this with the poor."

> "Look at what has happened since last year," Lindsay was saying. "They had had a King murdered, a Kennedy murdered and a cutback from Congress. Now the campaigns. Can't you just see it? Humphrey and Nixon. Not just now, August, and through the fall. But all beyond it, right through January until the inauguration. Nothing. All that time and nothing for them at all. Where do you channel the frustrations?" . . .
>
> The trouble of the cities can be found in the country's political lineup. When everybody wants something new, the two major parties intend to run two former vice presidents. When Richard Nixon talks about life in the 60s he sounds like a dog playing the piano.

By now the Tet offensive was over. More than 2,000 US soldiers had been killed between January 31 and the end of March. April was King. June was Bobby. War-crazed and realizing he had lost America, LBJ, the incumbent, on March 31 announced he would not seek reelection. And now the police in the City of Chicago where the Democratic

Convention would be held in the last week of August were preparing to work twelve-hour tours and learning to use gas masks at roll call. When it was over—after the barbed wire came down, the tear gas dissipated, the 12,000 cops working 12 hour shifts, the 6,000 soldiers, six thousand national guard troops and the FBI and Secret Service, had gone home—it was Nixon and Humphrey.

The TV anchorman, Eric Sevareid, described Chicago as a tourist spot second only to Prague, where a brief liberalization, the "Prague Spring," had just been crushed by Warsaw Pact troops.

Breslin attended the convention for the *Post* but his best writing on it came after he left the paper, in a *New York* magazine piece he wrote in the aftermath:

> Hubert Humphrey against Richard Nixon. In a political year that started last November, with John Kenneth Galbraith standing up at Cambridge, Mass. and introducing to a crowd, "My great friend, my dear friend, Eugene McCarthy"; in a year that went through the wet streets of New Hampshire, the night in Bobby Kennedy's apartment in New York, the shopping centers in Indiana . . . in the year of the balcony of the Lorraine Motel in Memphis and the kitchen floor of the Ambassador Hotel in Los Angeles; in a year like this we wind up with two former vice presidents running against each other. This is what the convention system has done to us.

## FEAT OF CLAY

Grief, despondency and chaos, money, newfound fame—these were not the only reasons underlying the rift. There was Breslin's phenomenal, unpierceable ego, of course. He had been egomaniacal for a very long time and now it was fueled by more than book wealth, more than the promise of movie wealth. It was fueled by ambition and the promise of a home where he could achieve it. What beckoned this "police station genius" was Clay Felker's *New York* magazine and a cast of bright, shining journalistic voices that had not been seen in such marquee lights before.

Even at the *Trib* there was the constraint of newsprint. Now there was the turned up volume of NEW! Now the pages were glossy. Bold. Set against a city establishment that was OLD! Literary ambition and journalistic freedom would soon be twinned with, and feature some of the same cast members, a quixotic political campaign based on ideas that were revolutionary: teach the Black students in the public schools, give the neighborhoods a voice, revamp the way policing was managed, and, to cap it all off, make New York City a 51st state. The campaign starred Norman Mailer and Jimmy Breslin. What could possibly go wrong?

So it was goodbye to the *Post*, welcome to the World of Clay. And through it would be the echoes of an enduring feud with both the editor and publisher of the newspaper he left. He and Mailer—who was himself Jewish—now seemed to view the *Post* with nonchalant antisemitism as the "Jew" press that was so predictably liberal as to not consider them worth covering. Welcome to the seriousness of Fun City.

The adventure that was *New York* had begun back at the *Herald Tribune* where the editors envisioned taking a staid Sunday magazine that was doing nothing to advance the new direction of the paper and turning it into something readable and exciting that could become the talk of New York. Clay Felker, recently of *Esquire* magazine, was brought in first as a consultant, and then as the editor. Soon it was packed with the prose of Breslin and Tom Wolfe.

The magazine got noticed. The writers got noticed. As the paper was folding, Breslin heavily encouraged Felker to buy the magazine and turn it into a free-standing entity. Felker borrowed $6,500 from the writer Barbara Goldsmith to buy the name from Jock Whitney. And Breslin helped cajole the investors needed to go from name to office space, writers, paper, advertisers and printers. He was named Vice President on the magazine's masthead.

Felker was the genius of zeitgeist. He could capture it. He could create it. He was an incubator of voices. He could identify them. He could nurture them. He invented the "City Magazine" though no one who would attempt to emulate it understood, to paraphrase one of *New York's* former editors-in-chief, the writer Kurt Andersen, it wasn't a magazine about zip codes. It was a magazine that captured the current of ambition that electrified New York.

Tom Wolfe was a marquee writer. Breslin was on the marquee. And on the masthead as a Vice President. Felker was rightly called a rock star editor, and "hyper ambitious." He helped Gloria Steinem launch

*Ms.* magazine. He attracted the young and the hungry. Writers who were hyperperceptive and hyperambitious.

Tom Wolfe explained some of this in a July 14 cover story that ran two weeks after Felker's death on July 1, 2008.

"As I recall, the first assignment Clay gave me was a story on the promenade *les chic* and *les chic-lettes* took every Saturday morning through the art galleries along Madison Ave from 57th Street to 79th Street . . ."

The story appeared. "And now *les* proto-*chic-lettes* came skipping and screaming . . . pretty young things in short skirts and jeans molded to their pelvic saddles. . . .

"As I say, I had never heard of this Saturday-morning art promenade before, but Clay had. He made it a point to hear about such things. . . . He was his own best reporter."

Breslin, as the novelist Philip Roth once said, was the resident New York City "police station genius." He gave the magazine, in the words of Gloria Steinem, street smarts.

"He was always street smart. Street smart means that you can inform and excite and invite readers from the street up. . . . He always had this nose for incredible characters. . . . He would introduce me. We were at *New York* magazine together or we would go someplace after work or something and he would introduce me to these characters that he'd been writing about.

"He also understood politics in other cities. I think, in my memory, he was the first person to say that what happened at the 1968 Chicago Convention was a police riot. You know, that the police had rioted. He and his friends who were cops were ashamed . . . because it was a blemish on the reputation of good cops. . . .

"The shocking thing for those of us who had been in Chicago . . . I don't remember if Jimmy was physically there or not. For those of us who were in Chicago, there was one reality. Then we left Chicago and people were blaming the demonstrators instead of the cops. We were just stunned by this because we'd been there seeing cops beating people up with lead-lined gloves and shoving people through plate-glass windows in the street. To come back from that and see that the demonstrators were being blamed was just shocking. I remember Jimmy as being a bridge between those two realities and trying to name what really happened."

Clay Felker's *New York* was a universe, with solar systems that revolved around its white hot suns: Gael Greene, on the snobbery of seating in high end eateries, "How Not to Be Humiliated in Snob Restaurants." Gail Sheehy in hot pants and white vinyl boots with her eyewitness account of the prostitution trade and the class structure within it. "Glo Glo" Steinem, whose *Ms.* was launched with unbuyable publicity when Clay included the entire first issue and Steinem's cover story "Sisterhood," as a pullout inside *New York.* According to published accounts, 300,000 copies were sold out in three days and 26,000 became subscribers. In residence were Peter Maas and Nick Pileggi, two of the best archeologists and historians of the Mafia. Ever. And of course, Wolfe, who seemed able in his magical, brilliant pieces to peel back any layer of society, such as he did in his notable dive into surfer culture, "The Pump House Gang." These solar systems would rub up against each other, and somehow the planets never collided. Steinem, Wolfe and Breslin were fiercely loyal to each other for decades even after their solar systems had moved out to different edges of the universe.

It was, looking backward, at the heart of the start of the last generation of Great. Voices. In American Journalism. Outside the magazine there were others: Murray Kempton, Pete Hamill, Gay Talese among them. Hunter S. Thompson in what might have been a parallel universe. Each of these reporters was an iconoclast. Each was intensely literate. Though Breslin seemed to hide his books in his desk drawers. Each a lover of their status, the company they kept, the trail they blazed and the bodies they left behind. Each invaluable in telling the story of a city and a nation.

Breslin wrote dozens of pieces for *New York* between his arrival in 1968 and his departure two plus years later over differences with Felker over what Breslin, according to one account, viewed as a magazine now essentially devoted to telling its readers where to find the best hamburgers in New York. This was far less true than it might have been after the magazine fell into Rupert Murdoch's hands for a while, then a series of corporate owners. Another version has Breslin discovering that that the writer Dick Schaap could barely get by on what the magazine, of which Jimmy was an executive, was paying him. Felker was robbing Schaap. Outrageous. But it suited Breslin's desire: To. Leave. And now Felker was on the enemies' list.

Some of his pieces were modestly titled, "How I Made Lindsay Mayor" and "My Triumphant Return to New York." Others were cheeky outlets for his perceived slights, "People I'm Not Talking to This Year" and "Jimmy's 1970 Black List" which appeared in the January 5 edition along with Judith Crist's Ten Best and Worst and Joe McGinniss on "Hustling a Best Selling Novel."

The cover's main headline "Who's Got Power in the City This Year" was by Ed Costikyan. And pretty much right then all that is good in

*BuzzFeed* and its listicles was born. There was a difference, of course, the journalism and the original voices were missing from the latter day incarnation.

There are two Breslin pieces worth singling out. Because they show what everyone who has ever been a police reporter knows, despite the breadth and depth of your knowledge, there is in effect a class distinction that essentially delimits reporters who speak in plain English. So even as Breslin in these pieces displayed a continuous depth, and breadth, and growth, he seemed destined always cast as the guy in the gumshoes, press card in his hat, reading through the police blotter and smelling of booze. To be fair, he cultivated at least part of that image. And to be fairer, this choice, plus his incredible flaws as a human being, perhaps helped define his limits.

The first piece is a wonderful, groundbreaking profile of Joe Namath, the football hero of the New York Jets at that moment. It is a textbook example, or *the* textbook frankly, of how to construct a profile of a bad boy. Rather than quote from it serially, just one or two portions.

But first the pull quote at the top, above the byline:

> ". . . The night before the Oakland game I grabbed a girl and a bottle and went to the Summit Hotel and stayed in bed all night . . . Same thing before the Super Bowl. It's good for you . . ."

Then this:

> They are trying to call this immensely likeable 25-year-old by the name of Broadway Joe. But Broadway as a street has been a busted-out whorehouse with orange juice stands for as long as I can recall, and now, as an expression, it is tired and represents nothing to me. And it certainly represents nothing to Joe Willie Namath's people. His people are on First and Second Avenues, where young girls spill out of the build-

> ings and into the bars crowded with guys and the world is made of long hair and tape cartridges and swirling color and military overcoats and the girls go home with guys or the guys go home with girls and nobody is too worried about any of it because life moves, it doesn't stand still and whisper about what happened last night. It is out of these bars and apartment buildings and the life of them that Joe Willie Namath comes. He comes with a Scotch in his hand at night and a football in the daytime and last season he gave New York the only lift the city has had in so many years it is hard to think of a comparison. When you live in fires and funerals and strikes and rats and crowds and people screaming in the night, sports is the only thing that makes any sense. And there is only one sport anymore that can change the tone of a city and there is only one player who can do it. His name is Joe Willie Namath and when he beat the Baltimore Colts he gave New York the kind of light, meaningless, dippy and lovely few days we had all but forgotten.

Of the era, it is like Murray Kempton's piece on Willie Mays that appeared in *Esquire* three years later: Unsurpassable sportswriting. It tells the story of a swinger who, the only times he didn't drink or have sex or both before a game, threw interceptions. There is no judgment, just a delightful night out with Joe.

And this:

> In the Super Bowl game, the Baltimore Colts were supposed to wreck Namath, and they probably were in bed dreaming about this all night. As soon as the game started, the Baltimore linemen and linebackers got together and rushed in at Namath in a maneuver they call blitzing and Namath, who doesn't seem to need time even to set his feet, threw a quick pass down the middle and then came right back and hit Matt Snell out on the side and right away you knew Baltimore was in an awful lot of trouble.

> "Some people don't like this image I got myself, bein' a swinger," Namath was saying. "They see me with a girl instead of being home like other athletes. But I'm not institutional. I swing. If it's good or bad, I don't know, but I know it's what I like. It hasn't hurt my friends or my family and it hasn't hurt me. So why hide it? It's the truth. It's what the ____ we are.

This profile, of a bad boy professional athlete, Tom Wolfe would note later, was the profile that became the template for all the "Bad Boy" athlete profiles that came after: "the John McEnroes, the Jimmy Connors." It is, as Wolfe says, "a priceless piece."

There are other such priceless pieces by Breslin and his cohort that played a significant part of redefining journalism. Two of them appeared in *Esquire.* One had appeared in the *Trib.*

# HOW TO WRITE A PROFILE

In 1966, *Esquire* magazine had published a wonderful piece by Gay Talese, the gifted writer, who as a young reporter was one of the few Italian Americans to write for *The New York Times*. Talese was the son of a tailor down on the New Jersey shore. Talese's prose was as impeccably tailored as Talese's own wardrobe:

> FRANK SINATRA, holding a glass of bourbon in one hand and a cigarette in the other, stood in a dark corner of the bar between two attractive but fading blondes who sat waiting for him to say something. . . .
>
> Sinatra had been working in a film that he now disliked . . . he was angry that a CBS television documentary of his life, to be shown in two weeks . . . he was worried about his starring role in an hour-long NBC show entitled *Sinatra—A Man and His Music*, which would require that he sing eighteen songs with a voice that at this particular moment . . . was weak and sore and uncertain. Sinatra was ill. He was the victim of an ailment so common that most people would consider it trivial. But when it gets to Sinatra it can plunge him into a state of anguish, deep depression, panic, even rage. Frank Sinatra had a cold. . . .

Talese's piece is beautiful. He reported it in the winter of 1965. *Esquire* gave him 15,498 words in the April 1966 issue. Three years earlier Breslin shaped his Costello piece in 1/15 of that and achieved a similar level of intimacy and as great an understanding of his subject in a little over a thousand words. They are equals in everything else.

In 1973, another such groundbreaking profile appeared. *Esquire* again published it. This one was by another man who would not have called himself anything more than a reporter, the great Episcopalian bishop of the dependent clause, Murray Kempton. It was a portrait of a baseball player, Willie Mays, who may have played one season too many:

> He was twenty when he began these voyagings, and he is supposed to have said then that this first trip around the league was like riding through a beautiful park and getting paid for it. Out of all those playgrounds, only Wrigley Field in Chicago is still used for baseball; everywhere else he is older than any piece of turf upon which he stands. All has changed save him. Before the New York Mets had ever played one game as a team, Willie Mays had already hit more home runs than all but six players then in the Hall of Fame.
>
> Mike Torrez, the Montreal pitcher, was not yet five years old the afternoon in 1951 when Willie Mays threw out Billy Cox from center field in the Polo Grounds, a ball traveling three hundred sixty feet to catch a fast man who had to run only ninety. Torrez paid his respects to this shrine by throwing two balls, the first wickedly close to the cap, the second evilly close to the chest. Willie Mays then watched a strike and another ball—he seemed as squat, as archaic, as immobile as some pre-Columbian figure of an athlete—then melted to protect himself with a foul tip and walked at last.
>
> Ted Martinez came up to drive a long ball to right center and two outfielders turned and fled toward the wall with a gait that at once informed the ancient, glittering eyes of Willie Mays that men run like

> this when they have given up on the catch and hope only for a retrieval from the wall. Mays gunned around second and then, coming into third, quite suddenly slowed, became a runner on a frieze, and turned his head to watch the fielders. He was inducing the mental error; he had offered the illusion that he might be caught at home, which would give Ted Martinez time to get to third.
>
> And only then did Willie Mays come down the line like thunder, ending in a heap at home, with the catcher sprawled in helpless intermingling with him and the relay throw bouncing through an unprotected plate and into the Montreal dugout. He was on his feet at once; his diversion had already allowed Martinez to run to third and he jumped up now to remind the umpire, in case he needed to, that when the ball goes into the dugout each runner is entitled to one more base.
>
> You remembered how often it had been said that Willie Mays knows more ways to beat you than anyone who ever played the game. But that was no more than comment; and here was presence; and all historical memory was wiped out for this moment when Willie Mays had paused at third as if to array himself as proclamation of an army with banners.

Kempton was as gracious as Breslin was boorish, his prose as difficult to parse as Breslin's seemed easy. He is too dense to quote in brief, and as he knew from long experience, he was too dense to edit in any meaningful way when he handed in his copy just as the clock ticked "DEADLINE." And the editor looked it over, shook her head: "Oh, Murray." Did her best and pushed the button. So to say *Esquire* gave him 2,400 words would not be as correct as saying Kempton handed in that many. He once declined a television interview by explaining that his sentences were longer than their segment. He delighted in the baroque.

In just a few paragraphs of these sentences he gives you in this article William Faulkner, Enos Slaughter of the Cardinals, the record *Farewell Blues* and Yogi Berra. This is a man who years later could come back from John Gotti's clubhouse, the only journalist allowed in that day that Gotti won in state court, and announce to his editor, his marbled pasteboard-covered copybook in hand, "I will not cheapen myself by writing about Gotti today. I am writing about Proust." Months later the Gotti story would come.

In the case of Willy Mays, Kempton's citation of remarkable accomplishments had a simple purpose in the end:

> Yet afterward his solitary gloom was impenetrable. It had been an afternoon to stir uneasy prospects. . . . all signs that the Mets would never know the comfort of being enough ahead or the resignation of being enough behind. No, it would go on all summer . . . until the familiar horror of those final weeks whose reiterated torment had brought him, as long ago as 1965, to confess how permanently drained he was: "No. There is nothing in baseball that can get me excited anymore." And yet there is not another Met who has known the ordeal of a close pennant race more than once in his career; and Willie Mays has been there eight times before. . . . and this would be another one of those cruel summers that, for just a little while, in the sun with the extra men, he had been able to entertain the illusion of escaping. Scowling, he strode through the children who had waited for him at the gate and alone he drove away, his face fixed in its contempt for destiny; everything that he had proved through all those years was worthless to appease him; nothing was ahead of him but the implacable duty of needing to prove everything all over again. Fuggin kids.

The Mets won the pennant.

In capturing how Mays faces his destiny he places us with Mays in a manner Breslin would use throughout his career. This *is* the way it comes to them all: they play a season too many, and then they stand alone with their destiny.

Breslin and Kempton, two giants, strode across the carpet tiles of two newsrooms together over the course of their careers. Theirs was an uneasy respect; the emotional, public, raging Irishman, and the aloof redhaired southerner, whose own daughter would describe his coldness. An uneasy truce between two who could find the flaws not in each other's work but in each other's thinking and who were both constrained by manners—easy for Kempton—to share compliments, if at times they were grudging. Because Kempton could be as biting in a newsroom aside as Breslin could be harsh in his bellowing.

Talese, well, he did not share newsrooms with these two and he shared little with Breslin except what amounted to a lifelong grudge. He would not speak of him for this book but he had the courtesy to explain why.

> dear Richard
>
> I'm glad [you're] busy with a book, and envy you as well. I'm struggling with a book I must finish by mid-August and fear I won't make the deadline of this patient editor of mine, who is also unhappy with my constant excuses.
>
> This is a way of asking you to forgive me in not making time to see you this summer, but there is another issue as well:
>
> We're told not to speak ill of the dead, and therefore I don't want to express my true feelings about Breslin. But I make no secret to you of the fact that I never liked him, and he never liked me, and whenever I was in his company in large or small crowds, I made every effort to

avoid him. By comparison, I loved many of the people he associated with, especially Pete Hamill and Tom Wolfe . . . but Breslin and me, it never could be a friendship.

Hope you'll understand . . . sincerely/Gay"

Gay Talese was not the only person who cited not speaking ill of the dead in declining to speak about Breslin. He was, though, as you might expect, the one whose sense of decency and courtesy and good manners required him to explain why to a fellow reporter.

Three men, Talese, Breslin and Kempton, equally regarded as brilliant, equally difficult in their own ways. Equally capable of portraiture that defined what such works would be like for decades to come.

Costello is 72 now, but he looks the same as he did when he was on everybody's television set back in 1951. There is a little gray in his sideburns, but otherwise his hair is still dark, still slicked straight back. Everybody says he doesn't do much of anything these days. He's up with the dog, then comes downtown for a little barbering, lunch early in his apartment at 115 Central Park West, walks at any of a few hotels, a turkish bath or a movie in the afternoon and then dinner some place and then home.

Now this sounds incongruous today, but in the Costello era there was an incredible looseness in government. There were some high officials in this town who, and perhaps this is wishful thinking, wouldn't last a week in office today under similar circumstances.

But all of this gone for Costello. He is out of it now, and he stays to himself and he wants no part of publicity.

He prefers to stir his coffee if you bring up a question. But as he finished up dinner and started to go home, he volunteered one more answer.

"Yes, I think I would say that I think I could put together an off-track betting system in New York and make it work." Which was an understatement. If there was anything that Costello ever did well, it was run gambling in this city. In the whole country to put it correctly.

"Anytime you try to get over 5 per cent for your money you're taking a risk," was his motto and he had risk takers going for him from coast to coast.

Now he's 72, and he's more than happy to leave the spotlight in the new crime hearings to Joe Valachi. Or Cago, as Costello knew him when they were on vacation together.

Kempton was ostentatiously erudite, Talese meticulous as his father, Breslin had a gift that is rarer than many others. He had a wonderful sense of humor.

# RUNNING AGAINST THE MACHINE

And then there is the police riot in Chicago, at the Democratic Convention at which one of the two vice presidents who would run for president, Hubert Humphrey, accepts the nomination behind coils of barbed wire while society howls for change outside the International Amphitheater. It is one of those crime stories where the crimes are committed by police and the crimes of omission are committed by the nominee for president. It begins with Humphrey, then goes to Mayor Richard Daley, the boss of Chicago, and then takes us to the streets. Humphrey makes one phone call during the week, to get one demonstrator released: the delegate for George McGovern, who has been handcuffed by police. After that, he sits on his hands and when it is time to ask Daley to tell his cops to ease up, the task falls to an aide. And nothing changes.

Breslin writes afterward:

> In Chicago, he left us with the police who were everywhere. Full bellies pushing against the blue short-sleeved shirts, round faces bulging under the helmets, the eyes wide open and burning.
>
> "They don't represent my kids," an Inspector says in a voice that is high in emotion. . . .
>
> "They don't represent my kids," he says again. . . . "They don't represent my kids, my kids are clean."

> "They represent somebody," he was told.
>
> "They shouldn't be in this town," he shouts. "The bastards."
>
> "It's a political convention," he was told.
>
> "They don't represent my kids."
>
> The cops had one thing on their mind. Club and then gas, club and then gas, club and then gas. In the afternoon, three of them, two in the back seat and one in the front, sat in a squad car . . . It was a hot, muggy afternoon but the three of them wore black leather gloves. The gloves were not thin gloves. There was something inside the gloves. The boxing people would call it a gimmick. Probably the gloves were lined with lead. . . .
>
> Late that night, very late, Katy Schefflien, 18, was standing in the hallway outside the 11th floor night court in the Chicago Police Headquarters building. . . . Her right eye was half closed. The discoloring ran down to her cheek. A sheet of blood covered most of the surface of her eye. . . .
>
> "What did they hit you with?" she was asked.
>
> "I don't know, I guess a fist," she said.
>
> Most cops, and most men anyplace, don't have the coordination and leverage to punch hard enough with their fists to do this to a person's eye. . . . To make the blood come out into the eye . . . and the blood will be there for weeks if I know my black eyes, to do this, you have to be an extraordinary puncher. Or you have to punch with a fist that is covered with black gloves that are gimmicked.

These kinds of people, Breslin says, are pigs in police uniforms. An alternate delegate was detained five hours after she was strip searched twice for guns, knives, and narcotics. Next time, Katy Schefflien said, she's going to wear a dress that buttons down the front; that way, she wouldn't have to completely strip. She felt sorry for Humphrey, who went under the shower when the tear gas came in through the open window to his suite. It's a long, detailed piece. And it would be easy to read it, as some read Breslin in general, and say, this man doesn't like cops.

It just isn't that simple. He had a cousin killed in the line of duty; he reminds us. He grew up with an uncle in the house who drank a lot and was a police officer who was almost killed in the line of duty, he tells us, when the car he was riding in with his mistress was launched by the car his tailing wife rammed into it. Across his career, among his closest confidants there were always cops. When we listen closely to what he has to say, we can realize that he knows, better than most, that police officers are unfairly asked to be the point on the spear for a failure of the political class to improve conditions, especially in the nation's cities which he understands deeply. He was an Irish Catholic living in New York, the Church and the Police were simply facts of life and part of what made a deeply flawed man a deeply insightful reporter and writer.

In Chicago, it was about the cops. As a reporter whose main event was the coverage of news, local and national through the 77-some-odd police precincts across the five distinctly different boroughs, with dozens of distinctly different cultures, it was often about the cops. And for a celebrity journalist about to launch a political career, it was, as it is for anyone who wants to get elected in New York: always about the cops.

"In Chicago," Breslin said, "a demonstration that should have been handled as if it weren't even there was turned into an international incident because police rioted."

In closing what is a careful analysis of the city's leadership, the use of the violence by Humphrey in an effort to carve out a law-and-order plank for his platform that could compete with Nixon's, there is an indictment that still holds true of just how political leadership uses cops:

> Actually, it is a crime that they are expected to handle a social or political matter at all. It is the job of the political leaders. But the political leaders do nothing and in the end they hedge off all the trouble to a cop who makes $8,500 a year and has a wife and three kids at home. It is unfair to the cops.

Mailer of course wrote *Miami and the Siege of Chicago,* his nonfiction novel based on his own reporting and sharp insights at both the Republican Convention in Miami and the Democratic Convention in Chicago. The book was lauded by many and seen as his significant contribution to the New Journalism. His significant contribution to the City of New York soon followed, beginning at the end of March 1969.

That was when Mailer and Breslin would launch their campaign: Mailer for mayor and Breslin for president of New York's city council.

It was seven glorious weeks long.

It began in Norman Mailer's apartment in Brooklyn Heights. The writer's domicile had those fabulous sweeping views of Manhattan across a wide, cobbled promenade that only those blessed by great talent or good fortune at birth could afford. Bisecting these two parts of the Imperial City were the East River waters, shimmering with light as that estuary widened and made its way to the sea.

It was March 31. Conditions in New York were bad and seemed to be tottering on the verge of worse.

In attendance were Gloria Steinem; Peter Maas, whose book *The Valachi Papers* had appeared to acclaim less than a year earlier; Jack Newfield, excellent if occasionally very biased dirt digger for *The Village*

*Voice*; light heavyweight champion Jose Torres; Yippie leader Jerry Rubin; John Scanlon, young and not yet having achieved wide fame as a bare-knuckled PR guru; and sitting on a stool in the back of the room, James Breslin, columnist, whose presence on the ticket, Steinem said, would give it street cred Mailer lacked.

The campaign was quixotic but Breslin, Mailer, and Steinem, who seemed to have a good deal of skill as a boiler room political fixer, fundraiser, and tactician, were serious about the ideas. There were plenty. One good one would have been more than the rest of the field could deliver. Winning, for Jimmy Breslin and for Gloria Steinem, and initially for Norman Mailer, one of the most financially successful writers in America, was not the goal. The goal was to bring fresh ideas to a city whose leadership was divorced from the needs of its citizens.

"The trouble is everywhere," said Breslin. "There are 1.1 million students in the New York City school system. . . . White people borrow to get children into private schools." And it could not be fixed, he explained when the decisions as to how to do so "Come from such as Perry Duryea ('a lobster peddler' and politician), who lives in Montauk Point, Earl Brydges of Niagara Falls (whose name is lost to most of us); and John Marchi, (whose name ought be lost) who is a product of the times when Staten Island was farther away from New York than Niagara. And the major lobby (the United Federation of Teachers) is led by Albert Shanker, who lives in Pearl River. They meet in Albany and discuss their own interests."

"How is one to speak of the illness of a city," said Mailer, who loved his words, and seemed intent throughout the campaign on pointing out he was every Jewish mother's dream, a Harvard-educated success story. (And this got worse after he was awarded the Pulitzer during the campaign.) "A clear day can come, a morning in early May like the pride of June. The streets are cool." Etc. "Yet by afternoon the city is incarcerated once more. . . . By the time work is done, New Yorkers push through the acrid, lung-rotting air and work their way home, avoiding each other's eyes in the subway. Later, near midnight . . . in the darkness a sense of dread returns, the streets are not quite safe, the sense of waiting for some apocalyptic fire, some night of long knives hangs over the city. . . ."

This prose, with statistical backing, appeared on May 18. The campaign was in high gear.

There is no suspense in the ending.

They lost. Were shellacked. Were beat upon by Breslin's old home, the *Post.* But if Mailer and Breslin could hardly be said to have had a sober breath between them while campaigning, their ideas were sobering: on education they called out the failure of the white-dominated, self-interested teachers' union to care about the Black students. They cited Benjamin Franklin High School, in East Harlem, as having a enrollment that would net from a starting field of 1,000 students 75 with an academic degree. They felt they could do better. Even Tony Salerno, the Genovese family mafioso who ran his successful illegal numbers lottery and bookmaking operation from the Palma Boys Club just across Pleasant Avenue and up the street from the school, could do better, without books. He could teach math.

The city was ill. It was a sharecropper for the state. It needed to be a state. A great city-state, with these curly haired *doges* for a short time at the helm. That was a core element of their campaign of ideas. The city would be better served using all the taxes levied locally rather than tithing a portion to a state whose residents for the most part seemed happy to take the money and turn their backs. They intended to bring power down to the neighborhood level. In New York City many of them are bigger than many towns but they had no power of self-governance, whether on schools, policing, sanitation—and they needed it. (*Running Against The Machine,* which was paid for by campaign funds and edited by Peter Manso, collects position papers, panels and appearances and many speeches in which these items were addressed.) And of course, the candidates had a position on policing. One of their public appearances was held at the John Jay College of Criminal Justice.

"Though Breslin had written columns about the cops, scolding them for their opposition to the civilian review board and the way they handled peace demonstrations, he also had been one of the few writers," Joe Flaherty writes in his book, *Managing Mailer*, "who had the insight neither to pronounce them pigs nor to plasticize them as saints, but to allow them a working-class dignity."

Breslin knew how to begin:

"I'd like the record to state that I'm here without a lawyer."

It was, according to Flaherty, to be the best speech Breslin delivered during the campaign.

"Though it dealt in part with race, it was essentially a class speech that united the white cop (substitute longshoreman, machinist, cabbie . . .) with the Black who is getting screwed equally by government institutions."

"I don't come here as a genius," Breslin modestly said soon after. "That's been well established early in my life. But I also have some views on policemen in this city which I'd like to express here. And before I decided to express them, I did look down to see that the chairs were bolted to the floor, and that's going to help. Because the way I see the city, and the way Mr. Mailer sees the city, is that there will be no more New York Police Department as we now know it."

"Our idea is to have the city become a state, have the various sections of this city become cities right inside the state, and let them run their own police. Let's get the wisdom of the neighborhoods."

He was as plainspoken as Mailer was rhapsodic. Fitting, probably, for a City Council president.

Steinem, closing an interview many years later, said, "One other errant brain cell rose up. I remember Jimmy speaking at Harvard atypically and, I don't think I was physically there, the first thing he said to the audience was 'How many of you have names that end in vowels? Hold up your hands.' There was hardly anybody and he said, 'No wonder you don't understand anything at Harvard.'"

Jimmy could talk to cops. And he could take it when cops talked back to him. But he certainly grabbed their attention this day with this statement: "I say the plan is far better, from a police viewpoint, than the way we're going, because in my estimation policemen today are being used. The police get blamed for all the mistakes of all the people who are supposed to be more important and smarter than us."

"Than us." He speaks like a column. And he brings himself to the cops. "You're asked to go out and take care of and patch up holes made in forty years of history by Congressmen from New York who sat still while federal housing bills were passed that didn't benefit us. . . . You're being asked to pay for the actions of union leaders who didn't do a thing for ghetto areas of this city and who have kept people jobless. And when they're jobless, they look to do things. . . . Now they created the problems. Now they turn to you, the policemen of the city of New York, and say: 'You go out and handle them.' In my estimation it's a disgrace. As usual it comes down to us—give it to the fellow on the bottom. Let him handle the problem.

"Now this city is in trouble, and the main thing we need is respect for law and its officers. But Black people never again will respect law under the present conditions."

It is a speech, if nothing else, about injustice. Breslin, like all great crime writers, knows that the greatest crimes are crimes of injustice. And just as in Chicago he talked about crimes by police, today he is talking about a grave crime against police.

And Breslin is a good speaker. "With that," he closes, "I think I'm going to step down, except for one thing—you had a class about bookmaking here first. I could bring in a guest lecturer for that anytime you want."

The campaign had plans, it had something of an ideology, it had smart people all over it who intended to wake up a city's body politic. That is what Breslin thought he was doing. Then one day he woke up, thought of Mailer, and said "This fuggin guy is serious." He tried and failed to quit and wound up riding it out to the end, when he has been famously quoted as saying he was ashamed to have had anything to do with an enterprise that required the closing of bars.

"People were taking it seriously," Steinem said. "I can't remember if it was Bill Buckley or us who first said—when asked 'what will you do if elected?'—'Demand a recount.' I don't know who gets credit for that line, but we were certainly saying it.

"Probably the book about the campaign by Joe Flaherty details this better but there was a profound difference between Mailer and Breslin and their working together and being in this campaign together was interesting in and of itself. Jimmy had much more grasp of street life. Some of the early meetings took place in my living room. Again, you should check all this but in my memory one of the problems with the campaign I thought was that it was pretty much all white. I invited some of the young honchos, political guys from Harlem. Not a lot, maybe four or five or six, I don't know. Mailer was astounded. He kept saying, 'Where did you find these people?' Jimmy of course knew them. It was like two different universes."

Another problem with the campaign was the marginalizing of women. Flo Kennedy, the radical feminist who was at the first convening of the campaign, was almost ignored, as was her suggestion to bring in the Black vote. Books on the campaign described Steinem as a "girl" from Toledo with honey-colored hair and willowy legs who had found the golden slipper in New York and become one of its glitterati. Those legs certainly served her well in 1963, when she went undercover for a month in Manhattan's Playboy Club and wrote a two-part series for *Show* that detailed the objectification and demeaning conditions a bunny had to suffer.

Now, as the first campaign conclave was being held, her groundbreaking article, "After Black Power, Women's Liberation" would be featured in a banner on the cover of *New York*. She shared the banner with Tom Wolfe on the etiquette of streetlights and Adam Smith on the creation of a supercurrency. The cover itself? Breslin's "Namath All Night Long," a bullseye design treatment with Namath's handsome, mustachioed, smiling face surrounded by six loungewear-clad, adoringly posed women.

That such a campaign was needed, that so many intellects across a broad spectrum embraced it, captured the boil under society's skin that needed to be lanced.

Steinem again: "In my memory. You know when you're in the middle of something you don't have a contrast. The dirt, pollution, crime didn't seem more than any other time. It just was a level of concern to ordinary people waiting to get their garbage picked up or worrying about getting to work while it was still dark in the morning. That kind of melded with the 60s movement atmosphere so there was a 'politics shouldn't be left to the politicians' aura. Why not just have a campaign that's not about getting elected but is about ideas?"

Mailer and his ticket received five percent of the vote in the general election. Incumbent John Lindsay, running as the Liberal Party candidate and with the independent ballot line as well, beat both the Democratic and Republican candidates. Breslin's later writing would reflect that at least Lindsay tried to give the city a fighting chance.

On a national level, since November 5, we had Richard Nixon.

# CRIMES OF A CENTURY

Is the coverup always worse than the crime?

That is one of many questions worth asking about two of the biggest crimes of the twentieth century in the United States. Each of those is the subject of a book by Jimmy Breslin.

The first is my favorite book by the author. It is called simply, *How the Good Guys Finally Won*. Its subject is spelled out under the title: *Notes from an Impeachment Summer.* It is certainly a candidate for his best book, though rivals can be found.

The second is for me the most painful book to read that the author wrote. It is titled *The Church that Forgot Christ.*

Neither is a big book in terms of pages. But each is a book that grapples with the biggest of subjects: Abuse. Abuse of a nation. And abuse of its children. And of course this is at the hands of the powerful. In Breslin's hands the examination of this topic is crafted by a master of modern reporting. By a man who helped shape the genre. And each makes the case that Tom Wolfe suggested when he examined the social strata of the literary classes and decided that beginning with the pre-cursor to the New Journalism *In Cold Blood*, by Truman Capote, the onetime underclass of that society, the scriveners, the journalists, had supplanted the onetime top aristocrats of the printed word, the novelists. Here is the lead paragraph to his February 1972 account "The Birth of the 'New Journalism'; Eyewitness Report by Tom Wolfe":

> I doubt if many of the aces I will be extolling in this story went into journalism with the faintest notion of creating a "new" journalism, a "higher" journalism, or even a mildly improved variety. I know they never dreamed that anything they were going to write for newspapers or magazines would wreak such evil havoc in the literary world . . . causing panic, dethroning the novel as the number one literary genre. . . Nevertheless, that is what has happened. Bellow, Barth, Updike—even the best of the lot, Philip Roth—the novelists are all out there ransacking the literary histories and sweating it out, wondering where they now stand. Damn it all, Saul, the *Huns* have arrived . . .

Writers such as himself, he goes on, "feature writers" if they had any idea at all when they checked in at a newspaper, had the idea that it was a sort of cheap motel on the road to final triumph. "The final triumph was known as The Novel."

What Wolfe writes is important when you look at Breslin's books and ask yourself the question: what is important in his long form work. Fiction. Nonfiction. In this estimation, the vote is for the nonfiction.

Although the "old dream," the novel, as Wolfe goes on to explain, never died. "As for our little league of feature writers [at the *Herald Tribune*] two of the contestants, [Charles] Portis [*True Grit*] and Breslin, actually went on to live out the fantasy. They wrote their novels."

The question though, in Wolfe's mind is the same question as when you read the body of Breslin's work: what's more important—the fiction or the nonfiction?

> And yet in the early 1960s a curious new notion, just hot enough to inflame the ego, had begun to intrude into the tiny confines of the feature

> statusphere. It was in the nature of a discovery. This discovery, modest at first, humble, in fact, deferential, you might say, was that it just might be possible to write journalism that would . . . read like a novel. . . . Not even the journalists who pioneered in this direction doubted for a moment that the novelist was the reigning literary artist, now and forever. All they were asking for was the privilege of dressing up like him . . . until the day when they themselves would work up their nerve and go into the shack and try it for real . . . They were dreamers, all right, but one thing they never dreamed of. . . . They never guessed for a minute that the work they would do over the next ten years, as journalists, would wipe out the novel as literature's main event.

Wolfe then goes on, at great and beautiful length, to show Breslin's key role, his very important role, in this new enterprise.

> . . . Breslin worked like a Turk. He would be out all day covering a story and he would come back in at 4 P.M. or so and sit down at a desk in the middle of the city room. It was quite a show. He was a good-looking Irishman, a lot of black hair and a great wrestler's gut. He looked like a bowling ball fueled with liquid oxygen. Thus fired up, he would start typing. I've never seen a man who could write so well against a daily deadline. I particularly remember one story he wrote about the sentencing, on a charge of extortion, of a Teamster boss named Anthony Provenzano.

We know the outcome. Provenzano, alone before the judge, the clock having ticked to the end of his reign. And we know it vividly because of the way Breslin wrote it.

He was there to bring you into a society, show you its strata and tell you the who, the what, the why, and the how come, which is in some way what literary fiction was supposed to do: immerse you.

Breslin wraps up this remarkable portrait of a labor caesar's tumble into the federal catacombs where he would ultimately die with a scene in a government cafeteria where the young prosecutor who worked the case is eating fried scallops and fruit salad off a tray.

> "Nothing on his hand flashed. The guy who sunk Tony Pro doesn't even have a diamond ring on his pinky."
>
> Well—all right! Say what you will! There it was, a short story, complete with symbolism, in fact, and yet true-life, as they say, about something that happened today, and you could pick it up on the Newsstand by 11 tonight for a dime . . .
>
> Among literary intellectuals you would hear Breslin referred to as "a cop who writes" or "Runyon on welfare." These weren't even intelligent insults, however, because they dealt with Breslin's attitude, which seemed to be that of the cabdriver with his cap tilted over one eye. A crucial part of Breslin's work they didn't seem to be conscious of at all: namely, the reporting he did. Breslin made it a practice to arrive on the scene long before the main event in order to gather the off-camera material, the byplay in the make-up room, that would enable him to create character. It was part of his modus operandi to gather "novelistic" details, the rings, the perspiration, the jabs on the shoulder, and he did it more skillfully than most novelists.

Wolfe goes on to make any number of points, enough for a two part series, in fact, that is dazzling in its erudition. At the heart of it for our purposes is the idea that he and Breslin, and the others of their ilk, were not going to lie flat and the let the people they wrote about "tromp" through the reader's mind while the writer maintained a flat, boring, dispassionate voice.

This may be a long way around to saying Jimmy Breslin's best fiction, his best literary fiction, was his nonfiction. Most of his fiction lacks one quality that his nonfiction has in spades: it is not important. It is—to use what must be or should be a cliché—the difference between "Three Blind Mice" and *King Lear.* Both are popular. But only one is important. In one a tail is lost. In the other, a kingdom. One is a nursery rhyme. The other is a tragedy.

*How The Good Guys Finally Won* is important.

It is a political thriller, and it is a tragedy, unfolding like a play. So it is a book for our times as it is about betrayal of the nation, not a burglary, not a cover up, but about little men, cloaked in respectability, who went beyond the grubby norms of political survival and tried to grab the country for themselves. They tried to raise a pirate flag above a democracy.

So, it is the scope and mechanism of Nixon's treason and the damage he caused to trust that is one of the many things that makes this book exciting and gives it great currency. Because Breslin writes like a crime writer, you can read it in an airport lounge. You can flip through pages filled with villains and unlikely heroes.

Richard Nixon, Breslin points out in the first part of the book, quoting one of President Nixon's last defenders, believed in nothing. "He doesn't believe in religion, or principle or anything," said John Dean, who served as Counsel to the President.

The heroes of the book are men and at least one woman who would prefer to not be heroes. They would prefer to be political survivors.

But in this instance, they stood up. They took the temperature first, of course, in the House of Representatives, and in the Senate. At the outset it was "racetrack suspicion" and not facts that alerted Tip O'Neill to the idea that impeachment might be warranted. But O'Neill, the House Majority Leader, came from the part of Boston where people of Harvard do not live and who was not a lawyer, thus was unencumbered by their books. He began by accruing power, and as word of his interest spread, Nixon's power began to be diminished. "The hugest wheel in the country, bureaucracy, was starting to turn."

In order to write his book, Breslin moved into the House Majority Leader's office: he spent the summer of 1974, the impeachment summer of the title, with Tip O'Neill, who was a Boston politician from the schools of the bricklayer, the ward healer, the saloon keeper and the neighborhood streets. The Gravedigger. O'Neill stood up. And that is the story Breslin tells. It is not a story told from inside a loser's locker room this time. It is a story told from the winner's lair. To tell the story Breslin brought you inside with him. There, Tip O'Neill, who began at 15 getting out the votes door to door in Boston, was now about to do the same. This time, he would collect them from the members of the House of Representatives and he would have his lair behind the doors to a long narrow cloakroom, with a ceiling curved like a railroad car's, with spittoons, and comfortable chairs and a dark corner to sleep in. He would wage it while smoking his Daniel Webster Cigars and drinking Manhattans. And he would wage it not with a great understanding of constitutional law, but with a great understanding of the only thing that could save the country: Votes.

Nixon's crimes are not strictly speaking the subject of this book. This is a book about political power: how to gather it, how to wield it and how one can lose it.

All political power, O'Neill educates Breslin, and ultimately Nixon, is primarily an illusion. If people think you have power then you have power. A good example is O'Neill's title: Majority Leader. There is no such position in law, Breslin explains. But there is a budget and with a title and a budget, there can be the "blue smoke" and mirrors that can allow the Majority Leader's power to grow. As it does, Nixon's declines, until, though he sits in the Oval Office he has no more power than a City Councilperson in Dayton.

It is drama, most of it, set inside buildings; courtrooms, cloak rooms, printing plants, supplemental office space and auditoriums. Some of it puts you in the backseat of car, in a smoke filled bar, and on planes and on golf courses; and, as it draws toward its final act, we are on the protagonist's Cape Cod lawn as O'Neill gathers up his wicker furniture to get the house on the Cape ready for winter. Breslin shows us how O'Neill must delicately balance the grubby business of political survival, money raising and the listening, listening, listening to his well over 100,000 constituents with this new undertaking which most simply can be put: how to kill a king.

While in Shakespeare, Henry Bolingbroke in Henry IV Part I answered the question by gathering armies offshore, then usurping a throne from a weak, arrogant Richard who was disliked by those he ruled, O'Neill must wield paper. This Richard cannot be shackled and tossed into prison by force. But the question of how you unseat a president, with the royal connotations Americans attached to that office, is as grave a matter in this story as it was then. Nixon, tyrannical Nixon, is the king. No one understood that better than O'Neill, than Peter Rodino, the Chairman of the House Judiciary Committee to whom the responsibility would fall and to John Doar, the quiet, patient, fifteen round fighter who had won legal battles in Selma, and in Mississippi and battles against poverty in Bedford Stuyvesant, Brooklyn, and walked behind Martin Luther King's casket and now would wage one against a man who had been steadily eroding the rights that had been hard won. Rodino was raised by an immigrant Italian father "to hold the president in respect second only to a statue in church."

These are the characters who Breslin, with intimacy and detail, introduces you to and who are central to the action. Among the challenges they would face would be partisan politics, bureaucracy, and appropriations.

This then is the story of this book: how to Impeach. And it unfolds beautifully in Breslin's hands.

Above it all is the Capitol Dome.

The book begins in the courtroom of Judge John Sirica, as serious minded a federal jurist as the United States District Court in Washington, D.C., had seen. It's a vivid opening to a drama that will now take us back to the start of this quest for political justice.

It is 4:25 P.M. New Year's Day, 1975. And the clock to the verdict has begun.

The events that got us here began on June 17, 1972, when a security guard, Frank Wills, 24, at the Watergate Hotel and Office Complex noticed a piece of duct tape covering the lock on the door to the sixth floor offices of the Democratic National Committee headquarters. He removed it and continued his rounds. When he returned there was more tape. He called the police. Arrests were made. The coverup began.

On November 7, 1972, Richard Nixon beat George McGovern in a landslide.

Nothing that surfaced as subpoenas and reporters exposed all the machinations of Nixon and his White House to cover up the administration's involvement in the June 17 attempted burglary of the Democratic National Committee offices in the Watergate Complex provided evidence that this act of a paranoid, vindictive administration did much to influence that outcome. Watergate, and the successful breaking and entering and installation of wiretaps on DNC phones that preceded it in May, were part of the most unnecessary suite of political conspiracies you had ever seen. The mendacity, grubbiness and acts of vengeance exceeded the norm even in the Congress of the United States.

Nixon announced his resignation as a result of the scandal on August 8, 1974, in a nationally televised address. On August 9, he handed his Secretary of State, Henry Kissinger, his letter of resignation, effective noon that day.

On September 8, 1974, President Gerald Ford pardoned him.

On October 1, 1974, the trial in Sirica's courtroom of five men implicated in the overall Watergate conspiracy—architects of policy and officials in the Republican National Committee—and coverup began. The trial was one of the many powerful scenes in the Watergate drama. Its final moments serve here as the dramatic opening to the story of events leading up to it that will unfold.

What Breslin gives us as he opens this book with the verdict is something that is usually only witnessed by stenographers, court clerks, court officers and reporters. The judge does not see it. Nor, usually, do television cameras. He gives us the sights and sounds against the ticking of the clock, just as he did with Tony Provenzano.

> It was 4:25 P.M. of an empty New Year's Day, 1975, and now it was all coming to an end.
>
> The windowless courtroom was too bright . . . This type of American ceremony has no richness to it; dark tragedies are played out in flat, harsh civil-service surroundings.
>
> It was 4:35 on and they waited in the courtroom.
>
> Haldeman, Ehrlichman, Mitchell, Mardian and Parkinson.
>
> Along the wall in the front of the room were two easels used for exhibits during the case. One of the easels had been tipped over. The large white card on it carried a heading, "White House Chart."

The squares showed which man was where in the times when they all thought the power they had was real and permanent. The card on the other easel said, "Committee to Re-Elect President." Titles out of the past.

Minutes went by. It was 4:40 now.

And "into the harsh light" comes the judge, John Sirica.

"Has the jury reached a verdict?"

"Yes they have."

At 4:48 a clerk brings a large brown civil service envelope containing the verdict to the bench.

Sirica opens it. At 4:49, Sirica is still reading.

At 4:50, Sirica nodded: "The clerk will read the verdict. Defendants stand."

Mitchell. Guilty. Six counts against him are read Guilty. Guilty. Guilty. Guilty. Guilty. Guilty.

Haldeman. Five counts. Ehrlichman. Four counts. Mardian. One count. Parkinson. Not guilty. John Mitchell mouths the word "Congratulations."

It's a scene with a great deal of similarity to the sentencing in 1963 of the racketeer Tony Provenzano. And this time it is the opening to a drama built on one million, five hundred thousand pages of Xerox paper; one tan-covered 718-page book of which 1,500 copies are printed; the work of thirty typists; and how all of this was used to collect the votes needed to get to August 8, 1974. And now the book will take us back to that summer and how we got there.

"The summer in which a nation forced the President of the United States to resign from office. And if we are going to talk about the end to Watergate, as we are about to do here, why don't we . . . step into the shafts of sunlight provided by some of the people who worked for their country, rather than against it. People who are so much more satisfying to know."

By the middle of this book we know them well, and we feel their pressures, their exhaustion, their pride and in the case of Tip O'Neill, his fundamental belief that it is always about the votes.

Though we are reading about treason and betrayal, Breslin has us see it through the eyes of the people who know what it will mean if they do not stop it and has us witness many of them wrestle the fact that they would like to survive this and stay in office.

Many of the devices Breslin uses are familiar in television drama: time stamps and date stamps, images of diary entries, and the cover pages of documents.

Then there is his gift of staying longer and capturing more detail than anyone else. Finally, there is the ability to recreate scenes and put you, the reader, in the room.

> On October 9, Peter Rodino, educated at a place you may never have heard of called Newark University, sent the impeachment material to the printer. On October 10, a 718-page book "the size of a quality paperback" with a tan cover, "House Document 93-7 IMPEACHMENT Selected Materials" is waiting for every member. There are 100 copies. O'Neill immediately turned to the last page. 718 pages. "It's fabulous work," he begins telling everyone. "We have to get more printed." He explains that everyone from constitutional scholars at Harvard on down wants a copy. There is no evidence that he or anyone else read this collection of impeachment materials, some of which had been out of print for a century. What is clear is now there was a book. And on its cover it said: Impeachment. "Keerist! This is gettin' to be important business now."

Now the paper, and the vote collection, and the battling over timing between O'Neill and Rodino, is well underway. Date by date. Detail by detail. Potential pitfall by potential pitfall. It is all there.

This book shows how slowly the hands on the clock must move, how carefully the paper must be collected, how O'Neill must continue to attend lunches and dinners—he may have gone to 4,000 such events in his career. What did he do there? He listened to those voices and what they might say about his own future.

Rodino has subpoena power now. He must select his counsel. He moves slowly. Too slow for O'Neill, who understands better the political clock. O'Neill gives him names. Rodino balks. O'Neill explains those names are just suggestions. They might give Rodino ideas for other names. Get the right name. Ultimately, it is the Republican John Doar who even the White House can find no fault with: if it isn't there, Doar won't find it, is the thought. It is a true one. Now the committee is bipartisan. This, O'Neill knows, is important too.

Doar builds a fortress for the paper he will collect. Bars on the windows. Alarms. Motion detectors. Steel reinforced doors. Smoke detectors. No one is breaking in here. And there will be no computers because Doar doesn't trust them to keep secrets. So no one is breaking in there either. Soon the piles of paper will become so great that the floor will have to be reinforced. And while O'Neill is out taking the sentiment of the House, watching whether the pace is too slow and sentiment might shift, Doar is building his files.

It is a drama you could only capture if you had spent your summer with O'Neill.

As the tempo builds Doar's team gets Nixon's diary. It shows a mind "so twisted" that "the effect of reading it was stunning," Breslin writes.

O'Neill goes to Wyoming, where 75 percent of the state went for Nixon. He goes because House Democrat Teno Roncalio has taken a great risk by supporting impeachment and he should lend whatever help he can as reelection looms.

"We are not happy. But we are strong in our hour of sadness," he tells the great and good of Wyoming. It is an important speech. He uses his important voice not his back room voice. "Our country is strong enough to survive. Jerry Ford will give the nation the stability it needs."

On the plane back O'Neill opines, "This has been over for months." Nixon has no support in staunchly Republican Wyoming. O'Neill will get his votes.

And we go back a little at the end, when he is still soon to be president, Gerald Ford, the House Minority leader, and there is a photo of him, walking down a golf course, his hand behind O'Neill's back, O'Neill's behind his. When Ford becomes president, they laugh. Because they know the power of a photo, whether or not they clash in the future, this will be the enduring image of the Democratic Majority Leader and the Republican President whom he will work with to ensure the stability that Nixon promised and did not deliver.

*How the Good Guys Finally Won,* like so much of Jimmy Breslin's nonfiction, is marked by his ability to make you smile. Whether in the odyssey of Sunny Jim across an archipelago of racetracks that began in the salty reaches of Far Rockway, or the improbable success of the Amazing Mets in a season of defeat that brought them closer to the fans in the bleachers than perhaps any team since, Breslin's wit and his laugh-out-loud humor even in the face of his protagonists' adversity shows us the humor in life and the ridiculousness at times of the all too American search for more. He delights us with Tip O'Neill's baritone, he amuses us even as we have a nation on the brink, and often, when he brings us moments of sadness, they too are leavened by his touch.

⁎ ⁎ ⁎

*The Church That Forgot Christ* is a different kind of book altogether. It is a story of a dark betrayal by the earthly stewards of the Roman Catholic God of their entire flock. The crime at its heart is hinged like a sacristy door. On one side is the abuse of tens of thousands of Catholic youths who went to the same Catholic grammar schools and Catholic high schools as their parents and grandparents. Who shared the immigrant belief that next to family and even before country came their God. And on the other side are the decades of coverups, across the country and extending to the Vatican in Rome, by the cardinals, archbishops, bishops, and monsignors who shuffled the abusers from parish to parish, diocese to diocese, of churchly lawyers who arranged to pay off the victims, in sums that could never be adequate for silence in the face of a pain that once begun will continue until death.

In this book Breslin, as so many who are educated to confess their sins on Saturday, go to church on Sunday and accept the Body of Christ into their own and adhere to ten Commandments, faces the fact that come Monday, children and youths had already been abused by clergy who were neither celibate nor chaste. It is the story of Breslin's own painful struggle, his crisis of faith and that of the believers across his beloved Queens. It is more polemic than reportage. It is more anguish than even anger.

Some of the earliest reporting on priestly sexual misconduct and abuse was done by Charlie Sennott, then of the *New York Post.*

Sennott is a bushy eyebrowed, broad shouldered Bostonian, the kind of kid when he was young that mowed the lawns of those that went to Harvard—the Bishops and Archbishops of the Northeastern elite; an elite that is important to this story. Charlie uncovered a predator as horrific as any pimp or human trafficker that plied the streets of "The Deuce," the area of 42nd Street and Times Square conveniently close to the bus terminal that at the time deposited plenty of strays and runaways on the streets of New York. The predator's name was Father Bruce Ritter. He ran a place called Covenant House. He built it into a 90 million dollar not-for-profit. And then he abused, and he had sex with his young charges and especially young men. He traded money, clothing, lodging, and comfort for sex. Just another pimp.

This is told well in Sennott's 1992 book *Broken Covenant.* Charlie got the story the old fashioned way: "Pick up line six" the 26-year-old was told. He did and then he listened to a story that to a Roman Catholic young man from a traditional Boston family, put him on edge and made him uncomfortable.

John Cotter, the *Post* Metropolitan Editor, listened as Sennott explained. "Welcome to journalism, kid. Nobody said it would be easy."

Ritter is one priest, but his story serves as well as any other to show how the forces of the establishment—the elite in government, finance, media relations, the news media itself and the Roman Catholic Church—all came together to cajole, question, and threaten Charlie and the tabloid. They came down hard: Suggesting Charlie was smelling a story that was tabloid gold, rather than accepting that what he was smelling was a stink of financial misconduct and sexual abuse that came off Ritter, who bragged that he controlled his charity with unchecked power. Attorney General Ed Meese had enlisted Ritter in a fight against pornography, President Ronald Reagan had cited Ritter as an unsung hero in a state of the union address, First Lady Barbara Bush stood beside Ritter. The *Post* stood by Charlie. And now he brought into the sunlight this heinous man, who used his Roman collar the ways fluke fishermen use strips of clean squid to bait their hooks. A man who was like many others in a church-wide scandal that cost billions of dollars in payoffs. It would all come out in the years ahead.

It was this simple: Ritter promised shelter and protection. And then he took advantage of young men. Next, the *Boston Globe* and its Spotlight team took on the hierarchy of the church and its political offspring, the government of the City of Boston, to expose the repeated rape and abuse of children, a massive crime and the massive coverup by the Cardinal of Boston, Cardinal Bernard Francis Law. The only difference between those cases and Ritter's was Ritter had no protection from a diocese. The similarity is what is important: these were among the more than 11,000 reported cases of sexual abuse and assault by the Catholic clergy in the United States.

In the end, with the possibility of indictment looming, Ritter, who publicly had suggested that Michelangelo's David could be pornographic as it showed male genitalia and that might provoke or stimulate, was forced out in a deal cut by the priests and lawyers of the "Powerhouse" as St. Patrick's Cathedral is popularly known. He resigned. He died in obscurity, except for a curious final profile by *The New York Times* that was almost exculpatory in its tone.

In the end, Bernard Cardinal Law became a Vatican citizen, and thus protected from any Boston subpoena. One had already been served to his residence the day he slipped out of Boston and fled to Rome. He was able to remain a force in Church politics and a Pope gave a benediction when he was interred beneath an old church whose beauty now rots from the foundation.

But what was exposed in Boston and what was exposed in New York essentially came down to the same thing: betrayal. Children and youths offered wisdom and promised comfort, safety, and understanding by men of God, were raped and abused.

Breslin's book is a book about the good Catholics of Queens. Some of his Catholics held their own religious services rather than set foot again in a Roman Catholic Church. Many of them had kept their abuse locked inside, where it festered and caused a life of pain and grief and hardship. It is the story of Catholics like Breslin. It is a story of faith betrayed. It cuts to the bone of every Catholic.

Breslin, at the time of Sennott's exposé, still had a hard time believing this could be true. That Ritter could be a monster. A priest. A monster. He called Michael Daly. The writer informed Breslin that the word on the street according to the homburg and bow tie wearing cop Jack Maple who worked The Deuce, as 42nd off Times Square was known to cops, was that Ritter was who Charlie said he was. He was what was crassly known as a "chicken hawk," though his New York empire had the sign of the Dove on its exterior wall.

Later, Sennott, now at the *Boston Globe,* was in the press room at the Vatican when Breslin burst in. Wearing a rumpled raincoat, a shirt stained by coffee, and his glasses down at the tip of his nose, "Charlie, Charlie," he said, his loud voice breaking the chapel like silence of the press room.

The Italian reporters, as they did at the time, were in polished shoes, creased trousers, good jackets and were fully credentialled. It was December 13, 2002, and The Pope would that day accept Bernard Francis Law's resignation as the Archbishop of Boston.

The *Globe* was less welcome than *Pravda* in the Vatican that year and Sennott was looking for a place to hide from Breslin's charge.

"'Charlie, Chaaarrrlieee,' he was asking loudly and slowly for me, by name. I was across the room at my laptop and on the phone and honestly thought for a minute about hiding."

"Jimmy."

"You were fucking right, kid. You were so fucking on the money on this. These lying fucking bastards."

Then Breslin did what he was known to do. He picked Charlie's pocket.

"A few 'how's Boston' questions," Sennott said. And then Breslin worked him over. "What I was reporting on. Who I was talking to. And knowing all of what I said would be in his column . . . As always, I gave him everything I could. After all, this was Breslin. Breslin in Rome."

And so, we come to Breslin's tale. It is uneven in places, and as a story of a struggle unresolved that is probably the way it had to be. Breslin, weak before alcohol, belligerent in a newsroom, betrayer of colleagues and those who thought they were friends, had through it all and a very long life, maintained as strong a faith in God as he did the people of Queens. Yet he had to wonder now: had God deserted him or had the church?

Like his Aunt Harriet, who knelt by her bed to pray before she joined her husband who was getting ready to possibly go to war, he was a Queens Catholic. He knew what it felt to genuflect and cross himself. And now he was at war with himself.

"She was twenty-one and she was going to use those prayers and belief in them to get through a war. Oh, this was no religious fanatic. She took a drink, don't worry about that and the best picture I have of her has her eating a hotdog in the grandstand at the old Jamaica racetrack."

Whether his Queens, or Sennott's Boston, for Breslin it always comes back to the people who are hurt. And Breslin's other people, the news media, somehow went years without paying attention.

> There have been four great movements in modern America that occurred without the news reporting industry knowing anything about them until they became a part of regular life. The first was civil rights, then the women and, third, homosexuals, and, last and suddenly, the

> crumbling of the Catholic Church. You can blame the church's condition on the Irish, who gave us total religious insanity. They are a race that sat in the rain for a couple of thousand years and promoted the most crazed beliefs in personal living outside of the hillbillies. The symbol is Edward Egan, cardinal, archbishop, who lives amidst the best Irish lace curtains on Madison Avenue in Manhattan.

This kind of writing found no friends among the those in the church or on the police who were bigots. Breslin would never be Grand Marshal at the St. Patrick's Day Parade.

He gets to what faith and the priesthood ought to be about in a scene that if Netflix or someone painted it in Queens would remind us of *The Last Supper.* It was the Mass for Rosemary Breslin:

> Then I saw Eugene Kennedy again, at Fordham, and as he spoke I remembered everything about an afternoon when he came to our house in Forest Hills and said mass at the kitchen table for my late wife. I keep the scene with me forever. He magnified love and needed no great cathedral to do it. Not even a small chapel.

A struggle with faith that brought Breslin back to the foundation of his own is an existential one that might not have occurred were it not for the rot that came from a priesthood required to be unmarried so that any riches they brought in would go, not to heirs, but to the vaults beneath the Vatican where historically they have been kept out of the reach of the poor. This book is a struggle for him. The lesson he learned in writing it is a powerful one:

> This final fear should be hurled out of our lives. The priest is not going to save your soul. Nor is the building he patrols, no matter the grandeur and the glory of it. You save yourself by honest work in the name of God and of the dead generations who have gone before us and from

whom we derive our legacy of compassion, of never being indifferent to the suffering of others.

Not the dead, as he reminded us in his epitaph for the great cop, Jack Maple, but the living.

This struggle for regular people, with all their flaws, flaws like his, to keep faith, find compassion, combat injustice and rise above themselves is the essence of his work and it is present in much of the rest of his nonfiction as well.

# THE NIGHT JOHN LENNON DIED

James Breslin was sitting at the assignment desk at Channel Five when the police scanner traffic went from staticky background chatter to an urgent, raised voice storm, pouring out of the squawk boxes. This told the desk assistant, Jimmy Breslin's son, it was time to put the cigarette out, take his feet off the desk and start dialing his bosses. Fast. The words "John Lennon" were starting to come over the air.

John Miller, the station's 21-year-old star police reporter, had just wrapped up a date that was going nowhere and swung the Channel Five car, a blue 1977 Buick LeSabre, by a motorcycle accident. You never knew who it could be. Might be a picture. Then he swung home, and when he got into his apartment on Madison Avenue all his phones were ringing.

Jimmy Breslin was home in Forest Hills, Queens, when James Breslin, having reached the news director, the anchor, and reached out to Miller realized, "I should call Dad."

"The scanners are going psycho. Squawking. Squawking. SHOOTING ONE WEST 72nd STREET. And you could hear the blaring sirens," James Breslin recalled. He called his father.

"I said, holy shit, there's something going on. And I'm hearing John Lennon's name."

"Get Froggy," Breslin said. Froggy lived around the corner from the Breslins. Another person impressed into service as a driver for Breslin and his considerable ego.

A few minutes later, Breslin was running out the front door half dressed as David Kasparian, a.k.a. Froggy, pulled up.

James Breslin was grabbing his coat and racing west, across Central Park from the Channel Five newsroom.

John Miller was back in his Buick and was racing across the park from his apartment just a few blocks from the television station.

The Emergency Room at Roosevelt Hospital, the entrance to the Dakota, the 20th Precinct. Breslin and Miller hit them all and what came out of it, from Miller, was the most thorough and accurate of television reports.

"One of the last things John Lennon must have seen was an overweight fan who had been pestering him for days," Miller reported in a measured cadence. "The last time he had been clutching a pen. But this time, he was holding a gun."

What came out of it from Breslin was deadline poetry.

The shots that killed Lennon had been fired at a few minutes before 11 P.M. Just a few hours later and in time for the Final Edition of the *New York Daily News*, his column was reported and written and handed to a reporter he would later betray but who this night typed it in to the rudimentary computer system where it was read by the editors. When Page Three of the paper was laid out it had the column with this quote pulled out:

> And a shaking woman, another victim's wife, crumpled into the back seat as Palma started for Roosevelt Hospital. She said nothing to the two cops and they said nothing to her. Homicide is not a talking matter.

And they put this headline over the work: "Cops Hear the Song Die on Streets of New York."

The column puts you at the Dakota apartment building where Lennon lay face down in his blood, and then it puts you inside two police cars that have arrived. One carries the victim across its back seat as it races to the hospital. The other was carrying the victim's spouse, who was soon to be a widow.

> That summer in Breezy Point, when he was 18 and out of Madison High in Brooklyn, there was the Beatles on the radio at the beach through the hot days and on the jukebox through the nights in the Sugar Bowl and Kennedys. He was young and he let his hair grow and there were girls and it was the important part of life.
>
> Last year, Tony Palma even went to see Beatlemania.
>
> And now, last night, a 34-year-old man, he sat in a patrol car at 82nd St. and Columbus Ave. and the call came over the radio: "Man shot, 1 West 72 St."
>
> Palma and his partner, Herb Frauenberger, rushed through the Manhattan streets to an address they knew as one of the most famous living places in the country, the Dakota apartments.

As the structure of the column unfolds, you recall "A Death in Emergency Room One" so many lives ago. But here there are only minutes until deadline. Here he files. Someone types it into the computer for him. And it will be in the paper.

> A car was there ahead of them . . .
>
> "Where's the guy shot?" Palma said.
>
> "In the back," one of the cops said.
>
> Palma went through the gates into the Dakota courtyard . . . A guy in a red shirt and jeans was on his face on the floor. He rolled the guy

over. Blood was coming out of the mouth and covering the face. The chest was wet with blood. . . .

Palma took the arms and Frauenberger took the legs. They carried the guy out to the street. Somebody told them to put the body in another patrol car.

Jim Moran's patrol car was waiting. Moran is from the South Bronx, from Williams Ave., and he was brought up on Tony Bennett records in the jukeboxes. When he became a cop in 1964, he was put on patrol guarding the Beatles at their hotel. Girls screamed and pushed and Moran laughed. Once, it was all fun.

As Moran started driving away he heard people shouting, "That's John Lennon!"

. . . Moran was driving with Bill Gamble. As they went through the streets to Roosevelt Hospital, Moran looked in the backseat and said, "Are you John Lennon?" The guy in the back nodded and groaned.

Back on 72 St., somebody told Palma, "Take the woman." And a shaking woman, another victim's wife, crumpled into the backseat as Palma started for Roosevelt Hospital.

Jim Moran, with John Lennon in the backseat, was on the radio as he drove to the hospital. "Have paramedics meet us at the emergency entrance," he called. When he pulled up to the hospital, they were waiting for him with a cart. As Lennon was being wheeled through the doors into the emergency room, the doctors were on him.

"John Lennon," somebody said.

That night, at that apartment building, you watched as fans quickly began to gather, and reporters who had raced from all over the city to get there were among them and were talking to police, with cameras, television cameras, microphones and pads. This crush of reporters was happening at the hospital as well. Breslin stayed with his simple part of the story.

Now Tony Palma pulled up to the emergency entrance. He let the woman out and she ran to the doors.

Somebody called to Palma, "That's Yoko Ono."

"Yeah?" Palma said.

"They just took John Lennon in," the guy said.

Palma walked into the emergency room. Moran was there already. The doctors had John Lennon on a table in a trauma room, working on the chest, inserting tubes. Tony Palma said to himself, I don't think so. Moran shook his head. He thought about his two kids, who know every one of the Beatles' big tunes. And Jim Moran and Tony Palma, older now, cops in a world with no fun, stood in the emergency room as John Lennon, whose music they knew, whose music was known everywhere on earth, became another person who died after being shot with a gun on the streets of New York.

## DIES THE VICTIM DIES THE CITY

On December 8, 1980, it was just under two years since the day—January 2, 1978—that Ed Koch, running on an anti-crime platform and promising to restore New York to its former glory, had been sworn in as mayor.

On that same day that the man whose music was known everywhere on earth was shot with a gun on the streets of New York, it had been just shy of four years since Sunday, November 14, 1976, when a box appeared on Page One of the *Sunday News* announcing: Jimmy Breslin, *Starts Today,* page 3.

In the box was a line drawing of hardworking Breslin, collar undone, tie pulled down, cigar in his teeth, smiling from his eyes.

That first column captured the state of New York as Breslin told the story of a young man shot in the back of the head on a Brooklyn street by a young gunman who wanted a coat.

> Dies the victim, dies the city. Nobody flees New York because of accounting malpractice. People run from murder and fire. Those who remain express their fear in words of anger.

By the end of 1977, Breslin's first full year at the paper, 1,557 homicides had been recorded. By the end of the month John Lennon died, there were 1,814 recorded for that year. Two decades earlier, in 1960, there had been 482. Koch's platform was on an EMS trolley racing to hospital emergency room doors. Here is how Breslin began the year:

> The first person murdered in New York in 1980 turns out to be Salvadore Vargas, 36, of Fourth Ave., Brooklyn who was shot at about 8 pm on New Year's Eve and then took so long to die that he tumbled clear out of the 1979 statistics and on to the top of the list of 1980. Vargas died on New Year's Day a clear two hours ahead of the next victim.
>
> Statisticians however were fighting over Vargas yesterday. I don't know why. Vargas was certainly not needed so desperately for the 1979 numbers . . .
>
> Nor was Vargas required to make our murder figures for the first day of 1980 seem impressive. Here in New York on New Year's Day, amidst our grandeur, our mansions in the sky, why right at the center of our absolute renaissance, we killed 13 people; shot them, stabbed them, strangled them, did everything but chew them to death.

Dies the victim, dies the city.

Breslin, with sadness, with wry humor, with fierceness; from that very first column gave the *Daily News* the voice that it needed to fulfill its promise to the city's residents. *Tell It to Sweeney* is how the paper once defined that voice in a book it published under that title. The book, written by John Chapman, the paper's drama critic since 1943, was printed at a time when the Sweeneys were the majority audience the editors and publishers aimed for. In 1980, the working class audience from the low rise neighborhoods in the demographically changing four outer boroughs of New York City remained an audience for Breslin. He looked out for those that took the longest rides in the world you could buy for a token; to get to Manhattan and stoke the furnaces, turn on the air conditioners, fuel the egos of the ruling classes: whether political or financial. He never took his eye off of you. The so-often powerless.

In the Bronx, fifty percent of the housing in forty-four census tracts had been burnt down in the 1970s. Ninety-seven percent had been gutted by fire in another half dozen places. President Jimmy Carter, who wore a yellow cardigan when he addressed the nation, encouraging us to lower our thermostats as we continued to experience an OPEC-driven energy crisis, went to the Bronx in 1977. What happened?

> A young woman carrying a movie camera walked in the warm sun across the desolation of Charlotte St. in the South Bronx yesterday, her feet clearing away the larger pieces of broken glass. She made her way to the top of a hill of debris and surveyed the desolation. A young man appeared . . .
>
> "We're making a film," the young man, Steve Brown, said. "The film is about archeology." . . . "Archeologists look for what gets left over when buildings and places are let go," Elle Nagler said. . . .
>
> What his archeologists would find someday are the fire-blackened bricks and beams . . . they also would find motor oil cans, beer cans, broken glass for wine bottlers, syringes, Styrofoam coffee containers, headless plastic dolls and under it all . . . the broken promise of the head of the government of the richest nation in the history of mankind.
>
> It was on Charlotte St. in the South Bronx that President Carter stood in 1977 and told the nation he would have this place rebuilt, born again as it were, in order to personally bear witness to the cities where so many live . . .
>
> Now it is almost the summer of 1979 and nothing has been done and nothing will be done.

"On Charlotte St., a Broken Promise Lies Among Ruins." That was the headline this column ran under.

Dies the South Bronx, dies the city.

During that time, even as Breslin's fame had grown, the newspaper's precipitous decline had begun. A decision would be made to cancel the evening "Bulldog Edition." Who was going to risk the dark and dangerous streets to walk their dog to the newsstand after 8:00 P.M. for a paper and cigarettes, a paper and ice cream, a paper and condoms, a paper and candy?

In May 1979, a young boy, Etan Patz, was kidnapped, to vanish forever, on the streets of Manhattan. His became the first face of a missing child on a milk carton.

In October the city gained one new, if temporary, resident: the Shah of Iran. With the help of powerful bankers, Mohammed Reza Pahlavi, removed from his Peacock Throne by the Islamic Revolution, had come to New York Hospital for cancer treatment. Just a few days later, Iranians stormed our embassy and took our diplomats hostage. This was a situation that went on for more than a year. Ronald Reagan was sworn in as president on January 20, 1981. On January 21, the hostages were freed.

By then, the city's population had dropped by nearly a million people from 1970.

In January 1980, Richard Ravitch, Chairman of the Metropolitan Transportation Authority, announced he would not have his 14-year-old son ride the subway at night.

The decision made by the Tribune Corporation that owned the *News* to cease publishing the Bulldog Edition was balanced by a decision to invest many millions of dollars in an afternoon paper called *Tonight* that would attract young, monied Manhattanites on their way home from the white world of finance, publishing, law, commerce, advertising and accounting that was still thriving. It would start in August 1980 and end with layoffs in August 1981. A failure. One that Clay Felker of *Esquire,* the *Trib,* and *New York* magazine had been brought in to help oversee. His magic could not turn blue collar subway and bus tokens into Manhattanite gold.

It was a failure that accelerated a decline in circulation that was matched perhaps only by the decline in the quality of life in the city itself. The *Daily News* was doing long takeouts on those who saw fit to arm themselves with licensed handguns, from ice cream makers to entertainment moguls to columnists; a memorable series that was a finalist for the Pulitzer titled "How Safe Are Our Subways"; campaigns against dogs fouling the sidewalks while their owners held their own noses in the air; reports that required counting the number of potholes in the city; the start of the state lottery and its impact on the state's coffers and the state of the numbers business, the most dangerous bus stops, the most dangerous street corners, the decision by the bosses of the Metro-North railroad to bypass the stops in the South Bronx because of the "urchins" on the streets there.

"Tell them he called them roaches," Michael Daly counseled a young reporter headed to the Bronx to get reactions.

In 126 columns in 1977, 107 in 1978 and 131 in 1979, Breslin cut to the heart of the matter with confident, straightforward prose, with bluntness or grace, humor or chagrin or sadness. He proved to be as incredible a reporter in early middle age as he was when he wrote his first book on Sunny Jim and his column for the *Herald Tribune.* In more than 1,100 columns published between 1977 and his departure from the paper, his prose shone even brighter than at his meteoric start at the *Trib* in 1963. Now his voice resonated, loudly when necessary, across the city, the state and at times, the nation. He used it to capture the rift between white New York and brown and Black-skinned New York. He shouted back at the white applause for a white man named Bernie Goetz when he shot four Black youths on the subway after they asked him for five dollars. He used it to capture the rent in the fabric of his soul caused by the death of his wife Rosemary. He used it to capture a most despicable crime committed by police, one that illustrated the divide between them and the communities they served. And he used it to tell the story of two big crime cases where he could offer a unique perspective. They were both committed by Jimmy's people: the crooks and crooked politicians of Queens.

# LUFTHANSA HEIST

In the last month of 1978, on December 11, the largest cash heist in US history occurred at John F. Kennedy Airport in the watery far reaches of Queens where the runways and landing beacons run right out to the edge of some of the finest fishing in Jamaica Bay with its grassy hummocks, deep holes, and skinny water filled with fluke, bluefish and striped bass.

Five masked gunmen circumvented the elaborate security measures at Lufthansa's cargo warehouse, Building 261, making their way through guards and security doors designed to set off alarms if you failed to close the one behind you before you opened the one ahead. The getaway driver waited outside.

They made away with $5 million in cash and at least $300,000 in gold and jewelry.

The story of the heist was another kind of gold: it was tabloid gold. The heist of the century and no one killed or injured. You could root for the thieves.

The gold would soon be covered in blood. A careless failure to discard a getaway vehicle prompted the beginning of the murders. Parnell Edwards, whose task was to drive the black Ford Econoline van to New Jersey and dispose of it, instead parked it at a fire hydrant in front of a girlfriend's house, where police found it two days later. And his fingerprints. He was shot and killed inside his apartment within seven days of the heist. There would be more killings. Fear that the exhibition of wealth might bring the FBI to the hijackers' doors, prompted someone believed to be Jimmy Burke, a Lucchese crime family associate and the mastermind of the heist, to continue the purge. What Burke's own paranoia did not encourage, his desire for a larger cut of the proceeds did, providing fuel to see a purge through to its bloody end. There would be nine or more murders directly or indirectly associated with the heist attributed to Burke's orders by the time it was over.

Feared on the streets as his homicidal nature was well known, Burke, dubbed "Jimmy the Gent," by Breslin, was believed to use the dirt beneath the floorboards of his own bar, Robert's Lounge on Lefferts Boulevard, as a graveyard. He used the bar of The Suite on Queens Boulevard, another place to plan and celebrate crime owned by Mob associate Henry Hill, to take out his anger on Breslin.

Henry Hill himself became truly a significant character first when he turned informant and again when he was put in the great crime writer Nick Pileggi's book *Wiseguy*, which became the basis for the movie *Goodfellas*. Until then his was a walk-on part as a government informant, which he became after his arrest on an unrelated narcotics charge. He could not help convict Burke in connection with the Lufthansa job.

Breslin had known Burke and drank with Burke for years before the heist. In 1970, reportedly unhappy with what Breslin had written about Lucchese capo Paul Vario, an Italian American mobster associated with him (and later the murder of Edwards after the heist), Burke grabbed Breslin by the tie, forced his head down onto a bar and slammed it repeatedly while choking him with his necktie. According to Sal Polisi and Steve Dougherty in *The Sinatra Club: My Life Inside the New York Mafia*:

> One of the legit regulars at Henry's joint was Breslin, the *Daily News* columnist who wrote a lot about the Mob. He used to stop in at The

> Suite all the time to have a drink. While he was at it, he'd drink in the atmosphere and pick up tips for stories.
>
> Later on I got to know Breslin a little bit from coaching his kid's football team. He was a good guy. He was also a celebrated character around New York—the classic hard drinking big-city newspaperman. He ran for mayor of New York with Norman Mailer in 1969, the same year his book about the Gallo Wars, *The Gang That Couldn't Shoot Straight*, came out.
>
> None of that mattered to Jimmy Burke. . . . because one night in 1970 he nearly beat Breslin to death right there at the bar in the Suite.
>
> Henry (Hill) said Jimmy was pissed about a column Breslin wrote about Paul Vario. But it might have been just because Jimmy didn't like the way Breslin was always making wise guys look like jerks. Anyway, nobody was sure what was said exactly; all anybody remembers was Jimmy grabbed Breslin by the neck and put a Kid Twist on him: He held Breslin by one hand and twisted his necktie till Breslin turned red and his whole head looked like it was about to explode. Henry thought he was going to break the guy's neck if he didn't strangle him to death first. Then Jimmy yanked down on the poor fucker's tie and started banging Breslin's face on the top of the bar.
>
> Breslin survived. He told people that he had a concussion, but guys who were there said he must have gotten a skull fracture at least.

He might have suffered a concussion. In at least one account, he suffered a possible fractured skull. In accounts collected decades later, the violence of the incident is downplayed. What is definite is that Breslin came home weary and worse for the wear.

"I'm all right," he said as he walked in the door. Then he went up to bed.

The incident did not end his relationship with the saloons of Queens. His range was that of a news shark: Pep McGuire's on Queens Boulevard, Robert's Lounge on Lefferts Boulevard, the Suite, and when he felt flush or puffed up with his own brilliance, the Copacabana in "the city" as people from Southeast Queens referred to Manhattan. In his 2005 book, *The Good Rat*, he explains the cost of their demise in a changing world of journalism:

> Among the saloons of the city today, there are no notorious places known as mob joints. And there are no more meetings between reporters and gangsters in places known for tough guys and neon and loud fun. News reporters get their information from Jerry Capeci's Gang Land on the Internet. When their work is done, you find reporters at health clubs or going home to some suburb where they drink wine and the contest is who causes more boredom, the wife or the husband. I stand on Queens Boulevard in front of what was once Pep McGuire's, and I recall nights and crimes, and I am certain that I hold memories possessed by virtually no one else alive. The owners were Norton Peppis—known as Pep, he gambled anything he had or didn't have—and Johnny McGuire, who appeared to have started life legitimately by going on the police force. He was in the Seventeenth Precinct and was posted at the door to UN ambassador Henry Cabot Lodge's suite at the Waldorf-Astoria. There had been threats. Officer McGuire, all tuckered out from a day at Monmouth Park Racetrack, took a chair in front of the suite's door and passed out. A flash from a *Daily News* camera woke him up. He tore down the hall after the photographer and begged him to take another picture to preserve his job. The guy gave Johnny a break and let him pose at the door. Beautiful, Johnny said. In the morning the police commissioner happened to differ. On his desk was the *Daily News* with a front page featuring Officer Johnny McGuire, uniform collar tugged open, hat and gun on the chair next to him. The partners opened a barren joint and filled the bar with stewardesses from the nearby airports and lugged in jockeys from Aqueduct, and soon the place was bedlam. Somewhere at the bar was Fat Thomas, drinking and yelling. There was a band, a dance floor, and people tumbling

around. You had Eddie "Lockjaw" Davis, saxophonist from the Basie band, drinking scotch and milk at the bar.

Nor did the incident or his columns on the aftermath of the Lufthansa heist end his relationship with Burke, whose affections could turn on a coin toss from murderous to munificent—but who, Breslin knew, was always bound to be a source of information.

"Because I came from Queens, which nobody in the history of New York newspapers ever wrote about or even saw, I was reputed to be streetwise and tough. Which was untrue. I didn't fight. I chased stories, not beatings. But I knew where to find people who were somewhat less than our civic best, and so editors clung to the illusion."

He wrote this also in *The Good Rat,* a book in which hanging from the golden transcript of the testimony of mobster-turned-informant Burt Kaplan in the trial of two dishonorable men, the "Mafia Cops," Mob hitmen who wore badges, are displayed the pearls of Breslin's knowledge, and the glittering charms that are remembered and then reworked from versions that appeared in columns and books he wrote over the course of decades. Autobiography may be a big word for "lies," and memory may be a thief, but in the hands of a storyteller with some roots in an oral tradition, they are the spine of life, repeated, polished, distilled for an audience that is waiting for them, an audience that includes Breslin, because, like some itinerant singer of tales, the words are the only way he can see.

The *Daily News* reported that the Lufthansa theft occurred at 3:15 A.M. when the thieves captured and locked the guards in a second floor cafeteria of the cargo facility on the northern edge of JFK's 4,960-acre property and then entered a 14-by-14-foot cinderblock room and exited it with thirty bags of cash and jewels. The detailed account by police reporter Bill Federici and rewrite man Owen Mortiz noted that the cargo area was bursting with cash as a Lufthansa flight had $2 million to $3 million aboard when it landed earlier, money earmarked for the Chase Bank.

The rest of the cash, jewels, and some canceled checks, which were worthless, was already on hand.

The Lufthansa shipment was not a regular occurrence. Someone had good information. It would turn out to be Louis Werner, an airport worker, who brought the information to Martin Krugman, his bookmaker, to whom he was in debt for a reported $20,000. Krugman to Hill to Burke. Because no one fails to keep a secret better than mobsters in bars, because one robber lifted his mask, because of the careless failure to properly dispose of a getaway car, the FBI was onto the Burke gang within days. For their efforts they watched bodies pile up, and no money was ever recovered.

"He was a stone killer," Steve Cerbone, the lead FBI agent on the case, said of Burke in an interview. "He was directly or indirectly involved in eleven or twelve murders in relation to the case."

But Cerbone and the FBI team that ultimately was given the case were not brought in for several days. Until then it was managed by the small airport squad and the local Port Authority Police. "By then they were able to get their stories straight. To be honest, it was just too late." The stories all synced up, Cerbone said. And the witnesses refused to talk. That plus Burke's brutal efforts at damage control stymied the investigation.

"A month after the heist," Cerbone said, "We got news that somebody was trying to kill him. He and his family were so hard core that his wife wouldn't let us into the house."

The FBI did manage to gather enough evidence to prosecute and convict Werner in 1979. By then, the Burke associates and airport workers who might have been able to provide information leading back to Burke were dead.

What Breslin did, over the course of columns beginning a few days after the heist and continuing through the Werner trial, was to bring everything to life in a way that could only be possible if you had drunk with, talked with, been beaten up by, walked the streets with and sounded, with your Queens accent, just like the men you were writing about who lived those fabled "second class" lives in the outer boroughs of the Imperial City.

Here he is in Howard Beach, which has not yet been made notorious by the mobster John Gotti nor had its deep-seated racism made public in "The Howard Beach Incident," in which a white mob chased a Black man to his death, when he ran onto a highway and was struck by a car. It also has not yet suffered the devastating noise of the supersonic Concorde airliner as it landed and took off from nearby JFK Airport. Howard Beach, therefore, was relatively unknown.

> It was dusk and the lights caused the ice on the edges of the canal to sparkle. . . . We were looking out at this from the bar of the clam shack . . . the two of us were having shrimp, mussels and calamari . . . The guy behind the counter asked me if I wanted a full apron instead of a napkin. I had dropped so much sauce on the front of my shirt . . . I was concentrating completely on the person I was with . . . My friend is a truck driver to the cargo area of Kennedy Airport, and he also is a thief.
>
> Police from four agencies feel he is involved in the $7 million holdup of the Lufthansa cargo terminal . . . So do I, which is why I intend to

> see him as much as possible from now on . . . I intend to become very famous writing about it.

This is Breslin, putting you inside the home turf of the robbers, and setting it up for the unnamed friend to speak. He is an interlocutor with a great sense of humor.

> The FBI calls up and they want to make an appointment . . . The major case squad needs something off me. They got a major case alright. I had my wife call them back. She told them that I went to the dentist and the dentist slipped and stuck the drill through my tongue. She told them I wouldn't be able to speak for a couple of months at least.
>
> "What happened after that," I asked him.
>
> "I went to the lawyer about it."
>
> "What does the lawyer say about this."
>
> "He says he hopes I done the robbery."

And now you know: Everyone in New York is cheering for the robbers.

In another column, published the day after Jimmy Burke declined to talk to the FBI and the paper reported that Burke was with Angelo Sepe, an associate of the Lucchese crime family and member of the Lufthansa heist gang, when the feds arrested him and charged him in connection with the heist, Breslin writes:

> Yesterday, a man on Jamaica Ave. who had witnessed the arrest on Saturday said that as the agents touched Sepe, Burke immediately started for them. That is in keeping with Burke's reputation: He never goes without a fight. He is big and active and has great resentment for authority that whiskey makes even stronger.

> But this time one of the agents told Burke that he was to go away, that this arrest did not concern him.

And now Breslin has shown us Burke in a way none of the other reporters can know him. He tells us about his youth hanging around the edges of the Aqueduct Racetrack. He tells us about the opening of Robert's Lounge near both the racetrack and the airport and how Louis Werner, also charged, lived around the corner and how Marty Krugman, his bookmaker, already deceased in between the heist and the column two-and-a-half months later, also drank there. And now we are in the barroom where the heist was planned.

By the next week he has put the heist in a context that his readers, rooting for the underdog, the robbers, understand.

> The announced figure is $5.8 million, but some people believe the Germans are underestimating their losses once more and that the true robbery figure is so high that it constituted the world's record take for criminals: legitimate people, of course, steal so much more that it is unfair to place your thief in a category with them.

And there we have it. The thieves and the outer borough second class citizens of New York City have common cause.

# DIES ROSEMARY DIES THE FAMILY

While the columns are being written, Breslin's wife Rosemary is dying. Breslin is seeking cures, consulting with doctors and attempting to manage his family, something foreign to him. On late night TV he hears of a possible cure. He explores it. The doctor who is supposed to have found the cure informs him that the television show's statements had no basis in truth. He had found no cure. The Lufthansa heisters, Burke and Burke's associates are aware of Breslin's struggles, which are also financial. And they seem to have learned of the same possible cure.

> Jimmy Grant came over. His wife, Dell, the singer at Pep McGuire's was Jimmy Burke's sister. Grant said "Jimmy has to talk to you right away. He's on the phone. . . .
>
> "You got to come down here," he said. "I got something for the cancer . . . Come down. I'm at the Villagio."
>
> That was a restaurant on Rockaway Boulevard that was owned by Dominick Cataldo, who was a nice little guy but had a terrible reputation for doing a lot of work. The expression "work" meant murder . . . I am faced with meeting Jimmy Burke and Dominick Cataldo alone on an empty sidewalk in the night. But why not? I know Jimmy a long time. He would never hurt me. Sure, I had written a lot about him running the Lufthansa robbery. That was business. How could I not write about a holdup that big, six million? . . . At the same time, he

> and his crew were insanely shooting anybody who could link them to the heist. The police were going crazy with bodies. . . . And now Burke had something he thought could help me. Something out of the nights of nurses and hospital and doctors . . . it still seemed only sensible to go down and to see Burke.

Breslin took a cab and brought along a friend who was a detective on the Queens burglary squad.

> As we were getting out of the cab, there was Jimmy Burke, alone, rumpled and loud.
>
> "Why is he here?" he yelled . . . "I'm not going to kill you."
>
> Jimmy then walked up to us. "I know Rose when you married her. The doctors know how to cure the disease. They won't do it unless they get paid. I got thirty-five thousand with me. I'll give it to you, and you give it to the doctor tomorrow, and he'll cure her. Don't worry about getting it back to me. I just want to see her cured."
>
> I told him thanks but we were involved with a whole hospital full of doctors and so I'll pass. "But I got to remember you forever."

And so he did, writing this in the book *The Good Rat*, which came over twenty-five years later.

We learn a lesson here that seems overlooked in many journalism classes. To write the truth and be able to look the person you write about in the eye is a guarantee that you will do your best to be accurate in your writing, and that guarantee will win the respect of any subject who is at least aware of who they are. Fewer reporters who pretend to work on the tough beats on the street do this than you might think.

Burke was never caught in connection with the Lufthansa heist, but he died in jail, nonetheless. He was convicted of fixing a basketball game at Boston College, which Breslin notes "was the alma mater of the federal prosecutor in Brooklyn, Ed McDonald, who never stopped until Burke was sent away for a long time. Jimmy had left a mountain of bodies . . . and they buried him on a missed layup."

Rosemary died in 1981. She was 50.

"Her death took the fun out of so much of the rest of life. No matter what," her son Kevin Breslin said.

Her descent into the final stages of the cancer came at the start of a decade that would be filled with some of the most powerful city reporting of Breslin's career. But it had begun years earlier, when he was drinking in the saloons of Queens. Heavily. Steadily.

"I was at New York University," Kevin said. "My father asked me to meet him and my mother at Desmond's bar on 53rd Street. Dessie Crofton was one of his best friends. It was in the afternoon. I guess she had just come from her first checkup. I remember my father told me that your mother has breast cancer and we're going to have to start dealing with it. It was sunny outside. It was spring but I remember a chill ran through my body and mind."

Desmond's was a small, dark place with low light. It could have been nighttime inside. Breslin was calm, and Rosemary had a smile on her face.

"He had a drink. And he was smiling. I was young at the time so I guess they were just trying to keep it buoyant but somewhere in my mind I know I didn't like any of it."

Now life became journeys to and from Queens to Dr. Kevin Cahill's suite on Fifth Avenue in Manhattan. And to many other doctors, anyone who might have a cure. Or an answer to "Why," which is really the question posed when the uncurable is unfathomable.

"When my mother died we were coming home at night on Queens Boulevard in the rain. And J.B. was just looking out the window and I swear he said . . . 'the Boulevard of Broken Dreams.'"

It could have been the same window he looked out of when he was waiting for his uncle to return from work to the house in South Ozone Park.

"He said to me after Rosemary died, 'Just go to work.' He was very stoic like that."

Where in the 1960s Breslin's lens was focused sharply on events that would shape our nation and its discourse for decades to come, in the 1980s he defined how to report from the five boroughs of America's largest city. He truly brought his City Column into its own.

At home: chaos.

"He was writing like mad. Kids were in school. It was a disaster," Kevin said. He was recalling the fact that even before his mother died, once she became incapacitated, Jimmy Breslin could not cope with life alone.

The first column now that she had died was simply his eulogy, reprinted by his editors:

> About a year ago, when she was unwell to the point where even she became unsure, she offered during prayer to her God a suggestion that she thought was quite good. Her youngest had experienced difficulty through the start of his schooling. Then suddenly, he had expressed great interest in attending one school. His mother developed great faith in the situation. And so, she proposed, give me this year while my son goes to this school. Let me try to help him as best I can. Then that should do it. He will be on his way. And I will be perfectly happy to be on my way. Providing the school works out.

Deals with gods, as we have known for centuries, rarely work out. But this one seemed to.

> Whatever she asked for, she appeared to be receiving. And now, the other day, from the depths of a hospital bed, with her body in revolt, she looked up and said, "The report card was pretty good. But now I don't feel like keeping my part of the deal." Which was her notion of fairness. For all her life, she believed that true evenhandedness meant that those in need always were allowed more. And now, at the end, she desired to follow her own counsel. So as she left us, she did so with that most elusive of qualities, a little bit of charm. We of her family who remain have a special burden. We have lived with nobility. She was a person who regarded life as one long attempt to provide a happy moment or so for another person. Always, she was outraged by those who rushed about, shouldering past others, their sides lathered with effort, horses in some cheap race, as they pawed for material success. She knew that life belonged to those who seek out the weary, sit with the defeated, understand the clumsy.

She was so much a partner, as well as an Italian mother, who cooked on Sunday, made sure the bills were paid, kept silence when her writer wrote, that in writing her eulogy he could have also been writing about himself. They shared these beliefs.

> She ran my life and those of her children almost totally. She leaves us with a tradition of decency that we must attempt to carry on. Her strength was such that even if those of us here today stumble now and then, I think the Rosemary Dattolico line of decency will reveal itself time after time in whatever generations there are to come.

"You never stop writing. You know that J.B. could never stop writing before it, and even after it even when he was crushed. After she died the house, empty and barren, just lost its soul.

"Even talking about it, trying to write a few words to you—just utterly heartbreaking." Kevin Breslin was 68 when he sent that email.

"We lived in such a unique world with Rosemary. She was 50 percent of the equation. Yeah he had the poetry. She had the poetry, humor and energy, love, and trust. That was an unstoppable combination."

She was gone. The paper came out every day. And his column appeared on its regular schedule. One wife. One death. One column.

> I work for newspapers, write a few books, and that's exactly what I should do, that's that for you, Breslin.
>
> I grew up being afraid of my feelings and suddenly my brain finds a way to make them my main strength. I replaced my feelings with what I felt were the feelings of others, and that changed with each thing I went to, so I was about sixty-seven different people in my life.

It was rare for Breslin to talk like this. And you really couldn't be sure if this was all of it. Or if he had peeled away just enough of the layers, once again, to let you see inside of a character. It is one that seems close to his core, though. He wrote it in a book that was rare, too: *I Want to Thank My Brain for Remembering Me: A Memoir.*

Rosemary Breslin died on June 9, 1981. Jimmy Breslin and Ronnie Eldridge were married on Sept 12, 1982. A year and three months later. There seems little time to waste in middle age. But seen through the prism of a child or a teenager or even a young adult who has lost a mother, it of course seems all too soon. Grief is so present. And now the six young Breslins would lose a childhood home as the father moved to Manhattan, which was where his new wife had spent her life. The animosity toward this second wife, a woman with a ready smile and a politician's ambition, would not end anytime soon. If ever.

If there are a few words you will see over and over in Breslin's work as he calls attention to his own condition, they are "broke," "money," "newspapers," and "drive." He identified himself as broke, he did everything possible to feel that way—making a mess of expenses, tossing his money onto bars, taking a car service wherever and whenever he could not find someone to drive him. In the chaos and sadness after Rosemary's death he remembered Ronnie, who he had met way back when she worked for Bobby Kennedy in 1968. He found her number and he called her. Things moved fast after that.

Marriage is a contract. And in every contract there are at least two sides. Love is written into vows. The partnership lies underneath those words. It takes nothing away from love. In Breslin's case, he was hopeless without a wife. Simply unable to live, let alone drive a car.

"We had a lot of fun," Ronnie Eldridge recalled. They would have had more fun without the kids, she might have said. This was around 35 years after the marriage vows.

And now that Jimmy was living on Central Park West, that other writer who never learned to drive and lived nearby, Murray Kempton, would stand on the sidewalk under the Breslin-Eldridge second floor window and they would converse before Murray remounted his bike and went on his rounds. A little fun there, too.

Joan Nassivera, who had been night city editor at the *News* when John Lennon died, later went on to be an editorial page writer. Before she went across town to *The Times*, she described Breslin succinctly.

"Yes, Jimmy was like a rare flower. He needed a lot of TLC. I will never forget the morning after Amy was born—actually the same morning as she entered the world at 12:18 A.M. and the phone next to my bed in the hospital room rang about 7, just as I was drifting off to sleep. Don't ask how he tracked me down, but the voice on the other end was unmistakable. Good thing since he never identified himself, just started right in: 'What's up. What's going on?'

"When I was working nights, Lou [Parajos, her husband at the time and an editor at the paper] often drove Jimmy around to wherever he needed to go for a column. So did I at times when I was free. I recall one Saturday taking him to Connecticut to a Sikorsky plant though I don't know what the column was about."

Driving is not in the normal job description of an important editor at a paper. But it was around Breslin.

And it was certainly in the job description for Rosemary, Ronnie, his sons, and his friends, as well as his editors.

Ronnie drove him, got him to events on time, arranged his insurance, his doctor and dentist appointments. Everything. And in the unwritten words beneath the vows, she got the power that came with being the spouse of a very powerful columnist.

But the partnership, according to a person who knew Ronnie, Jimmy, and all the kids both before the marriage and after the marriage and across both her political and his writing career, seemed to have no real room for the kids. Asked, there was no dispute on this point, nor that the father was a partner in this.

Childhood is always a lost country. It is for most, the first heist. It was so for Jimmy. For his children, who lived in sheltered chaos, the heist came late.

For the city of New York, while Lufthansa might have been the heist that delighted as the '70s drew to a close, the heists of the '80s were tales that included corruption and greed and fear and the theft of the public trust. In the post-Nixonian, post-Hope world, this was the landscape of New York.

When John Lindsay's first day in office as mayor was greeted with a transit strike, he was heard to say, "It's still a fun city." Dick Schaap at the *Trib,* when he sat down to write, turned that into the antithesis of a Chamber of Commerce appeal. "Fun City" was a city that at that time was already beginning to crumble. Now, nearly 20 years later, it was "Fear City."

# FEAR CITY

With it came Bernie Goetz.

On December 22, 1984, Goetz, who was white, boarded the downtown #2 train at 14th Street, the stop near his building on the same block. He shot four Black youths in the neck and in the back after one of them had asked him for five dollars. The case certainly called attention to the city's high crime rate. But more importantly, the case took the city's racial divide and turned it into a canyon far deeper than the 173 feet below ground of the deepest subway station at St. Nicholas Avenue.

Goetz was, for the moment, the subway vigilante, hero of the tabloids. He had shot four Black teenagers. Good. He surrendered to police after fleeing to Vermont for nine days. He got the best lawyers money could buy, for free in his case, and though charged with serious crimes, was convicted of carrying an unlicensed handgun and sentenced to eight months in jail.

Here, according to one Wikipedia account, is what Goetz said in a taped conversation with police: "Goetz told police that he felt that he was being robbed and was at risk of violence, and he explained he had been both mugged once before and nearly mugged several times . . . Asked what his intentions were when he drew his revolver, Goetz replied, "My intention was to murder them, to hurt them, to make them suffer as much as possible." Goetz also said that, after firing four shots, he moved to Cabey (one of the four) and said, "You seem to be doing all right, here's another," before shooting him again.

His words are eerily reminiscent of those of David Berkowitz, who when asked if he meant to harm his victims told the court, "No." Then, he explained, Son of Sam wanted to kill them.

Later in the tape, Goetz said, "If I had more bullets, I would have shot them all again and again. My problem was I ran out of bullets."

These remarks shot like electricity through the charged air.

> Before anybody knew anything about him, many people wound up cheering lustily on Christmas Eve for Goetz' act. As they cheered, one of Goetz' victims, a 19-year-old named Darrell Cabey, was discovering in St. Vincent's Hospital that he had no feeling from his belly button down. Bernhard Hugo Goetz' bullet had severed the spinal column.
>
> Yesterday, we learned a bit about Goetz, and his valor seems a bit questionable.

There is a lot more to learn about him and his actions. His admirers could dwindle as the facts present themselves.

This column was headlined: "The Gunner Grows Smaller as the Facts Mount."

On January 17, with Goetz still at the center of a storm of news coverage, opinion writing, and bar arguments, and front and center in the minds of all subway riders, Breslin took a leaf from the book of his own mayoral campaign, only this time with sarcasm that for once could be called effective:

> If the public decides to stop mouthing and to put its money and its votes behind Goetz, perhaps it can make this 37-year-old subway rider the Mayor of New York.

> One of the four shot by Goetz, Darrell Cabey, 19, went into his ninth day in a coma this morning. His backbone is severed because Goetz shot him in the back. New Yorkers claim they stand ready to cheer Goetz' actions. All right, then, let's go all the way. Cheer for gunfire and make Bernie Goetz the Mayor.
>
> So that people can express their support for Bernie Goetz, who as an expression of law and order shot four young Black people on a subway train, two in the back, and didn't even wing a bystander, we print today an important coupon.
>
> If you like what Bernhard Goetz stands for, then let him know. Put yourself on record. You don't even want Bernie Goetz tried. Forget law, lawyers, judge and court. Throw it out. Fill in the blank coupon and say that because Bernie Goetz shot people on the subway, you want him to be Mayor.
>
> Let's draft Bernhard Goetz for Mayor.
>
> No longer will I attack the public will. Instead I print herewith a coupon for the public to show whether we are in a new time, with Bernhard Goetz as your candidate and people applauding the coma of a Black he shot in the back.

What Goetz stole from the city cost it a lot more than five dollars. His bullets killed any hope of a sensible conversation about public safety and how it ought to be conducted, racial healing and how it ought to be accomplished.

Breslin's column continues, touching on each piece of what was stolen from its citizens by the city itself that led to Goetz and led to the applause for Goetz:

> He seems to be a hero at a time when the city has none. And he enters politics at a time when there is no politician around to challenge a Mayor who, despite his mouth that proclaims his invincibility, is quite weak because he has not done the work assigned to a Mayor.

Who knows more about subway shootings, Koch the Mayor or Bernie Goetz?

Who knows how to get things done, Koch the Mayor with his big mouth or Bernie Goetz with a good compact .38?

There are 26,800 New York City policemen and 5,800 civilian employes at a cost to taxpayers of $1,017,000,000 a year.

Yes, that is over $1,000,000,000 for police. Not including pensions.

Do you get $1,000,000,000 worth of protection?

And there are 3,820 Transit Police, with 338 civilian employes in that department. The cost to taxpayers is $144 million. This doesn't include pensions.

The total cost of these two police forces is $1,161,000,000.

And there was not one policeman on the No. 2 train when the four young Blacks approached Bernie Goetz on Saturday afternoon, Dec. 22, and he shot them all, two in the back, and one of them is in a coma and New Yorkers are cheering Bernie Goetz and paying $1,161,000,000 for police not to be on the train. . . .

Everyone knows that the most important part of the City of New York, the people riding the subway system, is largely unprotected. . . .

There is only one Bernhard Goetz. Where are these thousands of policemen? Who cost billions.

When we have Mayor Goetz in this city, there will be none of these questions anymore.

We will have only point-blank answers.

It is easy today to lose sight of a couple of things. One is just how important it was to have Breslin as a voice, a columnist on the pages of one of the largest newspapers in America, to speak out on these issues, hold a mayor to account, hold police to account and hold the reader to account. Today we have a badly fractured media landscape. There are few, if any, authoritative voices. Those that exist seem to serve as the clergy in a log cabin chapel, speaking only to the already faithful.

Though places like Axios, The City, ProPublica, and Politico all do a very good job of covering the news they choose or are able to cover, they do not offer a large voice and their audiences are so siloed as to often have little effect on government policy. TikTok had an US audience of about 150,000,000 in 2023, according to one estimate. One if four of those audience members were under twenty. while the combined prime time reach of Fox News, CNN, and MSNBC hovered around 3,900,000 at the end of 2023. Of those, only around half a million were under 55 years old.

# SIMPLY STUNNING

There are many ways to rip up a page of the social contract. Actions like Bernie Goetz's are just one of them. One of the most egregious comes when the part of the contract ripped up is that between police and citizens—which is to keep society safe for democracy, and citizens safe in traffic. It was ripped up by police once in Chicago during the 1968 Democratic convention and then it was very public—but now it was happening in New York, hidden inside housing projects and the grimy concrete holding cells of run-down police stations.

The Stun Gun case is a great example of how you can both do immediate harm, then harm the fabric of a city by breaking faith with the population and especially one large segment of it. The events leading up to it occur on a Wednesday night in 1985 when a young Black man and a young Black woman were seen talking on a corner in South Ozone Park and six white cops jumped out from an unmarked station wagon and came right at them. One in plainclothes. Five in uniforms. The allegation is that one of the young people was holding a marked $10 bill handed over by an undercover for the purchase of ten dollars' worth of marijuana. They were searched on the spot. First the young man. No such bill was found. Then the young woman. No such bill was found. Then the young woman again.

And that is where it begins at around 10 P.M. on Wednesday, April 17, 1985.

It is just under six months after an emotionally troubled, heavyset Black woman is killed inside her Bronx public housing apartment on October 29, 1984, with two blasts from a 12 gauge police shotgun. The allegation was that she was a danger to police. The police union highlighted this in ads that did little to defuse public anger.

It is a little over a year and a half after a graffiti artist named Michael Stewart dies on September 28, 1983, from what medical authorities deem strangulation while in police custody. There were no allegations that overcome the wail, "Oh my god, help me," that witnesses say they heard as a hogtied Michael Stewart struggled for life.

The steady, seemingly institutionalized tempo of apparent police brutality is now, with Breslin's sensational exposé, at a crescendo. The failure of police leadership is now in the spotlight.

> As Mark Davidson and Denise Memminger talked last Wednesday, a gray station wagon pulled up and, as both recall, six policemen jumped out, five in uniform and one in plainclothes. All were white.
>
> They searched Davidson for a marked $10 bill that they said had been given to him 10 minutes before by an undercover cop making a pot buy. Davidson insisted that they had the wrong person. He only had 26 cents in his pocket. . . .
>
> What six policemen were doing out on an alleged $10 pot buy is one small question. How six policemen could be involved in the sale and then manage to miss making the arrest on the spot is another. These points are quite small, however, compared to the charges about what happened next.
>
> The young woman was sent home. Mark Davidson says he was taken to the 106th Precinct. . . .

> Davidson said the tall man, who appeared to be in charge, took him into a room where, the teenager says, he then was punched in the right eye. Davidson had been to an eye doctor earlier that day for an examination and the doctor now certifies that there was no mark around either eye. Davidson then says that the tall man slammed his head into the wall twice. He says that the tall man then left the room and reappeared in street clothes and with a can of Budweiser beer. Davidson said the tall man again demanded to know about the $10. . . . when he did not answer, the man put something on his back which gave him an electric shock. He says that he yelled as loudly as he could when he was shocked.
>
> Davidson says he turned around and saw the tall man holding something that was black and fit in his hand and had two metal prongs about six inches long. The man then started to apply the prongs to Davidson's body, front and back, and sent shocks through him repeatedly. Davidson yelled. He says no other policeman entered the room to see what was causing the yelling.
>
> Davidson says that he believes the shocks went on for about 20 minutes. He says he yelled loud enough for anybody in the police station to hear him. He says that he asked to call his mother. The tall man with the instrument shocking his body refused his request, saying that they were not part of a television program. Davidson says the cop threatened to put the shock apparatus to his testicles. At that point, Davidson says, he made up the story about spending the $10 in a store. Davidson says that he made this up in order to get the cop to stop torturing him.
>
> The young man was taken to be booked at about 10 P.M. He was held until Thursday and a 7 P.M. court appearance.

There were twenty-two burns on the front of his body, twenty on the back. These were in sets of two as would be the case from a two-pronged prod capable, according to Breslin, of sometimes releasing up to 50,000 volts. And there was more: the electricity was also applied to his buttocks. In court, at the request of a prosecutor, the burns were videotaped. Though no one doubted the burns, there would now be an investigation into the cause, the torturer, and any accomplices. Afterward, in his office, his lawyer, Marvyn Kornberg, part of the defense bar aristocracy of Queens Boulevard and the criminal courts there, had Davidson hold up his shirt. The photographs were graphic. The burn marks ugly. Decades later they are still able to shock and disgust.

This was the start of the reporting. The *New York Times* picked up the trail the next day, and Breslin stayed on it, unrelenting in documenting each step of the aftermath.

By the end of the week, four police officers had been arrested, the Mayor of New York held a press conference to say the case "shocks the conscience," and the Police Department transferred the entire top command of the precinct. Queens District Attorney John Santucci told the media that his assistant who viewed the burns said they looked like fried flesh. Breslin returned to the precinct, the 106th (pronounced One Oh Six), and closed his first column by circling back to the tall man's offhandedly cruel remark about television drama as opposed to what happens in the real world.

> Yesterday in Ozone Park, on a lamppost in front of the 106th, there was a sign for a nonexistent cross-street. Hill St., the sign said. On any other day, this would have brought a smile. Seeing the sign in the gray morning yesterday only heightened the impression that the real police and those on television get confused in the minds of both public and police.

On the 23rd, Breslin's column takes us back to Queens and back to "Marvyn with a Y, Kornberg with a K," as the lawyer liked to remind reporters (and likely did at the press conference or afterward).

Somebody in the office asked him, "How clear did you see the faces of the cops?"

Kornberg interrupted. "That's for a court of law."

"How many times did you ask them to stop?" Davidson was asked.

"I'm not sure. It was a lot."

The questions were being asked by reporters, who leaned against office walls. Now photographers came in and Davidson was asked to stand up and show the burn marks. He stood and took off his shirt. A big strong handsome kid with these evenly spaced burn marks across his stomach and back. Forty two of them.

"You're a big kid. How did they hold you down?" he was asked.

"I was handcuffed behind the back."

The press conference ended soon after this because Kornberg and his 18-year-old client had an appointment at the District Attorney's office.

Inside, he would go over the photos of New York City policemen and try to pick out two who were torturers.

It was five o'clock by now, and from the regular offices of Borough Hall, from the sewer department and the real estate taxation offices, women streamed out and headed home.

One group, seeing the crowd following Davidson, stopped and watched.

"I know who that is," one woman, a burly blond, said. "That's the guy that the cops beat up."

"They didn't beat him up, they charged him up with electricity," the one next to her said.

"Could you imagine that?" the blond said. "Whoever heard of a thing like that?"

"And in Queens," her friend said.

> Upstairs, Davidson sat at a table and was shown a card on which were eight new color photos of policemen. He looked and immediately pointed at the second picture on the card.
>
> "He put the machine on me," Davidson said. "I don't have to look at anybody else."
>
> He then was shown a second sheet of photos. The finger went to one picture immediately.
>
> An officer from the Internal Affairs Division then pulled out an envelope, vouchered by the property clerk—obviously the result of a search—and took from the envelope a small black electrical device. The device had light fingerprint dust on it. The Internal Affairs officer asked Davidson if he had seen the device before.
>
> "I can't tell you, because I was in pain," Davidson said. "But that looks like it."

And now that a youth facing charges of selling a $10 bag of marijuana was no longer to be on trial, the city of New York and its police would be suspected of being capable of torture.

> Then Mark Davidson walked out into a wet Queens night and went home. He had to get up for school in the morning.

And Breslin continued to keep the case under a strong spotlight. At the beginning of May, just over a week after the first column, he explained:

> Kornberg stared at the burn marks and left Davidson and went downstairs and found an assistant district attorney, David Everett. He told Everett what he had just seen. Everett said that it should be reported to the Police Department's Internal Affairs Division. Everett called from the courthouse and was told by the division that this was a matter for the Civilian Complaint Review Board. Everett then called a special field

Internal Affairs unit. The answer was the same. . . . Everett decided that the district attorney's office would look into the case without the help of police. As Queens District Attorney John Santucci was born in the 106th Precinct, attended school there, represented it in the state Legislature and still lives there, only a few blocks from the stationhouse, there was no question about how intensive the investigation would be. There also was another dimension: If a case of this magnitude, occurring in his own neighborhood, ever got by Santucci, his present job—a very good job for a guy from Ozone Park—soon would be a memory. His future would be gone. Santucci, who likes both job today and promising future, had flames coming out of the sidewalks in front of the 106th. Here was a department which allegedly was responsible for an 18-year-old Black youth, handcuffed behind his back, being tortured with an electrical device by at least two white cops, with others present, in a precinct in Queens and would not even take a phone call of complaint about it.

In Queens, once so many were raised as the children of policemen, perhaps as many as five members of the Police Department of the City of New York could be under indictment on charges spreading from the alleged torturing with electricity of a helpless and handcuffed teenager in the 106th Precinct in Ozone Park.

Always in New York, a police scandal meant payoffs from bookmakers, prostitutes or the narcotics traffic. Commissions were established. Prosecutors had great careers and there was always a sort of hero cop who came forward with assorted tales which enchanted movie producers. But through the Gross bookmaking scandal and Serpico and the Knapp Commission, the problem was only over money.

Those policemen expected to be dragged into court in Queens would be there on charges of torturing citizens, an act usually associated with another century or continent. None of the policemen lives in this city. But they have made us all lousy.

Even looking at the event through a rearview mirror filled with other ugly incidents involving police officers, even in the aftermath of the sick and sickening August 1997 anal assault with a police nightstick on Abner Louima, this torture by electric shock of a handcuffed 18-year-old stands out simply because it is the kind of thing seen in dictatorships somewhere else.

Even after the July 17, 2014, death of Eric Garner in police custody when an outlawed chokehold was used to strangle his breathing.

Even after the May 25, 2020, murder of George Floyd by a policeman who pressed and held his knee onto a Black man's neck with no apparent sense of history, irony, or humanity.

Even after all these atrocities this burning of a young man's flesh, which happened inside a police precinct where dozens would have been on duty, stands out. In the aftermath the highest rank available to talk was a sergeant. The Police Commissioner was in San Francisco, junketeering. Even after these and the local and national and international protests we have seen, the attack on Mark Davidson remains high in the pantheon of deranged abuse of the only official power that matters on the street: the power of police. Because, on the street, the highest ranking government official you are likely to see is a police officer. Perhaps even a sergeant.

# BOULEVARD OF BROKEN SCHEMES

Michael Dowd, a Queens Blvd. attorney, last night told the United States attorney's office in Manhattan that Donald Manes, the Queens borough president, extorted money from him for a period of 18 months.

This revelation causes the city's Parking Violations Bureau scandal to detonate . . .

That was how Breslin began his column on Wednesday, January 22, 1986. It would run on Page One of Thursday's editions. Inside, accompanying it on the page where the column continued, was a news report by Barbara Ross that the editor, Gil Spencer, wanted there because it would stick simply to the facts, with no opinions, conclusions, or characterizations. It would balance the column with reporting and put it in a context.

A year that began with the January 1 inauguration of a euphoric Ed Koch for a third term in office as the mayor of New York, now saw that third term already unraveling, and many of the same honored guests who braved the cold that day to sit on folding chairs in City Hall Plaza and listen to what was reported to be a twenty-minute inaugural address, would now or soon be under investigation. They included Koch appointees and Koch political cronies. They included the political powerhouses of the Democratic machines in the Bronx, Stanley Friedman, and in Queens, Donald Manes. Meade Esposito, the lion of Brooklyn politics, now in his late seventies, stayed in the sunshine of Ft. Lauderdale, Florida. He too would be subject to an investigation. Another guest was a federal prosecutor. He already was pondering his case.

This, and so much more, is detailed in the comprehensive 1988 book *City for Sale* by Wayne Barrett and Jack Newfield. The investigative team noted that Koch in his first two terms as mayor, beginning just as the city's fiscal mess was ending, had done much to create wealth, power, and influence for at least one group of New Yorkers, many of whom were Manhattan dwellers for whom the word "more" ought to be attached to the words wealth, power, and influence, while not benefiting others in the working and middle classes. Many of those also were people of color. The third term would not be as lucky for Koch and his cronies.

There was another reason that Barbara Ross's byline was on that story: Ross had been working on the story since New Year's Eve, 1985, when she sat, virtually alone, under the white acoustic tiled ceiling of the *News* city room, poring over transcripts. And it was her knock on Michael Dowd's door, she said in an interview, that appears to have led the attorney and small collections agency owner to confess to Breslin on Friday, January 17, and to the US Attorney, a man named Rudy Giuliani, who had for months been working on this municipal corruption case. Ross's work and that of her colleagues at the *News* would help break open the sprawling case, and soon overlapping public corruption cases would be brought in state and federal court. They would come to include towing contracts; the Taxi and Limousine Commission, which oversaw valuable and scarce cab medallions; cable contracts; junkets; and the exchange of favors. Transportation officials and the head of the city hospital system would resign.

In a case that also had proximity to Ed Koch at its center, though was otherwise unrelated to the other cases, Bess Myerson, the first Jewish Miss America, who had played the role of Koch's campaign spouse, was indicted when she and her lover Andy Capasso, a sewer contractor who was married when their affair began, were investigated by the federal government. A judge's daughter had been given a job with Myerson. That judge had reportedly reduced Capasso's alimony payments from $1,500 to $500 per month. The interlocking fiefdoms of Koch's administration and the pay-for-play Democratic political machine that helped elect Koch and had used their power to award and steer contracts and obtain key city jobs for cronies began to be laid bare in the same cold sunlight of January.

How one probe led to another, one name led to another, and one crime led to another all of this, years later, can be viewed under the same umbrella name that Barrett and Newfield used as their title: City For Sale. The Parking Violations Bureau scandal was a perfect eye to this storm. You take too long eating your lunch. The meter runs out and you get a ticket. You forget to pay the ticket or toss it out. It goes to a collection agency. The agency sends dunning letters, and it gets a percentage of what is squeezed out of the taxpayer. To get these contracts worth millions of dollars, the collection company owners—Dowd for a time among them—pay bribes to politicians. It was a wonderful way to turn unpaid quarters into millions of dollars. This was better than even the best airport heist. You can only rob Lufthansa one time, and if you kill enough witnesses, you might never get caught. Parking meters, someone said, never grow old. They keep on earning.

In 1987, Meade Esposito was convicted in another public corruption case—providing a spa vacation to a Bronx congressman—in federal court in Brooklyn. Asked by reporter Phil Messing of the *New York Post* about his involvement in patronage, Esposito said, "Hey Phil, I didn't go into politics to become a poor man."

When Breslin appeared in the *News* on January 23, he would introduce the world to major characters in the New York case, which centered around his stretch of Queens Boulevard. that included Borough Hall; the Pastrami King restaurant where everyone who worked in the courts would regularly get something; a couple of bars that until the Lufthansa heist had only local notoriety; and a few second-floor law offices, the kind that always smelled damp with sweat and plea bargain deals and had dented file cabinets, not portraits of esteemed founding partners who went to Groton and Yale.

Overnight this stretch of concrete went from being the Boulevard of Broken Dreams to the Boulevard of Broken Schemes. Until that column, the Breslin stories and the reports by Ross and her colleagues including Brian Kates that had begun appearing on January 12 had been nameless, faceless, filled with hint and suggestion. Now they came to life:

> Michael Dowd, a Queens Blvd. attorney, last night told the United States attorney's office in Manhattan that Donald Manes, the Queens borough president, extorted money from him for a period of 18 months . . .
>
> Dowd, a light-haired, 43-year-old man who has spent his life in Queens, is one of the most important witnesses ever to step out of the crowd that always is silently and frantically shoving for better grabbing room at the junction of politics and crime in the City of New York.

The New York scandal, the pieces of which were there in Barbara Ross's transcripts and provided the underpinning of Giuliani's investigation, began with a probe in Chicago. Systematic Recovery Service (SRS), a collection company owned by a man named Bernard Sandow, had been paying bribes to municipal officials in order to win city contracts in Chicago and in New York. The government's informant and FBI undercover operative in Chicago was a killer named Michael Burnett, who worked for SRS. The audio and video he collected did not provide actionable evidence of a New York City crime, but made it abundantly clear that Sandow was paying off New York City officials. At the behest of the FBI, a reporter named Gaeton Fonzi, of *Miami/South Florida* magazine, held off publishing the information he had developed about the bribery scheme for nearly a year. In exchange, he had been allowed to sit in on investigative conferences and record government briefings. On December 20, he published. He then called Gil Spencer at the *News*. Spencer, who respected Fonzi's work, retained him. And the transcripts of the government briefings were put in the hands of Ross.

That is how she recalls the unraveling of a key element of the largest and most lucrative political corruption scandal in New York since William Magear "Boss" Tweed, who in the 1800s raked off so much city money and controlled so much patronage that his name is now synonymous with municipal corruption. Tweed, while he may not have sold us the Brooklyn Bridge, would not allow it to be built until he had a seat on the board of The Brooklyn Bridge Company.

At the outset, the *Daily News* owned the story. The discovery that several of Breslin's people, notably Klein the Lawyer; Borough President Donald Manes; and the small collection agency owner, Michael

Dowd, were at the heart of it both pulled the paper ahead, and caused Breslin, in his own mind, embarrassment. He had been betrayed.

"This is the scandal of our times and from now on I will bring it to you first and with the most fury because I am personally aroused. I have been betrayed on my own Boulevard," he wrote.

During his evening with Dowd, Breslin encouraged him to go and tell his story to the federal prosecutor.

It was a story Giuliani very much needed in order to solidify his case.

Although he had Sandow cooperating, until now, he did not have someone who could place Manes squarely at its center.

In a conversation that took place over bowls of clam chowder, Breslin told Dowd that in the free-for-all that is the process of gathering cooperating witnesses, he'd better get down to the prosecutor's office and get the first punch in.

This work on the part of Breslin led Guiliani to only a little grudgingly say to the *Washington Post* that Breslin "deserves a lot of credit for encouraging people to come forward and cooperate . . . at the core, Breslin is an idealistic guy. He holds public officials to a high standard." Breslin had some praise for the prosecutor as well, though years later he watched Giuliani fail to hold himself to that standard and described him as "a small man in search of a balcony," a characterization which only an accident will keep from being in one of the first sentences in Giuliani's obituary.

Ross, who could be mild and friendly as a neighbor or a colleague, was at heart an aggressive reporter who, when she was onto something, needed little sleep, little food, and no one to point her out the door.

She had continued, as she would for months to come, to work late and work through holidays. By the time she was done with her work on the PVB case, which would include sorting through hundreds of tips, fact checking, digging, and calling, she would have accumulated eight months of overtime. If you know newspapers, you know she was never paid.

On New Year's Day she came to the office and used highlighters to emphasize parts of transcripts she found interesting. She had started working her way through the names and the dollar figures and the hints.

But it only took two of those days to get enough for the first story, one that could say there was a public corruption scandal brewing in New York, and it involved the Parking Violations Bureau (PVB). By Thursday, January 2, she had called Rudy Giuliani. Minutes later, Rudy called her boss, City Editor Arthur Browne, and according to Barrett and Newfield, by the next day Ross and Browne were down at the US Attorney's office on St. Andrew's Plaza. Rudy begged for a week in which to keep building his case. Browne pressed for details, and the *News* finally agreed to hold off on a day-by-day basis, while the government continued its investigation. Browne and Ross knew, based on the transcripts in hand, the paper already had enough for a story. But they would wait.

Meanwhile, Ross and her colleagues, including Brian Kates and the political journalist Lars-Erik Nelson, continued digging.

"So first order of business was trying to put my arms around what we had," Ross said.

Then on Friday, the Queens Borough President, Donald Manes, "The King of Queens," was found weaving down the highway at about 1:45 A.M. with his wrist already slashed when he was pulled over by Highway Patrol officers and came to a stop against a wire fence that ran alongside an exit ramp on the Eastbound Grand Central Parkway. The stories published in Chicago and Florida had been enough to alert Manes and his cronies that their scheme was coming unraveled.

There were phone calls. There were meetings. Manes plunged into a depression.

"There was blood all over the steering wheel, the seat, and the floor, and it filled the pocket on the door where maps are kept," Barrett and Newfield wrote.

Later in the day, Ross told an interviewer, she turned to Browne: "So I poke him in the ribs and say, wouldn't it be funny if this story, the Fonzi story is related to that story, which is the Manes story, which was being done two desks away." She didn't have any facts connecting Manes to PVB. But she was still way ahead of any pack.

"Even Barbara Ross did not connect the slashed wrist of Donald Manes to the PVB story she was writing with Brian Kates," said Barrett and Newfield.

Giuliani honored his agreement and called Browne and told him he had learned another paper was onto the story.

The first story appeared on Sunday: "FBI Investigating Payoffs to City Parking Officials." It didn't name names, but it did set the municipal government into a tailspin. Bagmen, including the deputy director of the parking bureau, would soon be talking, big name lawyers were retained, Manes knew he was no longer the King of Queens and the bribes he had collected would soon come to light. His next attempt at suicide came later, and it was successful. He had plunged a kitchen knife into his own heart. There would be no extortion charges.

The parking meter collections contract component of the widening scandal, it would now become clear, had been orchestrated on Queens Boulevard, from the Borough President's office. Between that office and the bar once owned by the now-deceased city marshal Shelly Chevlowe, all of its players fed their egos and their pockets. Some for seven years or more. Breslin had spoken at Chevlowe's funeral service.

He had cried. Above a nearby bar, where Breslin, rogues, judges and lawyers drank, was the office of Klein the Lawyer, operating under his real name: Mel Lebetkin.

A call came into the newsroom after that first story appeared. Ross was tied up. Her colleague Don Gentile took the call and kept the caller on the line. Ross recalled that Gentile, a rogue even by tabloid standards of the time, was the only person in the newsroom who could convince someone to fall in love with him on a first phone call.

"I mean, that is a totally hilarious story where she I think fell in love with Don Gentile on the call," Ross said. "That's the only way to fall in love with him: one call."

By the time he was done, they had enough to grab their coats and head to the caller's door, which they would stake out overnight, drinking coffee and staying awake until she came out to walk her dog.

"Gentile and I went running out . . . and then we sat in a McDonald's . . . until the sun came up waiting for her to walk her dog so that we could grab her." The information she provided gave Ross fresh insight into the material back in the office on her desk.

"Now I've got this rule as a result of this story: all good stories start on napkins. Because I find a piece of paper and I'm writing. I'm writing names of these guys who were earning hundreds of thousands. And it's all on a napkin. It's the first thing I saw."

She showed the napkin to Browne.

"He said, 'That's Breslin's guy.' "

"And I said, which one?"

"He said, 'Lebetkin.' "

"I said, what do you mean?"

He said, "Klein the Lawyer." Then he pointed her in the direction of Breslin's office.

"I hadn't met Breslin. I was intimidated by Breslin. I walked in and I said, I am so delighted to meet you.

"Arthur Browne says this guy—and I handed it to him—this guy is, is Klein the Lawyer, is that right?"

At that moment, a colorful character who Breslin had portrayed as representing the guilty, misrepresenting himself to women, and failing to keep the women's names straight and who had provided delight since first introduced by Breslin was no longer a character. He was a person at the center of a criminal investigation.

In *The World According to Jimmy Breslin,* the editors reported: "It is Jimmy Breslin's proudest boast that one of the most successful and enduring of his newspaper column 'characters,' a grasping, impecunious counselor-at-law named Klein the Lawyer, first saw the light of print in the pages of *The New York Times*. . . . *The Times* was planning a special section of Super Bowl coverage and invited Breslin, who had once been a sportswriter himself, to send in a piece of fan reaction . . . Breslin chose to write about a group of guys watching the game on a television screen . . . the central figure of this little tableau being a person he identified as Klein the Lawyer. . . . 'Right there in the headline.' "

Now he was identified as Lebetkin. Right there on the napkin.

Ross grew up in a middle class household in Elmont, on Long Island, where the suburban County of Nassau kissed the sprawling borough of Queens. Her family got piles of newspapers on the weekend. She would have liked to read Pete Hamill, but her mother said Breslin made her laugh. Barbara Ross can still hear that laugh. She heard something else now. The Klein who could make you laugh was Lebetkin. The Breslin who could make you laugh remained Breslin.

"Fuck, fuck, fuck, fuck, fuck. He said it about sixty times in five minutes.

"I said, well, you know, I've been trying to call him and so far he hasn't called back. I just wondered, you know, what you knew about this? And he picked up the phone.

"You know, Breslin's style for the phone calls is not to say, hi, this is Jimmy. It's: 'They were stealing a fucking million dollars in the fucking city of New York. And you didn't fucking tell me, idiot. I don't know. Some c— walked into my office and told me.'

"I'm just like, my God."

She looked over at two other newsers who were present. They shrugged and told her not to worry: "He's that way with everybody."

She had her confirmation that Lebetkin was involved. And she filed Breslin's characterization of her in a forgiving place. When she later brought it up to him, he was embarrassed, and she now expresses the hope that perhaps it was the tumor already growing in his brain that caused the outburst. (The tumor later became the touchstone for his memoir *I Want to Thank My Brain for Remembering Me: A Memoir.*)

Lebetkin's roles as Klein, and as Donald Manes's secret partner in a collection agency, would be exposed a few weeks after Ross's visit.

By then, Breslin's role was one that mixed protagonist and author in a way he had not done since his run with Norman Mailer for city office in their secessionist bid in 1969.

Ross, thwarted in her calls to Lebetkin, was also rebuffed in her call to Michael Dowd a few days later.

She grabbed a cola, got in her car, gulped it down, drove to Queens, and rang his doorbell.

Dowd said he could not let her in. Okay, she said, but I've driven all the way here. I've drunk a whole bottle of diet soda. Can I use your bathroom? She did. And then standing in Dowd's living room, they talked, and she was getting enough to inform her reporting. She drove back to Manhattan.

By then Dowd had already called Breslin.

Breslin and Dowd met in Costello's bar at 225 E. 44th Street. It was one of those places, consigned now to history, which never should be seen in the light of day, but which at night had bottles that sparkled like Christmas presents and the wonder of words in the air.

The column began on Page One. It ran under a four word headline: "Manes Accused of Extortion."

Four words in thick, bold, black sans-serif *Daily News* Graphik type proved again why the blue collar tabloid continued to be a powerhouse that could shake government to its roots and why Breslin gave it a voice that no other newspaper could claim.

Under the headline, Breslin's logo, two columns wide.

> Before you judge the scope of this scandal, you might want to know how the politicians steal from you. . . .
>
> The "first placement" firms then keep from 35% to 40% of monies collected. One such firm, called Systematic Recovery Services, which is the long way to say "dun," owned by Bernard Sandow, who is another important federal witness in this scandal, earned $7 million in the last three years . . .
>
> Dowd entered this scandal as a partner in a collection firm. He now reports that he and Manes stood on a sidewalk after a funeral service at Schwartz Brothers on Queens Boulevard in Forest Hills, and Dowd says that Manes at that time told him who to pay and how much to pay. He said Manes told him, "See my friend Geoff." At first Dowd said he didn't know who Geoff was. Manes said, "My friend Geoff. Geoff

> Lindenauer." He then told Dowd the percentage of earnings that he was to turn over to Geoff. On Manes' sidewalk directions, Dowd says, the money subsequently was paid to Geoffrey Lindenauer, the deputy commissioner of the city's Parking Violations Bureau. Lindenauer was last seen in handcuffs in a hallway in federal court as he was being brought in on a charge that he took a $5,000 payment in the men's room of a restaurant, the traditional loading dock for New York politicians. Lindenauer is from Queens . . .

By the time this column is done, a congressman is named, and that powerful Queens Democrat is connected to Dowd, though not to the scandal; Manes has been put at its center; Sandow's information is confirmed; and a city official is identified as corrupt. It has all been spelled out very simply. And we are again on the streets of Queens that brought us many of Son of Sam's crimes, the Lufthansa gang's score, Jimmy "the Gent" Burke's nine or ten or twelve directly connected murders, the stun gun case, and Breslin himself. We were in Breslin's world that ended at the breakers of the Rockaways and the airport runways, and Breslin was angry. The biggest crime of all had been committed: Breslin's friends, who he drank with, laughed with, and wept with had conducted a years-long scheme under his nose.

"This is the scandal of our times and from now on I will bring it to you first and with the most fury because I am personally aroused. I have been betrayed on my own Boulevard."

Ross brought us the next installment on January 28 in a report on Page Four: "2d Lawyer Set to Sing," read the understated headline. No big capital letters here.

Under the headline we learned that Melvin Lebetkin, attorney, and collections agency owner, with a secret partner named Donald Manes, was willing to admit he delivered $100,000 in bribe money to the deputy director of the Parking Violations Bureau. And we learned that while Dowd was viewed by the government as a victim of extortion, and would likely not be prosecuted, Lebetkin, if he could cut a deal, likely would have to cut one that would send him to prison. It did not seem he made any payments out of fear. Greed seemed enough to motivate him.

On February 9, Breslin wrote about Lebetkin, but did not yet identify him as Klein. But he wrote about him with the intimacy that those familiar with his reporting had come to expect.

> Melvin Lebetkin arises in winter darkness each morning and like so many people on Queens Blvd., he puts on an all-news radio station, either 1010 or 880. Lebetkin never used to listen, but at this time, Lebetkin is part of the news; in fact some days, Mel Lebetkin is the news.
>
> At six o'clock the other morning, Lebetkin awoke and put on 1010, whose lead item was: "Federal investigators today say that a key figure in the parking violations scandal also has been linked to corruption in judges. Queens attorney Melvin Lebetkin . . ."
>
> "Oh, my God," Lebetkin said.
>
> He switched to 880 CBS all-news all day. It was only a couple of minutes after six, and CBS was into the world and national news: . . . Lebetkin relaxed as he listened to the world news. What Lebetkin did not realize was that CBS goes from 6 A.M. until 6:06 A.M. with its world and national report. And then at 6:06 A.M., it swings right into metropolitan New York coverage. And at 6:06, at the very instant that Mel Lebetkin was pouring himself coffee, the CBS show zipped from Manila to:
>
> "Federal investigators today, say that a key figure in the parking violations scandal has been linked to corruption in judges. Queens attorney Melvin Lebetkin . . ."

"Oh, my God," Lebetkin said. He switched back to 1010, where a newscaster soon said: "Repeating the headlines . . ."

"Oh, my God," Lebetkin said. He called a friend. "Get up right away."

"What for?"

"They are making me one step below Nixon!"

Probably, in this particular case they were.

As the owner of the Standard Collection company, Lebetkin says he was told to pay, and did, about $100,000 to Geoffrey Lindenauer, the deputy commissioner of the city's Parking Violations Bureau. But he became the man of the day in the city's news once the reports came out on the all-news radio. His secretary called him up. "They have a crowd of cameras and reporters out in the hall." Suddenly these days, news reporting has taken its billion-dollar technology and returned to the oldest methods of covering news: You now see television crews hiding in doorways and staking out hallways and restaurants. Ben Hecht with a microphone.

*The Times*, where those who once doubted Klein's existence dwelled, now became the news organization to identify him as Lebetkin. Any hope of keeping Breslin's character in business—the business of filling his column—was gone.

From late 1975 on, the character Klein the Lawyer was the property of this column and he did wonderfully well. He was a man who had trouble getting paid from the criminals he represented and then he had trouble with women in the bar downstairs from his office. . . .

Klein's real name never appeared: Melvin M. Lebetkin. He was a charming, popular attorney on Queens Blvd. and he liked the Klein name very much, and so did everybody else. At *The Times* newspaper, in the low-energy set, the Ivy League people, not knowing their own history, passed remarks about fictitious characters being used in newspapers.

That history, of course, included the doubter, A.M. Rosenthal, executive editor of that newspaper, having had his head berthed in the cleavage of a Lufthansa stewardess, turned believer, while Fat Thomas, whose existence he once had doubted, looked on. This is how Breslin later described the loss of his character:

> And so we came to the great New York City scandals, the largest in the nation's history.
>
> The scandals began right out on Queens Blvd. with the Parking Violations Bureau.
>
> "What do you think of this?" I asked my close friend, Klein the Lawyer, or Lebetkin.
>
> "I don't think much of it," he said.
>
> "Know anything?"
>
> "I'm glad I never knew what those guys were doing."
>
> And then it suddenly was disclosed that attorney Melvin Lebetkin had one of those collections firms that did work for the agency.
>
> "They better not tell any lies about me in the grand jury!" Lebetkin said.
>
> At that time, like everybody else in Queens, you could tell who was in trouble or who wasn't by background noise. Those in trouble had on the all-news radio, waiting to hear their names, and those with nothing to fear spoke with silence behind them.
>
> And so one morning at 5:45 A.M. the phone rang and I stumbled into the kitchen and picked it up and here was Lebetkin yelling at me over the sound of his all-news radio.
>
> "They are ruining me," he shouted.
>
> "Who?"
>
> "*The Times The Times.*"
>
> I grabbed the paper that morning and I found that *The Times* sure had done a lot of damage.

Not only did they have a major story about Lebetkin on the first page but they went ahead and identified him as being Klein the Lawyer.

"My character got stolen!" I wailed.

He sure did. Lebetkin now was in the flow of news. Which was a terrible thing for me, for in the years in which I must do this column, in the 1970s and '80s, there are virtually no characters in New York. . . .

Suddenly he was lifted away from me and I was left with only a man Lebetkin, who had to serve as a grubby news source. Klein the Lawyer, at least for the length of the scandals, was dead.

# A PRIZE NAMED FOR A PUBLISHER

In April, they awarded the Pulitzer Prizes. Jimmy Breslin had won in one of the fourteen categories, "Commentary."

Mutchie, the bar owner who had come north from the fish market area to Columbia University's World Room in 1964 when Breslin had won the Meyer Berger award—an award that Breslin noted was named for a reporter, not an owner—was not able to be present owing to the fact that he since had died.

Mutchie had ventured uptown then, wearing a blue topcoat and a well-pressed gray suit, it was reported by Breslin, "for a tour of the academic facilities and also to attend the Meyer Berger Award ceremonies . . . Mutchie is interested in journalism because so many newspapermen owe him money. He was very interested in the Berger ceremonies because one of the winners, who received 500 dollars, was one of Mutchie's prized debtors."

> "I brought everything with me," Mutchie said.
>
> "What's everything?"
>
> "All your tabs," he said. "One of them here goes back 13 months."

As a result of changed circumstances Breslin could now, come fall, view the Thanksgiving Day Parade from his windows looking out on the green expanse of Central Park. He was able to keep the $1,000 that came with the certificate that later would hang on the wall of his apartment.

The Pulitzer Board, which included a Pulitzer, Joseph Pulitzer III, who was a grandson of the great sensationalist journalist; a Black man; a woman; at least two bow ties and some of the most important names in journalism, said he won it for columns which "consistently champion ordinary citizens." If the word "ordinary" had been dropped, the sentence might have been less well rounded, but it would have had the two virtues of accuracy and brevity.

The columns on Bernie Goetz, the stun gun case, and a series on the AIDS disease told through one young man's struggle were cited by the jury as evidence of the body of winning work.

He appears, nose to the sky, cigar in a smiling mouth, flanked by the editor and the publisher on the cover of the next day's *News.*

Don Singleton, who in 1977 had smoothly reported in Saturday editions the coming of Son of Sam letters to Breslin in the *Sunday News*, wrote the story that appeared Friday, April 18, on Page Two.

"Breslin, a vigorous two-fingered typist . . . whose talent and energy are exceeded only by his self-confidence accepted the tribute with his usual grace," reported Singleton. " 'The truth?' he said when the applause had died down, 'I had won it in my mind so long ago I don't know what it's for. That's the truth.'

" 'It's something I'm glad came here at the *Daily News*. Anyone can win it at *The New York Times* or *Washington Post*—they give them out. . . . I think everybody got a piece of it because I had an awful lot of help with all the stuff I turned in.' "

"I've always been the best," the Associated Press added in its account. "They caught up with us today. Fine, good, I congratulate the Columbia Journalism School for giving it to me."

"Breslin is Breslin," *Daily News* Managing Editor James Willse told the wire service. "In a lot of ways, he is his own genre. People who have been reading Breslin over the years understand that Klein the Lawyer is, on the one hand, a mythical character, and on the other hand, he is totally real. Devices like that give Breslin the latitude he needs for what he does best."

He left the cheers behind in the newsroom when he spoke to David Camacho, the young man whose struggles with AIDS he told in a vivid way that conveyed the pain of a disease then shrouded in ugly bias and misunderstanding.

"I got the prize and you got chemotherapy," Breslin said he told Camacho. This account, buffed and polished and published, really captures both his gruffness and his warm heart.

# TRUTH, JUSTICE & THE COMICS

He had thrown himself across the long couch and he looked like a homicide detective, worn out but still smiling with his tie undone and still wearing his raincoat.

He alternated slapping through the pages of his reporter's notebook and tearing pieces of a fresh loaf of Italian bread and dunking the buttered heel and all that followed into a cardboard container of coffee, letting the crumbs fall onto his shirt. He kept smiling.

His head was back against one arm of the couch, his feet in black, thick shoes, were dangling off the side.

He had already been at work for several hours.

Sitting as straight in his chair in the corner as an American Gothic was Murray Kempton. His suit was neat, his tie was narrow, and he punctuated what he said with his cold pipe. An Episcopalian minister on a Monday morning, the Baltimore-born columnist was not yet too troubled by the writing of his next sermon.

In his thick suspenders, his dark colored shirt and too-wide-for-the-decade tie, behind the editor's desk sat Don Forst, Editor of *New York Newsday*. On the desk were a pair of glasses, a concession; they rested on their rims with the arms already out so they were easy to pick up and put on. There was also a conceit, his copy of *The Prince* by Niccolo Machiavelli by way of the Opinion Page editor, Tom Plate, who thought it never hurt to have a reminder at hand that it was better to be feared than loved.

Forst had been at work since 4:00 A.M. when he had pulled his first perfect cup of espresso from the gleaming wonder of the commercial grade espresso machine that held a place of pride in his Tribeca loft in the old Thread Building.

He knew full well how to manipulate love and fear and how to imagine, create, build and drive a newspaper. These were the things he knew how to do well. There were many other things he could not do well at all.

Each of these three men was complicated. One lived in chaos. One could be cold and distant. Forst, he was an editor. He had a dark spot on his soul that even those who admired him could not ignore. And he was single minded. Monomaniacal. Gael Greene, the restaurant critic who defined a genre and met him while at the *New York Post* said, with a great deal of affection, that she knew their marriage was over when he dropped her breast to pick up the phone for a call from Breslin.

And here was Breslin. He left a paper with close to a million and a half readers, where he had won a Pulitzer, to join one with a circulation that at around 130,000 was still growing from 25,000 to a peak of around 225,000. Forst had played a significant part in getting him to come. Why?

"Truth," Forst said. It was his mantra. "Truth is the ultimate con."

The three men had known each other since they were much younger, and each had played an important part even then in changing the way news and newspapers and city columns were reported and written. They were now going to do it again. That certainly may have been part of it.

"Let's reminisce about tomorrow," the man on the couch said. He finished ruining the pages of the notebook as he shoved it in his pocket and stood up.

The tall thin man in the corner picked up his coffee mug and carried it in front of him like a censer as he drifted archangelically toward the door. He turned as he stepped outside before vanishing into the quiet of his own small office with its archive of meticulously kept notebooks.

"Ha Ha Ha." Forst was alone again. Thinking about putting a bullseye on the reader's heart. In front of him he had two versions of it: his freehand sketches of the next day's front page. One of these would be the concept that had to be beaten to win the lottery and get on the cover.

Forst went for the heart. Not the head. One word, VICTORY, was better than two—WE WIN—which could be better than three—IRAQ WAR ENDS—but even when he used four to illustrate the knife a subway criminal had used (THAT'S NO BUTTER KNIFE), he still went for the heart. To do it, in Forst's bullseye school of page design, the words and the picture had to be united and in great tension with each other. Then you could sell a paper.

He would walk from the office looking at newsstands to see if they were selling papers sports side up or news side up. The vendors, he knew, knew their customers.

After winning his Pulitzer, Breslin lasted at the *News* for two more years. And why did he leave it for a startup? A paper hived off the immensely successful suburban Long Island *Newsday*, which had a virtual lock on that 118-mile island's lucrative two-car, some college, two-income demographic, *New York Newsday* intended to bring to New York vibrant, aggressive, in-depth reporting that would compete for the hearts of its readers.

If that sounds a little like the *Herald Tribune* of 1963, it is no small coincidence. That paper, knowing it could not compete with *The Times* in terms of completeness in its coverage, chose to compete with its writers' voices and its ability to bring its subjects to life. So did this one.

This one chose to dominate metro New York coverage. It hired an entire generation of the best and brightest young reporters—90 or so of them to do it, and a total staff of just over 230.

The paper was helmed by *Trib* alumni who staffed it with this vision of vibrancy, experimentation, humor and responsibility that Jim Bellows and Jock Whitney first had brought to the *Trib.* Forst, who became a Bellows protégé, had been an assistant City Editor there before going on to helm his own underdog papers and a long stint, for him, on the culture pages of *The Times.* Dave Laventhol, the soft spoken City Editor of the *Trib*, took his sniffles and went on to create with Ben Bradlee the Style section of the *Washington Post*, which was the first of its kind, then became editor of *Newsday* under publisher Bill Moyers, where he reprised his Washington success by redesigning Part II of that paper. He led the paper to four Pulitzers and he soon became its publisher. He launched *New York Newsday* in 1985 with a vision of bringing excitement back into news. He then became publisher of the *Los Angeles Times* and president of the parent company of both papers, the Times Mirror Company.

From that station he could coddle and protect his brainchild and Forst at the helm. Dennis Duggan, who was also a *Trib* alumnus, would become the paper's subway columnist, covering the travels and travails of more than five million commuters in a way that had not been done. *Serve the reader. Serve the city.* Kempton was there. And now Breslin. Kempton, Breslin and Pete Hamill were for a while in the company of Denis Hamill, Pete's much younger brother, bringing the voice of Brooklyn. By 1995, just before the paper closed, it took an eight-page press release to list the stellar staff and its accomplishments. The company Breslin kept would include that of the great gossip doyenne, Liz Smith; of Bill Reel, a delightful, gentle, general interest columnist; Mickey Carroll, Gail Collins, Sheryl McCarthy writing on politics, Jim Dwyer, Ellis Henican; Sydney Schanberg, who had left the soul-killing fields of *The Times*; cartoonist Doug Marlette, Les Payne, George Will, Art Buchwald (who also long ago wrote for the *Trib*). Sometimes it felt the paper had more writers than readers.

Breslin was not immune to flattery with a grounding in the truth. Nor to excitement. So Forst certainly played some part: he was promising Jimmy a better home.

But for Breslin there were several things that drove his writing: Fame, Money, Rage, as well as the need for a home. In this case, it was the money.

Paul O'Dwyer, the County Mayo–born civil rights lawyer and Democratic party activist, had cut him a deal too good to pass up: essentially a lifetime, no-cut contract for top dollars. With that, Breslin joined *New York Newsday*, a paper with a color front page, in a sea of newsprint that was still mostly gray, with deep and aggressive coverage of government and the neighborhoods, and the kind of thoughtfulness that branded it as a "tabloid in a tutu."

In a 1988 interview in the *Boston Globe*, Breslin told Karen Polk why he went to *NY Newsday*:

"Because they are giving me the most money paid in American newspapers. . . . Anybody who says they don't write for money is either a blockhead or an amateur."

The statement, echoing one memorialized in the 1960s at *The Trib*, certainly demonstrated consistency. Breslin to Jock Whitney, 1965—"When Our Circulation Began to Rise":

> When I started here, I thought I was just going to be writing for 300,000 people or so every day. And I approached my job with that attitude. But now I awake each day to find myself in an immense publication. The responsibility for going directly to over one million people each day is becoming awesome. It is clear to me that I need something to calm my nerves. . . . I need a raise.

Seen through another lens, Breslin's move resembled that of a perpetual journeyman rather than a star with a byline that could be associated with one organization for decades. His had been a career marked by one move after another, one disappointment after another, one gap after another, one home after another, one angry ending after another. He always, it seemed, was seeking the right home for his voice, always struggling with balancing his desire to create novelistic art with accepting the constraints of daily journalism that fulfilled two things: paying the mortgage and the household bills and feeding an adolescent need for instant recognition, instant gratification.

As Bill Graham, the impresario who famously founded the rock palace the Fillmore East, is reported to have said, repudiated or crushed when Mick Jagger dropped him as a tour manager for another representative who offered a better deal: "It's not the money, it's the money."

On May 22, 1988, Breslin's final column appeared in the *Daily News*. The city Housing Authority had moved to evict a woman convicted of killing her abusive husband, according to witnesses, before she had even been released from prison. Breslin took the trouble to point out that in the Jefferson Houses near 115th Street and Second

Avenue in East Harlem, this would hardly have been the introduction of a notorious Mob hitman into an Upper West Side senior assisted living home, but rather that of a slightly built woman into a complex with a significant number of formerly incarcerated residents, not so many of whom had committed only one crime. And her crime? The appropriate headline seemed to be the detective squad room saying: "He needed killing."

Following Breslin's arrival at *New York Newsday*, the *Boston Globe* took the trouble to write an insightful piece.

> But questions about his move or comparisons to his colleagues don't really interest Breslin. . . . He says that what he writes about and who he writes about are the same as when he was at *The News*, and at the *New York Post* before that, the *New York World Journal Tribune* before that and the *Herald Tribune* among others, before that.

Breslin compared himself to Joe DiMaggio, who never left anyone who bought a ticket feeling they had been robbed.

> "He got the best effort I know how to give," he remembered DiMaggio said. "If you start cheating on this, then you feel robbed yourself and you've robbed the readers. The reader knows he's been had.
>
> "As long as I tried the utmost to walk that last block or make that last phone call then I know I didn't rob them of their quarter."

So what had changed for him in 41 years in the newspaper business? The world. And not for the better. The writer Karen Polk asked him and his answer in the *Boston Globe* captured this ache with brilliant concision: "In 1964 Lyndon Johnson was president, Hubert Humphrey was vice president. The New York State Senators were Robert Kennedy and Jacob Javits. The mayor of New York was John Lindsay. There was some hope and with it some vocabulary in New York City and the nation where derogatory remarks about somebody's color was out of vogue, in poor taste. It was wicked.

"In 1988, what've you got? Reagan and Bush. [Sen.] Moynihan should know better and doesn't. [Sen.] D'Amato is a clerk and you've got Koch as mayor, who's an outright racist, and a governor [Cuomo] who has the ability to do everything and doesn't. And he's a friend." Balance? Fairness? Of no importance he tells Polk:

"I don't know what objectivity is. The truth is what's important."

And the truth, he tells her, is that since 1964, "It's been all pain."

The sadness shows in the eyes of the gray-haired man whose picture graces the Sunday, September 11, 1988, Page Two announcement "Breslin Column Begins Today." And the Page Nine column is filled with sadness at the senselessness that gave us crack pipe–sucking mothers and blind babies, babies born addicted, or with a sexually transmitted disease. It's all pain for which compassion is no match.

In his time at the *News* it wasn't all serial killers, unsurpassed scandals, and a police descent into the manners of an occupying army. Breslin elevated the stunt and the political caricature. There was one story in which he married the two into a gesture worthy of a true deadline artist. It appeared under the headline "Ed Koch, Home-Breaker" on Page Four of the Sunday, August 22, 1982, editions of the *News*. And it recounted the travails of Joseph Cruz, 55, and a World War II veteran, who was now homeless.

> Two years ago, he was thrown out of a single-room-occupancy hotel because his Veterans Administration check had arrived late. Cruz inspected the disgraceful chambers the city runs as shelters for the homeless and decided they were beneath his dignity. He became one of our street people, but a highly imaginative one.

Cruz moved to a traffic island underneath the FDR Drive at 61st Street and arranged his life.

> In this spot, with the roof over his head provided by the southbound lanes of the highway, Cruz set up full housekeeping, with bed, stove and chair. He washed body and clothes in a Parks Department building that is on the other side of the exit lane.
>
> . . . When Cruz' home was discovered by the brilliant Bella English of this newspaper, motorists stopped and handed Mr. Cruz money, beer and encouragement. In return they got a wave and a smile, giving the motorists perhaps their only cheer of the day. Sitting in his home, drinking his beer, reading a book, smiling as motorists yelled to him, Mr. Cruz never thought of himself as an aggressor.
>
> Oh, but he was. Mr. Cruz was an embarrassment to Mayor Koch, who runs for governor and whose car went past Mr. Cruz on the way to Gracie Mansion each night.
>
> The city bureaucracy kicked into high gear. Calls from City Hall landed on desks.
>
> "Why are they bothering me now?" Mr. Cruz said when he was told he might be moved. "I've been living on the streets for over two years and nobody cared."
>
> But that was before he became part of an election.

A psychiatrist was sent to see Mr. Cruz, who fled into traffic and this was enough to take Cruz, who had fought for his country, and have him committed to a psychiatric institution. He was a danger to himself and others.

> Mr. Cruz had been living on the island for months and there is no record of him ever endangering anything except an official reputation or so. But now the claim could be made that he was a nut who played in heavy traffic. So on Friday, a day in which several murders were

committed in the city, on a day when there were many armed robberies, here were six policemen pulling up to the traffic island to grab Mr. Cruz, dismantle his living quarters and take him to Bellevue and lithium.

Koch's office said that the mayor felt the action was "appropriate" but that Koch most certainly had not personally ordered the action. Which is another reason why Koch will soon be known everywhere as Copout Koch.

Breslin then turns the mayor's action on its head. He goes to the newly vacant traffic island, where there are now twenty large yellow barrels each filled with 100 gallons of sand set up to prevent any new occupant.

So yesterday I arrived at the traffic island with my friend Desmond Crofton . . . We turned over about a half dozen of the barrels, smoothed the sand and made a fine beach, a lovely beach, a cleaner beach than any beach in the East, and it was right in the middle of Manhattan.

I went to Crofton's apartment on 50th St., changed into smashing beachwear and returned to my private beach with an umbrella, beach chair, radio and book. . . .

I found my beach so thoroughly delightful that I remained for quite some time . . . and I intend to be there until Joseph Cruz is freed from Bellevue and returned to his home.

But it never should be forgotten that the temper, whim and nastiness of the city government, certainly reflecting on the desires of one man, Copout Koch resulted in citizen Joseph Cruz being taken by force of police and thrown into a mental ward on a summer weekend simply because he tried to live decently in New York.

Days later, city officials, lacking any rational answer or intelligent solution, were pulling out their hair. Breslin told the *Washington Post* why:

"The question of the homeless is going to become a major topic and a test of us as a people. What kind of a people are we if we have this? The answer is, we've lost the ability to assist, we've replaced it with a new standard, and the standard is greed.

"It's above and beyond this one guy," he said. "The traditional answer of the rich when they see vagrants is, the man must be mad, and they look to psycho them. They always say the man on the street corner is mad.

"The rich are uncomfortable at the sight of anyone homeless. The mayor has to pass there every night on his way to Gracie Mansion. They had the greatest show of bureaucracy trying to move one f— guy because he was an embarrassment. They drove the man nuts."

The writer Michael Kernan captured an essence of Breslin in his characterization: "Jimmy Breslin, you recall, is a larger-than-life figure who makes New York the setting for his life movie and its inhabitants the bit players. When Norman Mailer ran for mayor, Jimmy Breslin ran for the No. 2 spot, president of the city council. When Son of Sam wanted to talk, who would he talk to but Jimmy Breslin? As for his latest campaign, Breslin cautioned, 'Don't call it a crusade. Someone always gets killed in a crusade.'"

As a result of Bella English, and Breslin, homelessness, rather than his run for governor, was now sitting right in the center of the desk that Koch, like Fiorello La Guardia, used when ceremonially governing. It was right there in the *Daily News* in the picture of Breslin, in his cabana set, glasses set down on his Irish nose, cigar in one hand, book in another and towel around his neck and of course, a smile. Good on you, James Earle Breslin.

The theme of Breslin and his relationships with politics and politicians runs like a lead line through his column, where he measures their depth and the depths to which they are willing to sink to gain political advantage. He understood from the likes of Tip O'Neill that politics is about survival, and sometimes, sometimes more often than not, the public good is sacrificed on the altar of the ballot box. Votes brought Richard Nixon to impeachment. Votes put O'Neill in a place to collect those votes in the legislature.

There was Hugh Carey, a congressman when he elbowed up to the bar with Breslin and O'Neill in the days when Tip O'Neill was still collecting the votes for the impeachment of Nixon. Soon he would be a governor of New York and a confidant of Breslin. Until one day, he seemed more interested in dancing across the New York stage with his paramour, Evangeline Gouletas, a real estate mogul with a closet full of marital skeletons whom he wooed, squired, and married within three months of meeting her. He had slashed his way through New York's fiscal mess, uniting labor and management to help get the city back on its feet. He passed legislation to end the hospitalization of the disabled and mentally ill. Famously he united with the other Irish Americans—Edward Kennedy, Tip O'Neill, and Daniel Patrick Moynihan—to attempt to bring peace to Northern Ireland. Now he had dyed his hair red and, smitten, was using the state helicopter, according to Breslin, as a throbbing love seat. Breslin dubbed him "Society Carey."

Back in the art department of the *Daily News*, the gray spew from the airbrush was put to good use. Gone were the stripes from Carey's blue pinstriped suits, gone was the long tie, replaced with a bow tie that seemed crudely done until it appeared in the halftone cuts in the paper. And most important, now the lapels were those of a tuxedo. You watched in this way the transformation of a solid politician into a cartoon, whose last year in office was misery thanks to Breslin and the paper. And whose marriage to Gouletas he later dubbed perhaps his worst miscalculation.

Carey, Koch, and soon Giuliani and Trump would all be scorched by Breslin's pen. Of Mario Cuomo, who he called a friend, he simply said he did nothing when he could have done all. Of Breslin, Cuomo's son Andrew, himself a governor of New York, simply said, "Breslin was always a journalist first and a friend second." In this way they were two men who put their jobs first, almost obsessively. And they needed each other. Andrew, his father's campaign manager at age 18, had seen Breslin up close, in the chaos of the Breslin home, and in his own family's Queens kitchen where the columnist could put down a good portion of a bottle of scotch before Rosemary—"a saint, that woman"—showed up with the family car to carry him home.

A difference between Mario Cuomo and Ed Koch was that Cuomo did understand the difference in the job descriptions of an elected leader and a columnist: Breslin's, as he told Koch, was to inform and entertain. Koch's was supposed to be the running of New York City.

In the waning months of the third Koch term, after the PVB scandal had come to a head in January 1986, the city seemed a hellscape of disfunction. In June of 1986, Marla Hanson, an aspiring model, was slashed across her face by a jealous landlord. The disfiguring and career-ending wound required 150 stitches. On July 12, 1986, Police Officer Steven McDonald, patrolling Central Park, was shot in the head, throat, and spine by a 15-year-old and left a quadriplegic who lived, heroically and as a role model in forgiveness, until January 2017. In August, Robert Chambers, the Preppy Killer, choked Jennifer Levin to death, and tried and failed to escape punishment for the Central Park murder by using a "rough sex" defense. In December, there was Howard Beach. On December 20, Michael Griffith, 23, and two other

Black youths were attacked outside a pizza parlor in the predominantly white Queens enclave. Severely beaten, Griffith ran out onto a highway, was struck by a car, and was killed.

Crime in Central Park, cops shot, race hate—this was Koch's final term. Times Square, the crossroads of the world, felt like Beirut, crime was approaching a thirty-year high and the political machine that had elected Koch and fostered corruption while holding the reins of power was on the verge of being dismantled.

And as it grew to a close, there was Yusef Hawkins. This time we are in Bensonhurst, predominantly Italian and therefore, unfortunately, the domicile of mobsters who like to hide among the hardworking. It is August 23, 1989, and Yusef Hawkins and his friends have arrived to take a look at a 1982 Pontiac with an eye toward buying it. A group of 20 to 30 youths, who a mobster much later said were there to guard his home against racial unrest, attack Hawkins and his two friends. At least seven have bats. At least one has a gun. The reason given for their presence is that they were waiting in ambush for Blacks to show up to a party a neighborhood girl had invited them to.

Protest after protest followed. During one of them the Rev. Al Sharpton, an activist and quite a showman himself, was stabbed by a neighborhood youth.

But of all the racially charged cases, all the ugly police misconduct, all the vile racial undertones of Ed Koch's appeal to the working classes, the one that tore at the city's heart, the one with notoriety that raced around the globe as evidence of New York's depravity, the one that brought to light the blinders of the most liberal of reporters was the case of the Central Park Jogger. That was the name the victim of a sexual assault so violent that she lost consciousness for days was given by the media. In this case, Breslin's paper had one reporter whose source told him that he knew five youths arrested were guilty because they fell asleep in the holding cell. In that same paper, another reporter had a source who told him the youths were singing the "Wilding" song in their cell. Today few believe that characterization to be anything but shameful. Both the reporter and the source are dead.

The narrative at the time painted the youths as part of a gang or more than one gang who were rampaging in the park, coming down from Harlem and across the stone walls of the park like the hordes of Khan through the Great Wall of China to steal bikes, severely beat at least one person and push others around to which the youths added rape. The youths admitted involvement either as actors or witnesses in the other crimes. But the admission of the sexual assault was forced and tainted. There also was much prejudice, much implicit bias too, in news organizations comprised of mostly white reporters led by mostly white editors. Mostly.

The first narrative was filled with hate, fear, and the old story of Black men preying on defenseless white women. These young men had nothing to do with the rape. Their confessions appeared forced and were later recanted. A serial rapist came forward and said he had committed the crime—alone—this after years in jail for the wrongfully convicted youths. And that rapist's DNA was the only DNA found on the victim.

The new facts resulted in a senior Sex Crimes district attorney being let go by her publisher, a lead prosecutor resigning her post at a college in upper Manhattan, and a legal settlement by the city that paid $45 million to the no longer so young men.

# BRING BACK THE DEATH PENALTY. BRING BACK OUR POLICE!

The ad was signed with a flourish: *Donald J. Trump*. And its message was as ugly as it was simple.

> "Mayor Koch has stated that hate and rancor should be removed from our hearts. I don't think so. I want to hate these muggers and murderers. They should be forced to suffer, and when they kill, they should be executed for their crimes. They must serve as examples . . . I want to hate these murderers and I always will . . . I recently watched a newscast trying to explain "the anger of these young men." I no longer want to understand their anger. I want them to understand our anger. I want them to be afraid."

The ad appeared in New York newspapers on May 1, 1989. It rants on. And at the end, with a gift Trump was only then shaping and now has honed to an ugly point, he closed with his rallying cry: BRING BACK THE DEATH PENALTY. AND BRING BACK OUR POLICE!

It is in the fawning nature of some editors and some publishers and some reporters to press their noses against the windows of the wealthy and think there might be something there that we just don't understand, or how else could these ads have been printed? Simple greed is a good answer. And prejudice somewhere between the publisher and the head of ad sales. A prejudice toward money. It is that simple. Probably.

Breslin understood what was happening. He understood it while many were still largely coddling the upwardly mobile Trump.

His first column on the Central Park Jogger case pointed out, very simply, that this crime, whoever committed it, was not the biggest crime in the city. That crime was the cause of many crimes, perhaps even this one:

> The only reporting about these kids that could possibly help a reeling city at this time would be full disclosure of their education records, and some proof as to whether or not they can read and write. The rest of it, arraignments, trial, testimony, verdict, all has to do with the past. But at this moment, as long as the public attention is riveted on the magnitude of the crime, then the public must be shown what is actually happening in this city. There are tens of thousands of kids out on the streets, unable to read much more than a street sign, and yet capable, from age 10 and 11 and up, of being as dangerous as dynamite. Simply not enough people anywhere seem to understand this.
>
> Interest in the street language of this crime—wilding—is an example. The word has to be 10 years old. That most news reporting thinks it is something new shows that the news reporting doesn't even know the language of the most important story in the history of an American city.
>
> "How's the block."

This was his column on April 23. The rape had occurred on April 19. The jogger would be in a coma for another eight days.

Trump's ad came right about then, on May 1, so that the jogger would have something to see when she emerged into the light of life once more. And Breslin—who called him "Between you and I Trump," as that is how Trump speaks, not caring, says Breslin, enough about his own language "to learn the object of a preposition"—wrote. The headline on the column that appeared in the next morning's editions of *Newsday* and *New York Newsday* was "Beware of the Loudmouth Trump." In part, this is what it said:

> "I no longer want to understand their anger. I want them to understand our anger. I want them to be afraid."

Breslin quoted Trump so that his words could stand starkly against a different kind of language:

> Such violent language sounds as if it were coming from someone who walks around with bodyguards.
>
> Let us now turn to how the legitimate tough guys speak of violence. We had in Metropolitan Hospital the other night, at the bedside of the 28-year-old victim of the attack, the following:
>
> Her badly wounded mother, father and two brothers. Officer Steven McDonald, paralyzed forever by a bullet. McDonald was shot by a 15-year-old at a spot in Central Park only a hundred yards away from where the young woman was attacked. Also present was Father Mychal Judge, a priest who spends all his time with those dying with AIDS. All stood around the young woman's bed and held hands and prayed.
>
> The family of the young woman did not stop expressing their gratitude for all those who pray for their daughter.
>
> "Forgiveness," Steven McDonald said in a wheelchair he can never leave.
>
> "We must forgive or we cannot be," Father Mychal Judge said.
>
> The language of those who know.
>
> The curious thing about "Between You and I" Trump is not that he destroyed himself yesterday, for all demagogues ultimately do that, but why he became so immensely popular with the one group of people who are supposed to be the searchlights and loudspeakers that alert the public to the realities of such a person. That would be those who work in the news business.

Even the most unhostile of eyes cannot say that his buildings are not ugly. Yet all news stories say "imaginative" when common sense shouts "arrogant." Always, the television and newspapers talk of his financial brilliance, when anybody in the street knows that most of "Between You and I" Trump's profits come from crap games and slot machines in Atlantic City, the bulk of that, the slot machines, coming from old people who go down there with their Social Security checks. It also is an undeniable fact of life that gambling keeps bad company.

Yet with the one quality Trump has, amazing brashness—"I just bought the sky!"—he has overwhelmed the newspapers and television more than anyone we ever have had in this city. Barnum or Mike Todd used guile and chicanery, but Trump understood that this year, you can blind their minds by showing them a diamond. During a celebration of greed, he became toastmaster.

It would be comforting if "Between You and I" Trump was doing it the old way, by having half the reporters on a payroll someplace. But the News business today is so utterly dishonest that the people are below taking bribes. Instead, Trump buys them with a smile, a phone call or a display of wealth that so excites these poor fools that they cannot wait to herald his brilliance. "He let me see his yacht!"

And so "Between You and I" Trump, who runs crap games and slot machines, became an all-news person. Trump today bought a man a wooden leg! All candidates stand with sides lathered with excitement as they wait for Donald Trump's endorsement!

His thinking on anything was accepted. One paper—I think it was *The Times* but I have all these piles of clips around me and to tell you the truth I cannot read them—ran four separate stories on Donald Trump in one day.

Finally yesterday, in order to cash in on a young woman in a coma, to make an unedited statement, he ran his ad and showed himself for all to see what he was.

This is what James Earle Breslin saw and wrote in 1989. J.B. Number One.

As with many important things in life, it was overlooked. So when we ask how Donald Trump became president, those who wielded pens, notebooks, and computers and those who stood in front of television cameras first ought to look in the mirror and ask how they missed it and failed to call attention to it before it was far, far too late.

Years later, in the editions of October 22, 2002, Breslin wrote of the young men who became known as the Central Park Five and returned to the courts to ask to have their records scrubbed.

> Missing in court at yesterday's hearing on the five young men convicted in the Central Park jogging case was Donald Trump, who at the time of the crime perpetrated as lousy an act as he knew how, and that he can do . . .

This column was one that should chill anyone who thinks about what makes a person fit for office.

> Trump was seen yesterday on television in McDonald's commercials. Here he is, dead on the screen, with hair of swirled cement and strange color, and with a bad chin. . . . If McDonald's likes its Trump commercials then send them a message. Stay out.
>
> On April 19, 1989, a young woman jogging alone through the darkness at the north end of Central Park was attacked, beaten bloody, raped and left for dead. She just did live. Five young men, all of color, were picked up the day after the attack. A career-mad assistant district attorney whose name, Linda Fairstein, should not be forgotten, and five detectives, one of who still refers to the defendants as "mutts," had the five isolated and questioned for hours. Out of this came confessions that appear to have been coerced at least and maybe

> forced on them by detectives. . . . And then here came Donald Trump crying out to the lowest instincts, to the meaner parts of life. On the morning of May 1, 1989, Trump paid $85,000 for four full page ads that ran in *Newsday*, the *Daily News*, the *Post* and the *New York Times* newspapers and pulled them into the bottom of the sewer. It was the most inflammatory of newspaper advertisements. At that moment the city shrieked over five young Blacks who were under arrest for attacking a white girl. Were they guilty? Of course. How could they not be? Blacks on a white girl. As he ran his ad, it did not occur to Trump that they might be not guilty of the crime. In his life such a thing is dust for the maid to vacuum.

Breslin then reprints much of the ad before he closes with a summary that can be read again and again:

> That court session yesterday was about throwing out these old convictions because the evidence is fraudulent. If the woman jogger had died and the young men were convicted of murder and executed, and the evidence of being not guilty suddenly came out now, it would be murder by the state and Trump would be as good as an accomplice. The most you'd get out of him would be a shrug. Calling for the police to be let loose meant exactly what it said. Louima, Diallo. Let's go. Break their heads. Slam 'em. Find out what they did later. I'm Donald Trump and I want these people to suffer. The ad should be engraved on a wall someplace, the courthouse, a university, anywhere where it will stare down at the public and let them see this Trump for all he is and for the act he perpetrated on our city at a time when we were weak.

Six months and five days after Trump's ad, David Dinkins, when the votes were counted, learned that he would become the first Black man to become the mayor of New York and that on January 1, 1990, he would inherit this troubled hellscape of fear, hate, and economic anemia. Donald Trump was, of course, looking for tax advantages, according to Breslin, who deemed in a day when his mood was better that tax abatements were Trump's sole contribution to civic discourse.

Mayor Abe Beame in the 1970s was mocked for his height, for his fiscal failure, for the fall of New York; but always to his face. Dinkins was maligned in whispers behind his back: *psst*—he's a clerk. *Psst*: if he wasn't Black . . . *Psst. Psst. Psst.* And yet, against so many odds he brought his own tennis game—an education in itself to white New Yorkers—and the USTA's considerable money, money that still gushes into the city. He brought Restaurant Week. He brought Fashion Week. He brought in Police Commissioner Ray Kelly, who put his flag atop the thirty-year mountain of crime and said: Now we will begin to take this mountain down. His methods, especially later, were the subject of much legitimate criticism. But he and David Dinkins began to turn that tide. Dinkins did it in beautiful bow ties and perfectly tailored blazers. He did it with class. He redefined New York—it's not a melting pot, he said. It's a gorgeous mosaic. He certainly made any number of mistakes, and every one of those seemed to be leaked by Rudy Giuliani's team to the media. Ugly stuff. Rudy was becoming an ugly man.

Breslin was at this point earning $500,000 a year, according to a number of published reports. That in 2024 would be somewhere near or north of $1.3 million. He was living in Manhattan. He was living well.

# "ONE GREAT ACT OF BIGOTRY"

It is May 1990. He is in his office. It is one in a row along an interior wall of the 2 Park Avenue newsroom. Perhaps the cleanest newspaper office anyone who worked there had set foot in. Insurance company clean. Law firm clean. Spotless counters. Clean walls. Windows. Big, clean windows. Not the submarine interior of the *News,* nor the slum conditions of the *Trib.* Breslin has just published one of those columns that his editors and many readers had once found humorous.

A young reporter—recently an intern, according to executives at the time—did not find it humorous at all. She sent three sentences across an internal messaging system—this was before email and instant commentary became routine. She sent it to Breslin and a copy to Don Forst, the editor. "Finkery," a columnist of Breslin's generation wrote of the copy to Don Forst. The finkery was a violation of an ancient code from a time reporters battled only one another and when editors were left out.

With a keystroke, the message could have vanished. Deleted. This was not for J.B. Number One, whose readiness to rage seemed always just below the skin. He read the message in front of him.

Breslin broke out of his office and into the newsroom in an obscenity-laced rage, and ugly, vile, racist words poured out of his mouth and into the ears of every reporter, editor, and clerk in earshot.

"A yellow cur," he shouted, describing the Korean American reporter who had found his column sexist. "Slant eyed."

In 1986, when Barbara Ross, an admirer of his work since childhood, came cautiously into his *Daily News* office, holding the napkin that showed Mel Lebetkin, the Queens Boulevard lawyer who was the clay from which his character Klein the Lawyer was molded, was at the center of the biggest scandal in decades, he was able to shout and bellow "Fuck Fuck *Fuck* Fuck FUCK Fuck Fuck." It seemed like sixty times in five minutes to Ross, who was no newsroom ingenue. He dialed his phone. Slammed. Dialed. Slammed. Dialed. Slammed until finally he got Lebetkin. "You're stealing fucking millions and I got to learn it from this fucking c— who walks into my office." This had happened a mere four and a half years earlier. But that was in fact eons earlier in terms of how sensibilities had shifted, and it was in the coarser and still blue-collar tough confines of the *News*, not the late twentieth-century, pristine offices of *New York Newsday*.

Ross later sought Breslin out privately. No editors were involved. She attributed the behavior, she later hoped, perhaps to a tumor that might have already been forming in his brain. And the behavior, she recalled, was witnessed by only two other staffers.

At this newspaper, where diversity was sought for the reporting staff, and according to published accounts about 25 percent of the paper's readership were people of color, the racist and profane rant was heard by many. And editors could envision reader backlash.

"A yellow cur," he shouted. "Slant eyed." There was more.

While the object of his "one great act of bigotry" as it was described in commentary later was not in the room*, another Asian American

* The reporter who was the target of Breslin's ire agreed to be interviewed. However, after the reporter sent a list of 11 non-negotiable conditions the request to interview the reporter was withdrawn. The 11th condition was the right to add additional conditions.

reporter, Jessie Mangaliman, was there. A wonderful reporter, Jessie was driven to tears by this ugliness from the man who was one of the paper's stars. A man with a reputation of fighting bigotry, racism, and injustice. A petition was circulated. Many reporters signed it—more than forty, by one account.

In the old newsrooms where Breslin was raised, you didn't need secondhand smoke. You could suffer nicotine poisoning from touching any hard surface.

In the old newsrooms, desk men sucked down beer at their desks, drank after the first edition closed, and returned to their desks afterward. Here there were one or two who snuck cigarettes by a window and the smell of alcohol was virtually nonexistent.

Down at Police Headquarters, there was a plant in *Newsday*'s office. This was not the Police Shack at the *Daily News* where one young reporter had, late for work, picked up a coffee mug resting on a counter and took a swig before sitting down. He gagged. It was more vodka than coffee. When he had opened his left-hand desk drawer for the first time it was filled—to the top—with the damp-smelling butt ends of stubbed-out cigars.

A newer, less coarse world was forming. Breslin's was closing in on him.

The column in question was one in which Breslin used his wife, a city politician, as the butt of his gruff jokes.

> I hate official women!
>
> It is one thing when women have jobs that are not official and they act halfway decent because they're afraid of a man firing them. It is something else when they become official, get elected . . .
>
> Oh, this is all because of my wife, who is an official woman, don't you worry about that, and I'm going to tell you about it . . .

The column ran in the paper on Thursday, May 3.

In it, he tells this story about his wife while also passing judgment on a female court officer. It is simplified here just to show the remarks on his wife.

> I was still furious from all the trouble that started at home. It was caused solely by my wife, who was elected to public office, the City Council, in this city back in November and immediately, as an official woman, began to kill me in favor of herself.

In this pre-internet, pre-twitter, pre-blog era, it takes days for a cycle of anger, grief and action. On May 8, the newspaper announced to Breslin what he must do, and an apology was issued to the staff.

Don Forst and other executives thought that this slap on the writer's wrist in the form of an apology to the staff would be enough. A statement was issued on May 8. While it was not a gracious solution, it might have sufficed had Breslin not doubled down. On that same day he went on a call-in radio show that was itself a vehicle for anger and offensiveness. He ridiculed his own apology. And a meeting was called.

The paper's senior executives packed a conference room. The head of communications for the company was there, the publisher and the assistant publisher were there. The managing editor, assistant managing editors and many others. This was a business as well as an editorial decision. This was star talent. This was expensive talent. This was marquee talent.

Firing Breslin was put on the table. A number of other versions of serious punishment were debated.

The room was so crowded that the youngest editor in the room, the City Editor, sat on a credenza on a far wall.

"Suspend him," the City Editor spoke up into the din with the sureness of youth. It was a wonderful opening.

"Fine. You tell him," Forst said. "And you tell him he needs to write an apology for the paper."

No longer feeling so sure of himself, the City Editor returned to his realm to call Breslin.

"Jimmy, the paper is going to suspend you and you need to write an apology."

"Fuck you. You were a fucking clerk when I met you and you're still a fucking clerk. I know it's not you. It's that little Jew cocksucker Forst. Tell him I'll piss on his grave."

"You still need to write an apology."

"You do it."

The City Editor reported back. And then he sat down to write, a journeyman apology that is thankfully lost. Over his shoulder were public relations people, editors and others. It was a corporate apology. After a while, they were satisfied that it was okay to take to Breslin.

"No. Take this down," he said. "Once again I am no good. Breslin."

He was suspended for two weeks. A version of the apology he wrote appeared in the paper.

It is hard to remember ever seeing him in the newsroom again. Maybe he came in. Maybe he didn't. He wrote at home. He never talked to Don Forst again for the rest of Forst's life.

Loss and betrayal. Betrayal and loss. This was at the core of Breslin. It drove his anger. It drove him. It drove those around him insane.

## LOVE, BETRAYAL & LOSS

Why would he write a column like the one that triggered the firestorm? He had been writing about his family—how he hated his children, how his daughter couldn't get dates, for years. For all those years it had been more than okay. It was taken as his right. Even more tellng, why would he respond to a reportorial unknown the way he did? Why not pause? Because sometimes we do not see time passing us, a slow-moving freight now picking up speed as it leaves town without you.

Little Jimmy was lost without Ronnie Eldridge at home. A little boy betrayed. Humor masked anger. He was alone in the room again. Looking out the window, waiting for someone to come home. Humor masked anger, as it often did in these columns about those closest to him.

If love and work were for Freud the cornerstones of life, for Breslin the words chiseled into his heart were love and betrayal. He was more than capable of both. Of course, he also stole from his best friends. "I needed it," was a battle cry.

In this, too, he found kinship with Runyon, who he said was understood to be a poet, therefore capable of betrayal, and forgiven for it, even by gangsters, notably Arnold Rothstein.

"Of course it was understood that Runyon, as poet, was allowed to be friend or betrayer in the same hour, and it was the role of those around him, these subordinates, to accept this gracefully," Breslin wrote. And he demonstrated that he lived with this same expectation. He was the poet, you were the subordinates. As Joe Flaherty wrote all those years earlier during the campaign for city office: "Breslin's life . . . is starred in, written, produced, directed, and most important, publicized by Jimmy Breslin." Betrayal came with the turf.

- A friend, a friend who had provided Breslin with police information and knowledge for dozens of years, asked a favor. His son's first movie had come out to acclaim and success. Now there was a book backing out of it. Could Breslin write an introduction? "No. It's not a real book. Goodbye." That was the end of the friendship.
- Another friend, a reporter who Breslin called on for facts, for hard-to-get information, for a rundown of everything that happened overnight in New York that was worth knowing, asked for a simple favor: the paper where he worked was on strike. Could Breslin see if there was work at his paper until the strike was over? "Cross the picket line," Breslin said. Another friendship over. So over, that to say the other person despises Breslin would be wrong. To the other person, there is no Breslin. There is nothing to even think about. The man whose column on Lennon the person might have typed into the computer for him simply ceased to exist.
- His loyal secretary was another victim. Breslin was as disloyal to her as she had been loyal to him. Stuck for a column, Sam Roberts recalled, Breslin looked up and saw her talking on the phone with another reporter who might have been her lover. "All of a sudden he realizes there's his column." And he started

> typing. The secretary came from a country, Brooklyn, where betraying your husband in this way—even if your husband was away "on vacation," as a stretch in prison was called—was an unforgivable offense. "It's lucky it didn't get both of them killed," Roberts recalled.

In other cases, friendship and betrayal somehow became balanced bookkeeping entries.

Mickey Brennan was supposed to be somewhere else taking pictures, but tonight he was in Costello's bar on East 44th Street.

It was a big assignment. Mickey had plenty of those. He was in demand. This time it was Richard Burton.

But Mickey Brennan was happy drinking from a sweating glass in a bar filled with noise and smoke and the belly-bumping bragging of men in ties and women who carried notebooks in their purses.

On the walls were famous drawings by a man named Thurber. A Sistine Chapel reportedly created to pay a bar tab. Near the door there was a pay phone.

There was Breslin. And he wrote a column.

It began fine enough:

> Next to me at the bar as I celebrated turning in my novel was Mickey Brennan. Photographer. London *Daily Mirror.* The best thing about my novel, I told him, is that it is brilliant. As I had not been in a bar for some time I bought a drink. . . .
>
> On this night Brennan had so many cameras strapped about him that he looked like a human bomb. When he moved his arm to throw down a drink the cameras swung about. As I was afraid of being injured, I said, "Put your cameras behind the bar." He said he could not as he was about to rush to a theater and photograph Richard Burton and his bride.

I said to Brennan, "Burton can wait."

Brennan agreed. He then began discussing journalism, of which he is one of the better parts.

And that was how the night began. The discussion was of George Will, and a set of papers stolen from President Jimmy Carter which he viewed at David Stockman's house and said he did not use in preparing Ronald Reagan for a debate. This, Breslin felt, was a new tactic in debate preparation. He then took a little time to point out what kind of person Brennan was.

Brennan is a working man in journalism, although with a few flaws, one of which is he took a picture of me with a drink in my hand and promised to never show it to anyone except the bartender. I next saw the picture in the *New York Post* newspaper which used it as a bitter attack on me.

"I needed the money, mate," Brennan said.

What happened by the end of the column should really have been no surprise.

At 10 P.M. Brennan said, "Mate, I've got to go take my pictures of Burton."

"Stand fast and have another," I said. "I'll have him pose on the subway tracks if you want. He is a wonderful fellow. He will be happy to oblige."

At midnight I could last no more and left the bar. "What about Burton?" Brennan called. As I was going out the door, I said, "I'll handle it in the morning."

Morning arrived. Brennan awoke with no pictures and the London Mirror squalling.

"My rent is on the line, mate," Brennan announced on the phone.

> I put in a call for Brennan to Burton. Burton did not get back to us, but the message left for him noted that it would be a corporal work of mercy to receive Mickey Brennan and pose, with wife, for a few special Brennan portraits.

Walking down Second Avenue in midtown in the morning light, headed south on the East side of the avenue was little Mickey Brennan all swirling curls and undone tie and flapping sport coat, sputtering red with a hangover and anger.

"Look what your fucking mate did to me."

He slapped the paper at the young reporter.

"Look."

There it was. Brennan's career. In a column.

Breslin explained it. "I needed it."

Brennan doesn't care, except for one thing: "I wouldn't want anyone to think I had any bad feelings toward Jimmy."

They stayed in touch for all the years afterward. They talked with regularity. Jimmy gave him an introductory essay for a special edition of *They Must Fall: Muhammad Ali and the Men He Fought*, Brennan's book of iconic images of the champion and those he boxed. As is the way with publishing, Mickey needed something in writing in the way of permission to use it.

> Dear Mickey: I told you that you could use my piece. So now you have me writing a freaking note to say the same thing. What do I have to do next, put it in short story form? JB

Mickey Brennan understood the words "I needed it." Because he too had lived by that creed.

Breslin's daughter, Rosemary, understood how to avoid betrayal. Rosemary understood him and his need to consume everything in his world, anything in his world, extract meaning from it and put that meaning into words. This sometimes led to betrayal. She understood how to protect him from himself: don't tell him.

His book *The Church That Forgot Christ* includes this dialogue that shows he also had if not a full, at least a partial, self-awareness of this need:

> Suddenly, as I write I am interrupted. "Why are you saying that Mugavero was the best bishop?" my daughter Rosemary says. She says this as I write and this is why this book is so torturous to do. Not just because of her. Every phone call from victims and their families interrupts your whole life. This time my daughter has a printout of what I am writing in her hands and she is complaining. "He was such a good bishop he wanted ten thousand for an annulment." Her husband, Tony Dunne, had married a woman when they were both young and it didn't last. He and my daughter wanted to marry in a Catholic church ceremony, but the church doesn't marry anybody divorced. Only an annulment gets you to the altar. An annulment is purchased. "And the ten thousand was nothing," she said. "That's only money. What they wanted was for Tony and his first wife to send letters saying that they had not talked about having children before they were married and then afterwards she refused to have any. They wanted Tony to lie. Then they wanted him to get the former wife to lie. After you get these lies, you put ten thousand with them and you get an annulment. That says the marriage never happened. If you put up twenty thousand, they'll say that you never even knew the woman." "How are you so sure?" "Because I was involved." "Who was the money supposed to go to?" "The bishop. What are you, crazy? Never mind ten

thousand. The lies. They said you had to lie." "Why didn't you ever tell me?" "Because it was my business and you would have written about it and gone on to something else and left us in turmoil. Your business was to pay for the wedding." "What do you want me to do?" "Take out where you say he's the best bishop."

The book was published in January 2004, and in that year Breslin suffered another great loss: Rosemary the Younger, his daughter, died in June after bravely fighting a rare blood disease. She had battled it with poise, charm and an impressive workload. If she had a role model for suffering, you could say it was her mother, Rosemary One. Jimmy had to write a eulogy for a second Rosemary. In his obituary column, there was a father's poetry.

Rosemary Breslin, 47, died Monday from a rare blood disease. A writer who crafted scripts for "NYPD Blue" and wrote a 1997 memoir entitled "Not Exactly What I Had in Mind: An Incurable Love Story," Breslin was the third child of columnist Jimmy Breslin and the former Rosemary Dattolico, who died in 1981.

As it was with the mother who went before her, the last breath for the daughter was made before an onlooker with frightened eyes. First, there were several labored breaths.

And here in the hospital room, in a sight not distorted by passion, was the mother sitting on the end of her bed, as the daughter once had sat on the mother's in Forest Hills for a year unto death. They both were named Rosemary. When the mother's last breath told her to go, the daughter reached in fear, but her hand could not stay the mother's leaving.

By now, Rosemary, the younger, is married to Tony Dunne. He knew she was sick when he married her. He then went through 15 years of hospital visits, stays, emergencies and illness at home and all he wanted was for her to be at his side, day and night. His love does not run. And now, in the daughter's hospital room, as it always does, fear and deep love brought forth visions of childhood.

The daughter is maybe 4, sitting on the beach. She wants money for ice cream. The mother's purse had money to pay the carpenter at day's end. Earlier, the mother had tried to pay a carpenter by check and he leaped away, as if the check was flaming. The daughter plunged into the purse and found no change for ice cream. With the determination that was to mark every day of her life, she went through that purse, tossing large bills, the carpenter's money, into the air, digging for ice cream change. She sat there infuriated, throwing money into the sea wind. The mother was flying over the sand trying to retrieve it. Another labored breath.

Then I could see her later, and with even more determination. Typing a script with tubes in her arms. Writing, rewriting, using hours. Clearly, being attacked by her own blood. She said that she felt great. She said that for 15 years.

I don't know of any power that could match the power of Rosemary Breslin when sick. Suddenly, the last breath came in quiet.

The young and beautiful face stared into the silence she had created. Gone was the sound of her words.

The mother took her hand, and walked her away, as if to the first day of school.

# YOU NEVER LEAVE WHITESPACE

It did not matter so much, the issue of where Breslin wrote. What mattered was where his feet took him. In his biography of Runyon, it is already clear by page 61 in the hardcover edition that you are reading a biography of Breslin. Runyon, drinking a whiskey known as North Platte with the popular sportswriter Charles Van Loan after he had obtained a job at the Denver *Post* explained it this way, Breslin said: “All poetry gets written before you take up a pencil.”

Slap. Slap. Slap. The footsteps shaped the poetry.

“All of anything gets written before you write,” Van Loan said.

“But you still have to write it.”

He later brought Runyon from Denver to New York to replace him as a newspaper sportswriter when he went on to editing at a magazine.

And the bard who was Breslin, who described himself when he won the Pulitzer as unable to tolerate either criticism or compliment, was now avoiding on a regular basis a city room that could hold both. He was writing his poetry at home.

“He never talked to Don [Forst] again,” said Robert Johnson, the publisher of *New York Newsday*. “It was just an awful moment. But we really needed to suspend him, didn't we? I mean, there was no choice in that. No, unfortunately there wasn't. It was just wrong. She was naive as hell, but you know, she was like the newest kid in the world. You can't go and call people names like that."

But he was reporting solidly and his writing often was poetry. He wrote hundreds and hundreds of columns for *New York Newsday*—there would be, by his own count, 1,034 before the last one appeared on December 25, 1995.

Here is one week in 1991:

Sunday, August 18—Poetry, from the column "Trumpeting Best City Has to Offer"

> When it never looked worse, when the place seemed to have lost its footing, New York, just like some old champion, simply got up and threw a couple of those big rounds at you. And once more, the joint made the rest of the country look like Topeka. First, we had 750,000 people sitting on the grass at Central Park as Paul Simon sang his music. The only time the other people in this country can get a crowd this large together is for a war.
>
> And then, on the next night, on Friday, New York came right back at you, this time to demonstrate that it is the keeper of culture for the country. Here was Sam Koza, sandy haired and with gray eyes, in his white dinner jacket, warming up his cornet on the bandstand at Damrosch Park, in Lincoln Center. Sam comes out of Brighton Beach in Brooklyn and he started his music at 13 and he has done it all with a trumpet. Now, at 73, with the wife gone and the children out in the world, he helps protect one of those things that have ceased to exist in the rest of the country. Sam and 50 others formed the Goldman Memorial Band, which plays American music, marches mostly, at free outdoor concerts on summer nights, which once was an American tradition. . . .
>
> "In the summer, you can't beat a band," Sam Koza was saying. "A big living I've never made. But what a life I've had." He has done it all with a trumpet. He was in the pit on the opening night of "South Pacific,"

> playing for Mary Martin and Ezio Pinza. Here on the bandstand, he was talking about the excitement of it. . . . Because a musician does exactly what he must do to eat and pay rent, Sam gladly took a job playing "First Call" before each Thoroughbred race in New York. For 25 years, Sam Koza, once in the pit at "South Pacific," walked onto Aqueduct racetrack in a black riding hat and red velvet hunt jacket, brandishing a long Aida trumpet. He then played "First Call" twice before each race. He did that 18 times a day, six days a week. His dressing room was next door to the jockeys' room. "For the Lord's sake, don't bet horses," trainer Sunny Jim Fitzsimmons told him.

You may remember him from *Sunny Jim,* the first book Breslin wrote more than thirty years earlier.

> "Oh, I would never think of it," Sam Koza said.
>
> One day, all the jockeys were chattering about a horse trained by Hirsch Jacobs. Sam was unmoved. Then he heard one of them call out the horse's name: Chosen People. This was positively intoxicating for Sam Koza of Brighton Beach. He bet the horse, which paid $88. As he collected the first winning bet of his life, Sam Koza decided that he could do this forever. . . .
>
> And soon, on a cold day at the end of fall, among things for which Sam Koza had no funds, was a topcoat. . . .
>
> And in the finale, so full and thrilling, out of the trumpet section coming the best of Sam Koza, and that is very good music, with the percussionists quickening the heartbeat, the Goldman band finished with "The Stars and Stripes Forever," and the audience rose and cheered and clapped wildly on a soft night with stars seeming to cover the sky and the trees lining the sides of the park rustling softly in a breeze. I imagine it was hot and boring in Topeka and it was beautiful and exciting in New York. When it was over, Sam Koza went for a couple of beers with the younger musicians. Afterward, he took the E train home to the Van Wyck stop in Queens. He went straight to his apartment

and went to sleep. He had earned a gross of $83 for his night's work. Of course there was no more money than this. He may not have much under the mattress, but surely you don't believe that an artist such as Sam Koza was playing marches in Damrosch Park for money.

Tuesday, August 20—Politics, from the column "The Fall of Gorbachev"

You need be no historian or foreign relations prophet to comprehend the magnitude of the mistake that George Bush and his conservative Republicans made by not assisting Mikhail Gorbachev over the past months. When Bush was one of those helping supply the contras in Nicaragua, he broke the law of this nation as if it were some country club rule about extra weekend guests. If Gorbachev ever had received any of the fanatical devotion we gave to the contras in Nicaragua, perhaps we wouldn't be wondering where we are today.

Use your own common sense. Gorbachev took the atom bombs off our heads. Then he begged us for help and we treated him like a suspect.

Thursday August 22—Fury, from "CONFLICT IN CROWN HEIGHTS: Stripped and Beaten in My Furious City"

The incident that set off four days of uncontrolled rioting was the killing and severely injuring of Black children by a car driven by an ultra-Orthodox Jew.

Shortly after sunset on Monday, August 19, at about 8:20 P.M., the car, a Mercury Grand Marquis, according to published reports, driven by Yosef Lifsh ran a light, hit another car, jumped a curb, struck a several hundred-pound pillar which fell and pinned down two Black children: Gavin Cato, 7, who died and his cousin, Angela, 7, whose injuries were grievous.

The rumors were easy to believe if you knew New York and that neighborhood: an Orthodox ambulance service did not stop to give aid.

Nothing was further from the truth. But like the violence, the rumors started virtually immediately.

Rumors, violence, and police responses were all out of control by Wednesday when Breslin had hailed his cab and asked the driver to take him to an address in this neighborhood of Crown Heights, Brooklyn, where he might listen to a mayor, David Dinkins—who was Black, a first in New York, and ineffectual, not a first—to give a talk that might calm things down. It did not.

> We were going straight up Utica Avenue. We went past the 77th Precinct station house and then past blocks that were serene in the soft early evening. Now, the cab went up a couple of more blocks and suddenly on the left, at Sterling Place and Utica Avenue, here was this crowd of young people coming along Sterling Place and then dancing onto Utica Avenue, looking up toward Eastern Parkway, trying to see if police were coming.
>
> The cab driver stopped the cab.
>
> "I'm not going up there," he said.
>
> We had two blocks to go to Eastern Parkway, where my original intention had been to hear the mayor address a meeting at a grammar school.
>
> "Back up, then, and we'll try another way," I said.
>
> He started to back the cab up Utica Avenue.
>
> On the corner, somebody looked at the cab and called out, "White man." "White man," somebody else called.
>
> "Where?"
>
> "In the back."
>
> I then strongly urged the cab driver to increase his speed in reverse. Now from the left came a young man in a tan shirt and running as fast as any car in Brooklyn. He was grabbing for the door. The cab driver made a short stand, trying to push the young man off. At this point, for the purposes of the story, it must be said that the cab driver

> was Black. The passenger in the back seat was, as reported on the street, white.
>
> Now, the kid in the tan shirt was at the rear door, leaning in the window, holding out his hand. "Money, money, money."
>
> A couple of faces looked through the open window on the other side. "Gimme it. Gimme it. Gimme it."
>
> Now, there were young people running from every direction. In an instant, there was a crowd of over 50, at least. Both doors were yanked open and fists flew in, though not as strong as you would expect.

Breslin's friend Michael Daly recalled turning on the television that day and seeing a yellow cab in flames and thinking, "Who would take a yellow cab to a riot?" And answering his own thought with a smile: "Breslin." The scene from a riot he saw on TV that day came from a furious event known already as "The Crown Heights Riot," for the neighborhood in which it occurred.

The day had been, for Breslin, prior to his cab ride, one that included watching the continuing television coverage of the beginning of the end of the Soviet Union: an attempted coup that found Mikhail Gorbachev under house arrest and things like *perestroika* and *glasnost* in about the same shape as they now were to be found in Crown Heights, New York.

> The kid on the hood swung the baseball bat with as much speed as you could want and with a look on his face that told you all you ever want to know about life in New York at this time. This was no loss of reasoning or momentary blindness to the world, this was one angry young man . . . On his third swing, the entire windshield shattered and the glass fell into the cab. . . . There was no way for him to get at me, for there were so many piled into the back seat, throwing punches, holding me, ripping at my clothes for the only thing they wanted, the money. . . . Somehow, I got out of the cab on the right side. . . . There was a restaurant on the corner and a man and woman were in the doorway,

and I figured they would be glad to let the working press in. But as I reached the storefront a metal gate came rolling down electronically. I now am what you might term cornered. I have no clothes on me, save for a pair of shorts and somehow by primeval instinct, I still have a green working press card.

"Cab driver?" somebody yelled.

"No, I'm a reporter," I say, thankful that I had the chance. The answer was a right-hand punch from one side and a left hand from the other. . . . I then was hit with the best punch of the evening, and I went down . . . and I knew I had best get on my feet.

As I did, the guy with the baseball bat took one swing for my head that would have been memorable if I hadn't ducked the least bit. The bat went over my head and with that, some guy pushed through the crowd and grabbed my arm.

"Leave him alone," he said.

Another guy came through with a knife in his hand, a big one too, and he told everybody to get back. The crowd did not like being asked to leave but the two were adamant. They then started walking me down Utica Avenue toward the police precinct.

One of them said to me, "Do you know me? My name is Joe Williams." I told him I did, which was the truth. I couldn't place him for a moment but I believe I once met him in a bookstore on Fifth Avenue, where he was working at the checkout counter. If this is true, then the omen presented here might have been worth the entire night.

The other guy said his name was George Valentine. He was 35 and he lived on Herkimer Street. He is a slim guy who seemed sad about what had happened. He has no job and washes cars for anybody in Bedford-Stuyvesant with any money.

"They were mad," he said.

"What have they been doing all summer?" I asked him.

"Hanging around somewhere, just waiting for a time like this to let off some steam. They got a lot of steam to let off. It isn't just you. They don't like white people. They sure don't like white cops."

By now, we were on the corner by the 77th Precinct. A group of cops stood outside and looked at me. I had the usual few scratches and I also happened to be not wearing any clothes.

"Nice people," one of the policemen said.

"How do you like them?" another police officer said.

Which is what helps to keep things going.

And then George Valentine put me into a gypsy cab driven by John Juin, who is 35 and married and has three kids, and he drove me home. And that is the end of my story for today.

It is the end of the story as he filed it, which he did on the evening it happened. He filed it to Ellis Henican, a gifted columnist in his own right, and Ellis made sure that it was undiluted Jimmy that appeared in the *New York Newsday*.

But, as ever, reporters and writers make decisions on what they will put in, and what they will leave out. Here is what Breslin did not file to Ellis:

The cop who said "nice people" with his dangling helmet and his utility belt, was walking to a precinct that had already been made infamous by a corruption scandal that came out in 1986 and that showed how this precinct had been running an extortion racket of the most invidious kind: they shook down drug dealers and sometimes took their drugs too, and then they resold the drugs in the same neighborhood they were paid to police.

What the cop actually said was, "How do you like your n— friends now?" according to one of Breslin's closest confidants.

✶✶✶

The next riot took place in 1992. Looking back now at the start of this decade, the 1990s, we are twenty-five years away from Selma. We are nineteen years from Barack Obama sitting in the White House. We are thirty-one years away from January 6—a date, like 9/11, that seems to need no year. And that cop's ugly sentiment is again on display.

It is September 16, and the police are rioting at City Hall. And here is Rudy Giuliani with a megaphone, looking more like the man we saw after January 6 than the man we thought we saw after 9/11.

David Dinkins, the first Black mayor of New York, is being attacked with his City Hall under siege because he has decided a Civilian Complaint Review Board is needed. Ten thousand mostly white cops have marched across the Brooklyn Bridge. Racist signs. Obscene signs. Violence.

> They had beer and they wore guns and they all thought it was great to be young and drunk and ignorant. They were screaming that the Mayor, this Black mayor, wants a Civilian Complaint Review Board.
>
> And they put it right out in the sun yesterday in front of City Hall. We have a police force that is openly racist and there is a question as to what good they possibly can be in a city that will be famous forever as existing grandly with every color there is between here and Mars. . . . this frightful rabble, this armed suburban trash, vicious and rebellious, broke through barricades and rushed up the 10 steps to the doors of City Hall.
>
> They were urged on by the noxious words of Rudy Giuliani, who seems not to care if towns burn.

It is a column of power and beauty and significance, and it has been quoted extensively since the beginning of 2021. It is quoted again here.

> They drained cans of beer and pushed and screamed and shook their fists in the air and shoved people and kicked them and threatened them. Some waved toilet plungers and others held up a sign saying, "Dump the Washroom Attendant."

You saw calendar pages ripped off and torn into the air from Harlem to Selma to Dr. King, to Bobby, to Crown Heights, and land like litter under the feet of this horde.

> . . . and some of them climbed along the front of the building and began to bang on the windows of a place they never could reach on their own abilities. . . .
>
> They take home about $1,100 every two weeks. In today's job picture, there is little to match it. And they get a month's vacation and sick leave and chances at overtime. They work for only 20 years and then they can retire at half pay, and what that is all about, letting a guy go home with your money and he's only 45 or so, is a mystery.

One threatened a female TV reporter: "Here, let me grab your ass." Another "calling across the top of the beer can held to his mouth," went after Breslin: "How did you like the n— beating you up in Crown Heights . . . Now you got a n— right inside City Hall. How do you like that . . ."

Other reports have them kicking a reporter in the stomach. Breslin reports a Black delivery person pushed into the street. He calls the rioters Hessians from faceless towns on Long Island. An occupying army.

He had committed one great bigoted act as his world was shifting, but in Crown Heights, and again on Sept 16, he is reporting as he always has on race hate, bigotry, and the ugliness of politicians like the one Giuliani has become.

*BAM. SLAM, BANG, BANG. BANG. KABOOM. BANG, SLAM.* . . . This is how Jimmy Breslin types. Denis Hamill wrote that in 1977, during the Son of Sam frenzy.

Breslin was in his late 40s. Now he is what has been called late middle aged; he is in his early 60s. And columns like this one, that stand up to history, can be the result.

His audience, strong in 1977, had by now peaked, and Queens Boulevard was changing. Klein the Lawyer's alter ego had been indicted in federal court in Brooklyn in 1987, and by 1998 Pastrami King would move away from the state courthouse on Queens Boulevard. There would be other places to eat, and the boulevard would start to become unfamiliar looking.

Maybe, but you keep writing. A story he tells in his book on Runyon, and which he told Sam Roberts years earlier when Sam thought he might have a cold, sums up the ethic:

> "My friend, you never leave white space, you always fill it," Runyon said. It was 1925. He was talking to Wally Pipp, veteran first baseman for the Yankees. And he didn't think Pipp understood. "I am owed many days off by the newspaper. I could just as well get out right here and walk home. But I would be leaving white space. This man here (sports editor Edward Frayne) has white space blocked out for me in tomorrow's paper. If I do not fill it, he will get somebody to do it. Fella, the thought of that makes me uneasy. So I am now going all the way downtown to sit and write and most likely finish late. But I will finish. Don't ever leave white space. . . . You will feel better in the morning."

Pipp didn't listen. Sam Roberts did.

"I think it says it. [It] just tells the story. [It is] 1977 with all the Son of Sam pages, with the blackout in Bushwick, with the Yankees,

Dysfunctional Yankees, with George Willig, with the '77 mayoral election and Bushwick, with every crazy thing that was going. I remember one day, telling Jimmy I was coming in at 5:30 in the morning—I lived across the street, which was too close. I said, I really don't feel that great, I think I may come in later. I may even take the day off.

" 'I have two words for you.'

" 'What are they?'

" 'Wally Pipp.'

"And I said, 'Who's Wally Pipp,' I really didn't know and he said, look it up and I did and you know, Wally Pipp had a headache and he decided to take the day off and for the next 2,100 games, Lou Gehrig substituted for him. So I never missed a day of work after that." And Sam kept a picture of Wally Pipp on his desk.

*New York Newsday* closed its doors in July 1995 and the city was the worse for it. Unlike the *Trib*, it was the owners who killed it, a paper that kept the other news outlets honest by the aggressive, interesting way it covered the news. It spoke truth to power.

There were hundreds and hundreds more columns for the Long Island *Newsday* before Breslin's last regularly scheduled column in 2004 and his occasional ones after. Now, writing for a paper whose large readership lived almost completely in two suburban counties east of New York City, in a very real way he had left his audience behind. Yet the writing itself was in no way diminished, and many of those Long Island people, or their parents, had come from "the city." So at least they could say, in that nasal, Long Island way, they were familiar with what he was writing about. In fact, these readers were the circulation list descendants of the readers of the *Long Island Press*—the newspaper on the southeastern edge of Queens where he had worked as a copyboy and on April 19, 1949, published his feature article on how a television hanging on the wall was changing the nature of a barroom.

One of those columns distills so much of Breslin's soul into its few hundred words. It is one of eleven published in *Newsday* in 2001 between September 12 and September 30.

> I stand on the street corner in the darkness and wait for her, but for another day she is not here.
>
> I don't remember the first time I saw her. I know the hour, between 5:45 and 6 A.M., because I already have finished swimming at this health club and she comes walking along on her way to the gym for her exercise. . . .
>
> She was young and had short black hair and a face that was delicate and filled with energy. She had a fast stride. Quick-quick-quick.
>
> This went on for a long time. One morning I was late or she was early and I was still on Columbus Avenue, almost at the corner of 68th Street, when she came around the corner with that fast walk. People who barely recognize each other and suddenly meet at a strange place exhibit warmth. She smiled a little and her lips said hello, but I did not hear her voice. I nodded.
>
> From then on, when we would see each other on the familiar 68th Street, she would smile and I'd nod or smile back. But I still went to the other side of the street.
>
> This went on through so many months of darkness and cold and morning rain, when we both walked with heads down, and then at times when the sky lightened and spring arrived and after it summer heat. Always, a nod and a smile and then I parted and she went on.
>
> I never spoke to her, nor did she ever speak to me. I never got her name or where she was coming from at such an hour and what job she was going to for the rest of the day. She smiled, I nodded. Month after month.

I don't know when I realized that I had not seen her. It was 10 days ago, a week ago, but suddenly in the morning I noticed that she was not walking on the street at about 6 A.M.

. . . I never knew where she came from. She just materialized on the street, walking so quickly. And now I did not see her all last week.

I found myself irritated. "Where is she?" I said aloud.

The days and nights of my working life had become one of hurt women asking in strained voices for lost men, and so many young men in tears standing in a hospital doorway and asking if the woman of their lives might possibly be inside.

And there was nobody. Not in the wreckage at the World Trade Center, nor at the hospitals. The morgue was empty. There were 6,453 listed as missing, all of them in the sky forever from the moment the building blew up.

And this young woman no longer passes me going the other way in the morning.

Not only do I not know her name, but I never saw her with anybody else. I have no one to ask.

Yesterday morning, on the 14th day since the catastrophe, I was around the corner on West 68th Street at the appointed hour. She was not there. She was not in the dimness on the other side of Broadway. When I reached the corner and looked uptown on Broadway, she was not one of those coming through the light of the outdoor newsstand on the corner of 69th.

She was not here in my morning.

I stood on the corner in front of the Food Emporium supermarket and looked for several minutes. Maybe she moved, I thought. Maybe she got married to some nice guy. Or maybe some nice guy she is already married to had a new job and they moved. Maybe she has a new job and her hours changed. Maybe she comes to exercise later in the morning. Maybe there is a pleasant reason for her not being here in the morning. Maybe she will simply be here tomorrow and not have the slightest idea why I am upset.

> Right now, as I stand on the street corner in the early morning, this young woman, whose name I do not know, whose voice I have never heard, is part of the overwhelming anxiety of the days of my September in the city.
>
> The butcher from the supermarket came out, holding a container of coffee.
>
> "What are you looking for?" he said.
>
> "Somebody."
>
> "They'll come," he said.
>
> "I hope so," I said.

There turns out to be more to this story of loss and betrayal and anger.

In 2002 *Newsday* and the Tribune Company published a book, *American Lives*, with an introduction by Jimmy Breslin. And it is there we find the rest of the story.

> The mornings turned into days and weeks . . . I am turning onto Broadway at the same hour, five of six, and it is now 14 weeks since the catastrophe and I am about to go inside the supermarket and buy a paper and I happen to glance up Broadway.
>
> Deep in the January darkness, moving along quickly. An arm swinging. I stand there and I watch as she comes closer. It is the left arm swinging. Here she is, walking quickly. Quick, quick.
>
> Here coming out of the shadows is the face, smiling as she sees me. She comes right up to me.
>
> "Where have you been?" I say to her.
>
> For an instant she doesn't understand.
>
> "I thought you were gone," I said.
>
> Now she knows. Her face changes.
>
> "Oh, I'm sorry. I'm sorry."
>
> "What am I supposed to think? You disappeared like the others."

"I'm so sorry. I just stopped coming. I had two friends who were missing and we went looking for them. We had pictures and everything. I just didn't want to go anyplace else."

She starts to leave with a smile.

"One thing."

She stops.

"I'm glad you're alive."

She turns and walks off, quickly.

When I went upstairs, my wife looked at me and said, "What's the matter?"

"I just saw a ghost," I said.

And you felt so much of what every victim feels. And what everyone whose hopes are answered feels. For Jimmy: It is personal. Always.

On November 2, 2004, James Earle Breslin, 75 and sure that writing 840 words three times a week left room for nothing else, announced, in his *Newsday* column: " . . . I quit. Beautiful." He thanked his readers "for the use of the hall," and closed the column.

His editors added a note informing them that Breslin would continue to write "from time to time."

This would prove to be different from all the past times when he had quit newspapers. There would be still more columns for the paper in 2005, 2006, 2007, though the numbers would diminish. And he would be back in the *Daily News* from 2011 on, writing for the Sunday paper, but he would never again be a regular fixture, and the columns themselves became increasingly difficult to edit.

By any measure, he'd had a great, musical, run, already longer than *The Fantasticks*' forty-two years. He summed it up himself when he wrote: "I had a column once . . . and started a great run, and continued it wonderfully well and for a long time, and sometimes when I think of this I am so delighted that I could sing a song. And you better do the same thing. For if you do not blow your own horn, then there is no music."

And the one-time bugler summed up his method in an interview: "In newspapers? Work. That I did do, work—incessantly. And you don't stop working until the job is truly finished. Then you can. At one time I would go for a drink. No more now. I just go home and get ready for the next [one]. And—that's it. That's the only way to feel good too."

There would be, however, even as the number of grandchildren grew to seven, more heartbreak: Rosemary the wife, Rosemary the Younger, and now Kelly, the blonde daughter; she collapses in a restaurant and dies in April 2009. The writer himself develops diabetes. At least once he falls at home. Another time in public. Ronnie does her utmost to keep him on track. And somehow in his 80s now, becoming physically frail, he knows there is one more story he must own, and he must tell, to you, the reader.

# HE FINDS SELMA IN ZUCCOTTI PARK

Breslin this final time rides his "tabloid horse," as *Politico* dubbed it, into another battle of great importance. He rides it to Zuccotti Park, where Occupy Wall Street was being born. And once more, his words would be the ones that stood out. They appeared in the *Daily News* four times. On Sunday, October 9, 2011, the headline spanned the full page:

SPIRIT OF SELMA IS REBORN ON BROADWAY

In the morning, I climb the steps out of the subway and onto lower Broadway, whose new history is starting. The outcry today is from the 99% who start this day of work against the 1% whose rich comforts include acceptable theft.

The future of today's Broadway inherits the past that suddenly is living so fully in memory. I am on Broadway, abuzz with buses and cabs and chauffeurs driving people to work.

For the unemployed, the jobs are nonexistent.

The contrast comes at a time of rising national opposition to Wall Street. The politicians have not recognized that the gathering against the government of the rich and uncaring is only the start of a national outcry.

They all cannot see the start of a future that will make history.

The crowds today at a small park on Broadway and Liberty are perhaps the most pleasant, uplifting scene that we've had around this city for so long.

They set up life in a park on Broadway and then had a march of great democratic health. . . .

The small place where all this started is Selma, Ala., the place historians call the basis for all the rallies and marches that those in New York have now recognized as the same outcry for change. . . .

I now go to a notebook stored in a closet and take out this half a century later. I get pained thinking of how long I have been out on the streets in this business. But I was there in 1965, and this is something I found . . . Patricia Anne Dossiage, 10, stood in the red dirt and twitched her toes . . . and looked at the people walking on the road.

"I know why you marchin'," she said. "I know it good."

Fifty years later on Broadway the issues are different, but the cause remains the same. One percent of the country gets the best of everything. The rest gets the shaft. Funny how some things never change.

On Sunday, November 6, he began again at the subway station, this time descending.

I am starting the day reading the paper while I'm walking to the subway to go downtown to cheer a new gathering of the Wall Street protesters. The entire city is just starting to be convinced that these crowds are going to change things and forever. Just follow the numbers and energy of the people.

Still, the people you thought would be first to tell the country all about this are news people. But they have stayed seated in the office. These desks in a warm office save some newsmen from going out to the site where they would have to get cold and push through the crowds of protesters. That is work—and they are not so busy at that.

Instead, they're telling another kind of story.

> The New York Post had a front-page headline on Thursday for the city:
>
> "Enough! Post Editorial. Mr. Mayor, it is time to reclaim Zuccotti Park—and New York City's dignity."
>
> The paper's ownership comes out of Australia and London. The owner is Rupert Murdoch, who is friendly with New York politicians who fall down when they get a glimpse of his money.
>
> On Friday, the New York Post runs a front page that screams:
>
> "Occupy Wall Street animals go wild . . ."
>
> I am standing in the middle of Eighth Ave. reading the start of this paper. I became busy reading other parts while standing there. A bus had to stop dead or leave me in the same condition.

Breslin then captures how the paper tells its readers what is happening: pages of fights and people being called morons. This is not, he assures his readers, what is actually happening.

> . . . actually walking around Zuccotti Park you find the scene pleasant and moderate. The large crowds coming here now are filled with children walking in front of their parents.

It is in this context of the whole that he includes some of the uglier elements of the protest. And then he closes the column with a woman from the East Village, knitting, as she does each day until it is too dark to knit.

> This is molestation? Lawlessness? These are animals? Morons?
>
> That's another kind of story. All right.

The mood in the news media and in official New York was as unsympathetic as Breslin was understanding. In 1991, on his way to Crown Heights, he starts his column looking for the taxi that will take him to the riot. This time he took the subway to the protests, which had been marked at times by some bottle and rock throwing, some knocking down of mailboxes and trashcans and some running through the streets, but on the whole, it is a peaceful protest crowded into a park, hemmed in by steel and glass towers, the media, and the police in blue uniforms, their bosses in white shirts with gold bars or stars on them.

As the nonprofit news organization *Gothamist* noted on October 16, "Famed New York City journalist Jimmy Breslin, who has spent his long, storied career highlighting the plight of the common man, has visited Zuccotti Park and mingled with the Occupy Wall Street protesters. Not surprisingly, he approves. Calling the protests a 'human rights movement' that's 'threatening to become historic,' Breslin writes in the *Daily News*, 'Each day, the crowd grew larger and there came a moment in a city newsroom when somebody picked up his head and wondered if they couldn't begin to cover the News.'"

On Mayor Michael Bloomberg, and his views on the park, the news outlet notes, "Breslin uses his plain, matter-of-fact style to cut the politician to the quick," and quotes his column:

> He has an arrogance that, as always with the rich, comes with the poorest knowledge of people. I don't know how the city made him mayor. It also turns out that his lady friend is on the board of the real estate company that handles Zuccotti Park, and that wants to push and con the protesters out of the park. Great surprise! The mayor wants the protesters to beat it out of the park. Bloomberg seems to stand with the people in New York who don't stand for all of the city.

And that detail about the mayor's girlfriend is all you need to know about Jimmy Breslin, reporter, hovering on the northern edge of 80 years old, a newsman from the age of 18. Not counting *The Flash*, of course.

"Yes. I remember how excited he was by what they were doing when I talked with him after he filed the column," recalls Kevin Convey, who was the Editor-in-Chief of the *Daily News* that year and who, with senior Managing Editor Stuart Marques, were Breslin's editors.

"And that was distinctly different from the prevailing tut-tut tone of the media at the time. I was happy to have that viewpoint, and Jimmy, in our paper, especially as the *Post* was ripping the protestors."

Just as there were friends who worried when Jimmy was writing for suburban *Newsday*—opining that writing for the suburbs was a mistake—there were several good friends who were concerned that Breslin was continuing to write at all at this point. They were concerned, perhaps understandably, that age and injury had taken away more than his fast ball.

"Pretty sure I edited that column. Truthfully, I didn't know Jimmy prior to 2010-2011, so maybe he had degenerated by that time in a way I could not measure. I attributed whatever he had lost off the fast ball to age," Convey said. But it was what he had that mattered, not what he might have lost, he added.

If they are very good, major league pitchers can regularly put fastballs across the plate at 90-plus miles an hour as measured by the radar gun. Hurling it from the mound to the plate at more than 100 miles an hour is much rarer. And the analogy is probably as good as any for journalism—where there are plenty of very good pitchers, but only a few who can regularly put it across the plate with a speed well north of 100. That was Breslin at his absolute no-hitter best.

But here we are in 2011, and Convey was still seeing a lot of speed on the ball. And that speed came with the kind of knowledge that a Willie Mays could bring to the game—a player who, as Murray Kempton pointed out, had played the game before some of the pitchers he faced were born.

So Breslin, who had been playing for decades before these protestors were born, dug out his notebooks from his coverage of the marches from Selma to Montgomery, Alabama, in 1965.

> Fifty years later on Broadway, the issues are different, but the cause remains the same. One percent of the country gets the best of everything. The rest gets the shaft. Funny how some things never change.

Joe Pompeo raised a question in his article in *Politico* on October 10: "We wondered who Breslin thought he was writing for in the tabloids today, and whether he thought his readers shared his sympathy with the protesters, so we called.

"'You got me there,' he said. 'I don't know. I hope they read what I write.'"

Pompeo puts you there much as Breslin might. And he quotes enough of Breslin to follow J.B.'s thoughts on how he covers a story and what the other coverage was like.

"'A lot of these places,' [Breslin] said, referring to newspapers, 'even when they're finally gonna come around, they say, "You gotta get the other side." Well, there is no fuckin' other side to this.'"

Whether the protest, even as it spread across the nation, was a full-blown success, a failure, or something in the middle, was a matter for continued debate.

How to cover news, and how to cover the crime of not covering it properly, is, for Jimmy Breslin, not such a matter. Tell the truth. And make it present. Breslin explained that to his readers one day shortly after Nelson Rockefeller died in 1979.

Chen Ping—who was also called Bo Ghee Lo, which was said by Breslin to mean "newspaperman" in Cantonese—pushed a shopping cart with eight different Chinese language newspapers to the Gold Coin Restaurant as he flapped one copy like a pigeon in the night air of the always busy midtown canyons. It was in the best, time-honored tradition of the New York newsie and he was one of the last, he and Firpo, the newsie down in the canyons of Wall Street whose name came from the fighter who almost beat Dempsey and who, it was reported, flew through the ropes and on his way down to defeat landed on a journalist's typewriter. Bo Ghee shouted in the present tense and flapped the thin pages as he wheeled bundles of them in a shopping cart to Bill Chan's restaurant at 994 Second Avenue, just ten blocks up from the *Daily News* Building, a gilded shrine to alcohol and New York–style Chinese food where Breslin and the editors of the paper would drink in deep thoughts.

"People don't want to fool around, they want big news. They don't want nothing to happen, make them read."

"Like what?"

"War."

"And?"

"Big Guy Die."

"Make people read."

# BIG MAN DIES

The church was on a side street.

His kind of street. His kind of church.

It was the church he and Ronnie Eldridge were married in at a time when religions found it hard to rise above themselves like this and bond two people of different faiths in public in a sacred space.

The Church of the Blessed Sacrament at 152 West 71st Street. And in many ways it was his kind of crowd: New Yorkers who packed it on Wednesday, March 22.

The governor's mother, Matilda Cuomo, came. Her boys and girls grew up with the Breslin family.

The governor came. For a governor, he came quietly. His security detail was discreet and in the background. He came, Andrew Cuomo said, as the elected representative of the Cuomo family. His mother was there, of course, as the matriarch.

His father, Gov. Mario Cuomo, and Jimmy Breslin—who met as adults—also grew up together politically: defining, discarding, and refining their thoughts and feelings on social justice, on politics and on the body politic.

Chris Cuomo came, network-TV-tall-and-handsome, and the governor's younger brother, came. He stood in the back of the church. Quiet. Keeping himself out of the picture.

Former Police Commissioner Ray Kelly came. Alone. In a black overcoat, a white shirt, and a perfectly knotted silver tie. Fit. Face tight. A former Marine.

Book agents came. Writers came. Politicians came.

And yet it was a simple memorial service on a quiet side street. The kind of street and the kind of church you could find in the neighborhoods off Queens Boulevard and even here off Columbus Avenue.

A grandchild read the Prayer of the Faithful:

### PRAYER OF THE FAITHFUL

Lord, blessed in many and various ways, we have gathered to celebrate the death and Resurrection of your Son, placing James Breslin in the midst of that celebration. That prompts us to ask of Your mercy these gifts:

. . . for James Breslin...that having used the gifts given in Your service, he may now be admitted to the fullness of eternal life . . . we pray . . .

. . . for journalists . . . particularly in print media—the Fourth Estate—that neither political pressure nor fear of reprisal will alter their presentation of the truth . . . we pray . . .

. . . for a spirit of common concern in our City...that the various injustices that Jimmy railed against might be eliminated by our demand for integrity and honesty . . . we pray . . .

. . . for the poor and overlooked, the discarded, the unwashed and unwanted...be visible to us as we walk the streets of the City . . . as we imbibe some of the "rage" that was Jimmy's gift to us all . . . we pray . . .

. . . for humor, for 'tis a sin to bore...we pray...

. . . for my grandfather, he who believed in God and the goodness of people, now he might enjoy the peace that God has promised to those who strive to be faithful . . . we pray . . .

> . . . for our family and for our grandmother, we are experiencing great loss, that we might find comfort in the words that he wrote . . . we pray . . .
>
> . . . for the world in which we, his grandchildren and children, and all gathered here will live, together let us raise our voices in a prayer for peace . . .

The governor spoke. Mostly in a quiet voice. You couldn't call it a eulogy for Jimmy, really. It was more of a eulogy for a passing of the telling of the truth as part of the discourse in our society. One of the best tellers had passed, and with the passing some of the ability to call "bullshit" when it was heard or seen went with him.

"He was the quintessential New Yorker. He was irritable and he was tough, but he was an authentic voice for New York. He was the people's voice. I think we are losing that more and more in journalism, frankly, where when you read a Jimmy Breslin column, you knew who he was and what his values were. . . . he brought a perspective to journalism and he gave people comfort."

Thomas Ridges, Special Counsel to the Staten Island District Attorney, also spoke eloquently.

"The speaker before me said that Jimmy knew without this city, he would not be anything. Well, I'm here to tell you that without Jimmy, I would not be anything. . . . This story began in 1980 when I was 15 years old, living in the Sumner Housing Project in Bedford-Stuyvesant, and I was introduced to Jimmy Breslin by Michael Daly.

"I, at that time, 15 years old, didn't know whether to thank Michael Daly or to hate Michael Daly. Think about it. For those of you that have been intimidated at times by Jimmy. I was 15 years old at the time. I am now 51. In a couple of weeks, I'll be 52. God willing. So that means Jimmy has been in my life for 37 years and Jimmy dared me to do better, to be better.

"He saw something in me that I did not think at that time. I saw a lot of people around me that were dying, going to prison, no hope, and he told me that 'doesn't have to be you.' Jimmy wanted me to do great things. He was with me through high school, through college, through law school, through the loss of my parents six months apart. I just wanna say I, I'm glad he saw and he looked beyond the headline, that he saw more than a 15 year old Black kid from the projects, Jimmy saw people for who for they are. And that's why day in, day out, when I make decisions about cases, when I talk to people, I think about the person, not their status, not what they look like. I ask myself, what's the right thing to do? . . .

"Jimmy knew. And until the day I die, I will not let him down. So whenever I'm faced with a hard decision going forward, and I know it might be sacrilegious to say this here, but I will ask it myself—not what would Jesus do, but what would Jimmy do . . . A lot of people talk about Jimmy being behind the headlines. It wasn't about the headlines. He saw the story behind the story. The headlines back then were about crime and, and the projects and all these negative things. He saw me behind those headlines.

"I want to state to the family. I thank you for sharing Jimmy with me."

And Michael Daly spoke. Someone who had known him since they were young and able to laugh watched Daly stand on the altar and hold up the one sacrament that mattered: a press card. The writer was as close to tears as he would allow. One had to wonder, as Tip O'Neill said when JFK died, whether he'd be able to laugh again.

"Nobody ever brought more honor to this pass than he did."

Almost everything was said that needed to be said and then Ronnie Eldridge, his wife of thirty-four years, spoke the words you had waited to hear: "Thanks for the use of the hall."

A Big Man had died. No longer would a reporter, lying in bed beside her husband, be awakened in the night with the shout, "I'M BIG." And the hang-up.

# CODA
## A GOODBYE TO JIMMY BRESLIN, TELLER OF TRUTHS
## BY MICHAEL DALY

In a time of fake news and alternative facts, we have lost Jimmy Breslin, a brave and brilliant teller of deepest truth.

Early Sunday morning, this 88-year-old genius newspaper columnist and novelist roused his wife, Ronnie Eldridge, with a question.

"How do you open a can of soup?"

She got up and the two of them spent a magical hour together, sipping soup and talking. They finally returned to the bed and he reached for *The New York Times*, which he always read so he could declare it unreadable. She drifted off after asking him not to get up again without letting her know.

He of course disobeyed her and was up and around when she woke up again shortly before 7:30 A.M. He approached the bed and she asked him how he felt. He told her he felt terrible.

He then pitched over onto the mattress.

On thousands of other days, Breslin had set out with pad and pen to cover the latest story, often pulsing with the adrenaline burst that comes with a tight deadline, pushing himself yet again to do his very best, hyper-focused so as not to miss the telling details, opening himself up to feel what the subject was feeling, almost becoming the subject, composing the narrative in his mind even as it unfolded.

He had been the doctor on duty when John F. Kennedy was rushed into a Dallas emergency room and the gravedigger who prepared the president's resting place and a scared young soldier in Vietnam and Mafia boss Vincent "Chin" Gigante and a young woman waiting for the results of a life-or-death medical test and a family living without heat in cold so bitter the walls of the apartment were covered with ice.

He had also been a father of a murdered cop and a detective who captured a famous serial killer but then had to go to his second job lugging birdseed at a warehouse because he needed the extra dough to make ends meet and a Mexican immigrant who traveled to New York to feed his family and ended up drowning in a sub-standard cement pour and a little girl who proved to be the toughest kid in Brooklyn, sitting down at a murder scene and doing her homework for the next day.

Breslin would then hurry back to write if time allowed. If it did not, he wrote the column by hand and got on a phone to dictate it, often coming in at exactly the right length. He in all circumstances paid particular attention to verbs and to the sound as well as the sense of sentences so they expressed the feeling as precisely as the action, just as his favorite poet Yeats would.

The result was a joining of letter and spirit that is truth. His particular truth ran even deeper because he sought it in people who are often overlooked or ignored. Editors who did not understand what he was doing would call it color or an angle. Anyone attentive on the scene would know that he had chosen his latest subject as the best way to tell the full story.

But now, on Sunday, Breslin was at his own death scene and there was nobody for him to be but himself. And this was one story that a lesser talent would have to write.

Two uniformed cops from the Midtown North precinct responded to the Breslin apartment. Representatives of the Frank E. Campbell Funeral Home arrived in the late morning and showed the same kind of respect as that long-ago gravedigger as they set to work. They placed the great bard in a blue velvet body bag and zipped it up. He was rolled in a gurney from the bedroom and into the foyer. His novels and non-fiction books were on the shelves. Framed pages from a hand-edited draft of a Yeats play hung on a wall.

If there is an afterlife, Breslin will surely be communing not only with William Butler Yeats, but also with Fat Thomas Rand, the 400-pound bookmaker who had often appeared in his columns. Some Breslin detractors insisted Fat Thomas was a fictional character. Among those who could attest otherwise were the hotels in the south where he checked in during a tour in the civil-rights era, registering as Martin Luther Fat and liberating shoeshine stands by sitting on them.

"What's doing?" Breslin would have said on reuniting with his friend Fat Thomas in the hereafter.

"How do you like it?" Fat Thomas would have replied.

And you can be sure that Breslin would give the cry that those of us who love him so well remember.

"J.B. Number One!"

If there is only the here and now, Breslin still lives on in work that really does make him J.B. Number One as a result of hard work and brilliance rather than the bluster his imitators copy. And he leaves a pantheon of people he introduced to us in his continuing quest for the true greatness of America and therefore the human spirit.

They prominently include Thomas Ridges, who grew up in toughest Brooklyn and was a teen when he first met Breslin more than three decades ago.

"He was a true gentleman, he judged people by who they were, not what they looked like," Ridge said. "Think about it. I was a 15-year-old black kid from the Sumner Houses and he gave me the time of day. Instead of just writing about me, he spoke to me. He mentored me."

Ridges graduated high school and college and joined the NYPD. He served with the Emergency Service Unit while he went to law school. He ran short of money at one point and he had only needed to call Breslin.

"I was able to finish law school and look at me now," Ridges said.

Ridges went from being a prosecutor in Brooklyn to his present position as the 51-year-old special counsel to the district attorney of Staten Island.

"For me that story became a happy ending," Ridges said. "A positive about the Sumner Houses. Anybody can do a negative."

As Ridges grieved in his present home in Staten Island, the funeral home representatives were wheeling the gurney bearing Breslin's remains down a hallway in his Manhattan apartment building.

Upon reaching the elevator, they discovered that the gurney was not going to fit in the usual position. Breslin's son, James, watched as they gently and respectfully tipped the gurney and his father upright.

James understood that his father would have been delighted.

"He left his residence standing," James said.

The funeral home representatives continued on to the street and a waiting hearse. There will be no story about a gravedigger for Breslin's place of rest. He was to be cremated.

# A TIMELINE OF SIGNIFICANT EVENTS

**October 17, 1928**
Born in Jamaica, Queens, to James Earle and Frances Breslin

**1939**
Editor and publisher, *The Flash*

**1947**
Graduates John Adams High School

**1948–1951**
Copyboy, *Long Island Press,* while attending Long Island University, 1948–50

**1951**
Short stint as a writer, *Nassau Daily Review-Star*

**December 26, 1954**
Marries Rosemary Dattolico

**April 1959**
Sports reporter, Newspaper Enterprise Association Sports Syndicate

**April 1959–1960**
Sports reporter, *New York Journal-American*

**1960**
Quits *Journal-American*

**1961**
Receives Best Sports Stories Award for "Racing's Angriest Young Man"

**1962**
*Sunny Jim: The Life of America's Most Beloved Horseman, James Fitzsimmons* published (Breslin's first book)

**1963**
*Can't Anybody Here Play This Game?* published (this book about the hapless New York Mets' first season caught the attention of the *Herald Tribune*'s publisher, Jock Whitney)

**May 1963**
Joins the *New York Herald Tribune*

**November 24, 1963**
"A Death in Emergency Room One" and "It's an Honor" published by *Herald Tribune*

**March 27, 1964**
Receives Meyer Berger Award, $500 and a plaque

**May 1967**
*Herald Tribune* closes

**March 11, 1968**
Joins *New York Post*

**1968**
TV commentary for New York ABC and NBC affiliates (various dates in 1968–69 and 1973)

**February 1, 1969**
Quits *New York Post* ("The placement of my column in the paper was poor, I got lost between the girdle ads.")

**1969**
Joins *New York Magazine* (writes articles 1969–1971)

**March 31, 1969**
Norman Mailer and Breslin run for New York City mayor and city council president, respectively

**November 1969**
*The Gang That Couldn't Shoot Straight* published

**1970**
Attacked and beaten by Jimmy "the Gent" Burke at The Suite (then owned by Lucchese crime family associate Henry Hill)

**1971**
*The Gang That Couldn't Shoot Straight* opens in theaters

**1972**
Delegate to Democratic National Convention

**1973**
*World Without End, Amen* published

**1975**
*How the Good Guys Finally Won: Notes from an Impeachment Summer* published

**November 14, 1976**
Joins *New York Daily News* (first column, "On Slay St., and Atrocity Ave.")

**May 30, 1977**
Son of Sam Letter addressed to Jimmy Breslin arrives at the *Daily News*

**1978**
*.44* published (with Dick Schaap)

**August 1980**
*I Go Pogo* (voices the character P. T. Bridgeport)

**June 9, 1981**
Rosemary dies

**September 12, 1982**
Marries Ronnie Eldridge

**1982**
*Forsaking All Others* published

**1984**
*The World According to Breslin* published

**1985**
Wins George Polk Award

**October 1986**
Lands his own twice-weekly late night talk show, *Jimmy Breslin's People* (disgusted because the show is often delayed or preempted, Breslin takes out a full-page ad in *The New York Times* announcing that he is "firing the network")

**1986**
Wins Pulitzer Prize for Commentary

**May 17, 1986**
Hosts Season 11, Episode 17, of *Saturday Night Live* (with Marvin Hagler)

**January 1987**
*Table Money* published

**January 1988**
*He Got Hungry and Forgot His Manners: A Fable* published

**February 17, 1988**
*The Queen of the Leaky Roof Circuit* opens at the Actor's Theatre in Louisville, Kentucky

**May 1988**
Final column appears in the *Daily News*

**October 1988**
First *New York Newsday* column appears

**May 13, 1990**
After a colleague describes one of Breslin's articles as sexist, he retorts with racist invective, appears on the *Howard Stern Show* to double down on his outburst, is asked by *New York Newsday* city editor Richard Esposito to write an apology, and is then suspended

**January 1991**
*Damon Runyon: A Life* published

**August 19, 1991**
Crown Heights riots (Breslin is torn from a taxi, robbed, beaten and left with only his underwear and his press card)

**December 1995**
Stops writing regular column for *Newsday* (*New York Newsday* ceased publication July 1995)

**1996**
*A Slight Case of Amazing Grace: A Memoir* published

**1997**
*I Want to Thank My Brain for Remembering Me: A Memoir* published following his brain aneurysm in 1994

**June 1997**
Returns to writing a column for *Newsday*

**2002**
*I Don't Want to Go to Jail: A Good Story* published

**2002**
*The Short Sweet Dream of Eduardo Gutierrez* published

**June 14, 2004**
Daughter Rosemary dies from a rare blood disease

**November 2, 2004**
Quits *Newsday* ("I'm right—again. So I quit. Beautiful.")

**2004**
*The Church That Forgot Christ* published

**2008**
The Library of America selects a Son of Sam column for inclusion in its anthology of American True Crime writing.

**2008**
*The Good Rat: A True Story* published

**2009**
Daughter Kelly, 44, dies after a cardiac arrhythmia in a New York City restaurant

**March 2011**
*Branch Rickey* published (Breslin started his career writing sports books, now his final book is grounded in sports and civil rights)

**November 5, 2011**
"Occupy Wall Street"—his last significant piece of journalism

**July 24, 2012**
Receives honorary degree from LIU Brooklyn

**November 14, 2013**
Inducted into the New York Journalism Hall of Fame

**March 19, 2017**
Breslin dies

**March 22, 2017**
Breslin's funeral

# ACKNOWLEDGMENTS

Write a book that, at its heart, is about news—a thing that is said to be a first draft of history—and by the time your work is done you will want to thank everyone who worked in the business of reporting it across the time, in the places, and at the organizations—most notably newspapers—the book concerned itself with. So, thank you everyone. If in the following acknowledgments I forget a name, forgive me.

Among those who must be thanked for their contributions to my understanding of the man at the center of this work and my understanding of how his story might be crafted, there are four whose assistance was so great that I need to single them out: Michael Daly, Denis Hamill, Mitch Gelman and Ellis Henican. Thank you for your unstinting sharing of your time and your knowledge.

To all the other friends, colleagues, experts, witnesses, and participants in history who also shared their time and energy across the years, beginning in 2015, I am deeply appreciative.

There is a debt of gratitude that cannot be repaid to: James Breslin; Kevin Breslin; Dan Barry; David Black, my agent who was there from the start and helped envision this book; Mickey Brennan, a wonderful photographer; Ed Burns, Sr.; Charlie Carillo; Steve Cerbone; Chiara Coletti; Kevin Convey; Andrew Cuomo; Robert Dembo, who built

NBC's Investigative Unit with me, pushed hard for this book, and is a great friend; Mike Downing; Martin Dunn; Steve Eisenberg; Ronnie Eldridge; Bill Farrell; Ed Faye; Michael Gross, who graciously shared his Mailer–Breslin mayoral campaign memorabilia; Pete Hamill; Ken Jacowitz for his invaluable archival research that included unearthing Breslin's work from newspaper morgues and libraries across the United States; Robert Johnson; Richard Kluger, whose magisterial work, *The Paper*, was an invaluable resource; Murray and Gloria Loew for unflagging interest as I slogged on; Stu Marques; Morty Matz, who at 99 years old maintained his sense of wonder; Marie McGovern; Frank McLaughlin; Diane McNulty; Phil Messing, who was always ready with a fact or an anecdote; John Miller, a news reporter of uncanny ability who was always there when I needed him; Bob Nardoza; Dick Oliver; Patrice O'Shaughnessy; Otto Penzler, the publisher who believed in this book and its importance; Michael Regan; my good friend Clem Richardson; Tom Robbins; Sam Roberts, who was my first city editor, sitting right under the big clock in the *Daily News* newsroom; Barbara Ross; Myron Rushetzky; Howie Sann; Louis Schiro; Charles Sennott; David Starr; Gloria Steinem; Gay Talese; Curtis Taylor; Peg Tyre; Tom Vallely; Dick Wald; Pete Williams; and Tom Wolfe.

Tom Wickersham was a wonderful editor whose suggestions added immensely to this book.

My debt extends to my colleagues from NBC Investigations: Tom Winter, Mark Schone, Jonathan Dienst, Matthew Cole, and Andy Blankstein for their support and encouragement.

In my heart, there is a special place for the never-departed, enigmatic, and often difficult Don Forst, the editor of *New York Newsday*.

Don taught me how to become an editor, manage a newsroom and to edit a newspaper.

Closest to my heart, there are two more people I cannot begin to thank: the woman who gave of her wisdom, her days, nights and countless weekends, and who read the drafts, my wife, Karen Loew, to whom this book is dedicated. And the woman who was always there for her father when his energy or confidence flagged, my daughter, Tati.

And then there is Ted: This book could not have been written without Ted Gerstein, the consummate reporter, who collected, collated, researched, interviewed and shared countless burgers and cups of coffee with me. Ted was a partner on this book, during more than ten years' worth of *Nightline* episodes that we produced beginning shortly after September 11, and on the book that came before this one. Ted could not have been there were it not for his wife, Christine Rannazzisi-Gerstein, and her tolerance for the hours he spent locked away on this project, and her faith in him and in us. Thank you so much Chris.

City of New York press identification memorial card, courtesy the New York City Police Department.

# INDEX

## S



## T